Finance
and World Power

A POLITICAL COMMENTARY

by the same author

MASTERS OF INDECISION
An Inquiry Into The Political Process (1962)

MERCHANT BANKING
Practice And Prospects (1966)

Finance and World Power

A POLITICAL COMMENTARY

GEORGE K. YOUNG

NELSON

THOMAS NELSON AND SONS LTD
36 Park Street London W1
P.O. Box 336 Apapa Lagos
P.O. Box 25012 Nairobi
P.O. Box 21149 Dar es Salaam
P.O. Box 2187 Accra
77 Coffee Street San Fernando Trinidad

THOMAS NELSON (AUSTRALIA) LTD
597 Little Collins Street Melbourne C1

THOMAS NELSON AND SONS (SOUTH AFRICA) PROPRIETARY LTD
51 Commissioner Street Johannesburg

THOMAS NELSON AND SONS (CANADA) LTD
81 Curlew Drive Don Mills Ontario

THOMAS NELSON AND SONS
Copewood and Davis Streets Camden New Jersey 08103

First published 1968
© G. K. Young 1968
17 153036 5

Printed in Great Britain by
Thomas Nelson (Printers) Ltd, London and Edinburgh

Contents

Preface

Since credit creation is almost as old as human settlement and rests on confidence, issues of financial policy are ultimately questions of consciousness, race, language, and culture. In this book, the subject has been treated in the broadest framework of history, and no one should be put off if his eye catches numerous statistics, usually in nine figures, or frequent percentages. They are given for general comparative purposes and require neither memorizing nor analytical attention. Readers who take more than a passing interest in the financial pages of daily newspapers should find no great difficulty in following the discussion of monetary matters. Anyone encountering an unfamiliar financial expression is advised to read on: he should find it explained later in the text. For currency comparisons, it will be sufficient for British readers to divide dollar amounts (pre-devaluation) by three and French, Swiss, Dutch, and German currency amounts by ten to have rough sterling approximations.

The figures themselves are generally taken from OECD and EEC publications, Bank of England, Board of Trade and Federal Reserve bulletins, and IMF reports. So as not to interrupt the narrative with too frequent references or footnotes, I normally give sources only in cases where the authority for the figures could not be regarded as conclusive. As a former civil servant concerned with policy-making in the Foreign Office and the Ministry of Defence, I suffer from the usual handicap of the Official Secrets Acts, at least in discussing affairs of state up to and including 1961. I also have to observe due discretion over the confidences, professional and private, expressed at various times by central bankers and officials, especially at meetings of the European League for Economic Co-operation, where Dr Otmar Emminger gives his lucid periodic summaries of the course of monetary reform.

For historical and background material I am indebted to Prince Fugger-Babenhausen, Geheimrat Wilhelm Vocke, Messrs Oscar L. Altman of the International Monetary Fund, Fred H. Klopstock of the Federal Reserve Bank of New York, Guy de Mowbray of the Bank of England, R. V. Palin of N. M. Rothschild and Sons, Stewart Pixley of Sharps Pixley and Co., Hans Hagnell of Svenska Metallindustriearbetareförbundet, and John MacArthur, head of Kleinwort, Benson's research department. Any opinions about men, institutions, and policies are naturally my own.

Since the completion of the manuscript, we have had the sterling devaluation of November 1967. This and subsequent attempts by central banks to retain control over the international gold market serve to underline the shifting emphasis of power. The devaluation in itself represents neither turning point nor cure for 'the English sickness', has saddled the United Kingdom with a further £500,000,000 short-term liabilities, and reduced the United States Treasury's stock of gold to $12,143 millions, the lowest level since 1937. Whether the pressures on sterling again become critical in 1968 or 1969 depends primarily on the confidence placed by Western European Governments in Britain's conduct of affairs.

The last increase of Federal Reserve international 'swaps' to some $6,500 millions also stretches the Bretton Woods monetary system to its limits: for the unresolved United States debate in 1967 between Executive, Congress, and Federal Reserve on the issue of more taxation or higher interest rates threatens to undermine the hitherto successful American financial diplomacy of persuading foreign authorities to hold a growing dollar component in their reserves. And it is even less likely than in the thirties that a United States administration in the face of increasing social tensions, could sustain the political consequences of a severe deflation. The United States do not have limitless room for financial manoeuvre.

The wider power issues remain open. If the 1967 IMF conference and top changes in the U.N. Food and Agricultural Office point to a stronger European assertion, the 1968 UNCTAD preliminaries indicate the persistence of the liberal-universalist fallacies which have diverted Western thinking from the realities of human affairs. Mrs Indhira Ghandi's announcement in December 1967 of a 'holiday' from Indian planning should have exploded some of our obsessive notions about aid and development; it passed almost unreported. Throughout history power has been lost rather than seized. This can still be tomorrow's outcome.

December 1967

1. New wealth from old skills

Wealth as authority

In September 1961 there was a special air of pageantry about the annual conference of the International Monetary Fund. The venue was the Vienna Hofburg, former residence of the Hapsburgs. The gay display of flags of participating nations was dwarfed by the gilt crown and imperial eagles of a power which had disintegrated forty-four years previously. But they were in keeping with the world character of the occasion. Twice a day, as the hired Cadillacs rolled up to the entrance, the loudspeaker called out the names of Asian and African delegates, while Viennese newspapers carried long reports of the high-minded speeches in which British and United States Ministers promised generous aid to the underdeveloped.

In closed meetings, quite a different subject dominated. The then British Chancellor of the Exchequer, Mr Selwyn Lloyd, was ruefully admitting that selling pressure on sterling in the world's money markets urgently required emergency support arrangements. In return he had to listen to pungent views by the representatives of Continental European countries on Britain's methods of running its economic affairs. Even more incongruous was the appearance on the mat of the United States Secretary of the Treasury for not bringing his country's $3,000 millions balance of payments deficit under control. And all this in the palace where, only six years before, the hoisting of the Stars and Stripes had evoked a collective sigh of relief from occupied Vienna— the sign that the 'American Month' had come round once more at the Four-Power Kommandatura and that the inhabitants of the central districts could sleep soundly without fear of a Russian knock on the door.

For Britain the confession of monetary weakness was particularly galling. It came only three years after the British Government had announced full convertibility for sterling. Although the United States Government could claim that its problem was of a different order from that of Britain and was the consequence of military and economic expenditure incurred in the general interest of the non-Communist world, there were ghosts of past global financial crises, such as 1931, which were not so easily laid. In spite of the agreement reached in Vienna to prepare emergency measures against future sterling crises and American assurances that their deficit would be brought under control, the difficulty of laying the ghosts was illustrated by the unmistakable 'Gold Rush' which developed from 1961 onwards.

Did this reflect some rationally based apprehension? Had there been a fundamental shift in financial power and influence? Or was it a return to primitivism—an atavistic need to hoard one of mankind's oldest measures of value, the surest safeguard when confidence in a ruler's ability wanes? For when fear displaces trust, the basis of a community's strength is eroded. When temporal authority can no longer command confidence in its conduct of financial affairs, its power and influence are sapped as disastrously as if its armies had mutinied or sedition spread among its subjects.

Five years after Vienna this seemed the fate of Britain. If Mr James Callaghan, as Chancellor of the Exchequer, denounced France's financial ideas as 'primitive barbarity', the Republic was able—thanks to gold reserves of $5,000 millions—to make its voice heard effectively in international affairs. As far as 'barbarity' was concerned, the world's oldest civilization, that of China, was, at the very moment Callaghan spoke, actively buying gold in London's bullion market.

Even in small and primitive communities where power can be exerted through personal influence, wealth and the opportunities wealth gives for ostentation add to the effective means of command. And once wealth, in the form of a surplus of production, actual or potential, can be combined with an acceptable medium of exchange and a reliable system of communications, a new factor comes into play. The hoarded surplus becomes true 'capital' and its investment in future ventures is made possible. With the material advance of civilization, those who represent authority in human consciousness thus acquire new instruments of power. Given mankind's need to find identity in durable and stable things, even in enduring myths, the sources of power of past ages can persist with later generations as symbols of authority.

Deliberate use of the coinage as an instrument possessing a power over and above the market value of its metal, either as a medium of exchange or as a store of wealth, found full application under Imperial Rome. The emperor's style and the official deities on the coins reinforced the prestige of public authority, as well as providing proconsuls, tax-gatherers, paymasters, and traders with uniform instruments for arbitration and enforcement, for official awards and guarantees. In the third century after Christ, when Rome itself fell into crisis and anarchy, debasement of the coinage and collapse of the monetary system were the outward symptoms of a malady which infected the furthest province. As Diocletian and Constantine restored imperial authority between A.D. 284 and A.D. 337 by the creation of a new centralized administration, they set up a new currency system based on the *solidus* of pure gold, approximately the size of a half-sovereign, weighing in Roman terms twenty-four carats. It remained the basic unit of account and measure of value in Europe throughout decline and fall, during the folk movements of the 'Dark Ages', to be taken over by the feudal kingdoms which emerged as new incorporations of power and authority.

With the dispersal of power, coins still appeared bearing the names of Frankish, Gothic, and Vandal rulers, but Europe had entered an era where, although the peasant and land-owning economy was not entirely one of barter, power was mobilized by mustering men and forging weapons under feudal pledge. Where human beings were the most desirable form of wealth, slavery, serfdom, and other types of thraldom flourished. Untilled lands exceeded the cultivated areas even in what had been the most populous regions of the Roman Empire. Kings and merchants may have accumulated considerable personal hoards and had their chests of gold, but these were not their effective instruments of power.

European transformation

Yet with the growth of large-scale commerce in the fourteenth and fifteenth centuries there is a transformation in kind. It was not a mere quantitative increase in wealth, nor a revival of urban trade as it had existed in the ancient world. The chandlers, wine-merchants, oil-vendors, and retailers whose shops can be seen along the roofless streets of Pompeii, Leptis Magna, and Jerash had never dominated the governments of their communities: power had lain with those who controlled the imperial revenue, estimated by Gibbon as £18,000,000 yearly in Augustus' reign.[1] The merchants of the European Middle Ages were a new breed. Their profits derived from the growing farm surplus brought about by higher skills in animal husbandry, improved iron tools, axled wheels, and water mills. The purchasing power of land-owners, yeomen, and peasantry called for better quality manufactures, cloth, spices, and products of other lands.

[1] At present consumer prices this would amount to £120,000,000.

3

Though the gold and silver mines of medieval Europe, functioning under royal control or charter, supplied regular quotas for minting the increased circulation of ducats, thalers, marks, crowns, and florins, the merchants' bills of exchange had become as important as gold coin. The credits these represented stimulated economic advance far from their own towns, encouraged Gascon vintners to produce wines for England, Baltic barons to plant wheat for the Low Countries, Cotswold farmers to improve their wool for the weavers of Ghent and Bruges, Turks and Berbers to plan their harvests to suit the market needs of Europe. The merchants financed complete trading expeditions, arranged the supply and transport of armies, raised loans for monarchs, bought privileges for their guilds and cities, and hired soldiers to defend them. Safeguarded personal privilege and legal equality served the medieval merchant's interest better than dominance of his fellow-men, although when the weavers of Courtrai defeated the knights of Philippe le Bel at the Battle of the Spurs, commerce demonstrated that in case of need it could mobilize its own power. The revenues of the *domaine du roi* which, until the thirteenth century, had sufficed for the needs of central government, could no longer meet the increasing cost of armies and administration.

How uniquely European was this process is apparent if one turns to the civilizations of Asia. The merchant classes of Arabia, Persia, India, and China wrested no such privileges from their rulers. They could hope for the sagacity of kings, who saw the benefits of protecting the prosperity of their subjects and were mindful of the precepts of Islamic law or ancient custom. The traders of the Levant and India may have enjoyed wealth as great as that of the European guildsmen: but the privilege it conferred was that of having to pay a higher price for the favours of capricious rule. The Western European process was a subtle interweaving of new privileges, stronger strands of commercial credit, and increasing political participation. 'Liberty' may have been one facet in the process: 'power' was another.

The process was not without its setbacks for the participants. Europe, too, knew the caprices of rulers. The rise and fall of Jacques Coeur, the Bourges merchant who managed the French royal mints for Charles VII and administered crown rights over mining, illustrates the risks of serving princely power. At the height of wealth and fame, Coeur made loans to Charles of up to 200,000 gold crowns, more than a fifth of the annual royal revenues, for the successful prosecution of the war against the English.[1] After 1451, when the English had been expelled

---

[1] 'Rise and Fall of Jacques Coeur', A. R. Myers, *History Today* (July and August, 1966).

from France, Coeur enjoyed trading privileges in the reconquered provinces, possessed papal licences to trade with the infidels of the Levant, and throughout the three realms of France, Anjou, and Navarre had a network of three hundred factors, some twenty great town-houses, and twenty-six estates. If his total fortune cannot be estimated in present-day terms, the fact that the king hoped to mulct him of 500,000 crowns gives an idea of his mobilizable wealth.[1]

Coeur's success was his undoing. His debtors among the nobility, seeing no hope of ever being able to repay him, brought accusations of every kind, from poisoning the king's mistress to helping the infidel and minting false money. After three years of prison, interrogation, confiscation of his estates, and threats of torture, Coeur escaped in 1454 to Anjou and then to Rome, and died two years later in papal service in charge of an expedition against the Turks.

Fate was kinder to the most famous of the medieval banking dynasties, the Fuggers of Augsburg. Established as merchants in Augsburg in 1367, the Fugger financial ascendancy coincided with Hapsburg supremacy in Germany and Western Europe and with the alliance between emperors and popes. Under Kaiser Friedrich III, Jakob Fugger the Rich was ennobled, and under Maxmilian I and Charles V, the family acquired vast estates in Southern Germany. Their surviving bills and ledgers reveal the Fuggers as financiers to Catholic commanders in campaigns against Turks, Swedes, Italians, and Netherlanders. Their Antwerp office extended credits to Henry VIII of England while still Defender of the Faith, and later to Bloody Mary during her usurpation, but discreetly withdrew as bankers to the English Crown when hostilities broke out between Philip of Spain and Elizabeth; an account for the Duke of Alba was opened in their books.

The working capital of the Fuggers came from their merchandising, mines, and lands, while the banking deposits originated from the revenues and funds-under-transfer of the German prince-bishops. Virtually all European rulers, including Ivan the Terrible, have entries in the ledgers, and the 1527 inventory of assets, written in Anton Fugger's own hand, shows a total of 2,132,791 gulden. Twenty years later these had risen to 3,760,000 gulden—in today's purchasing power equivalent to £50,000,000. The Fugger house disposed of some twenty branches or 'counters' extending from Leipzig and Vienna to Antwerp, Rome, and Venice, with regular correspondents in Budapest

[1] Allowing for the difficulty of comparing like with like, 500,000 crowns would have a purchasing power of approximately £2,000,000 in terms of today's consumer prices.

and Madrid. The Thirty Years' War, the decline of the Holy Roman Empire, and the rise of nation-states gradually disrupted Europe's first Continent-wide banking venture, although the Fugger family remained in enjoyment of its own estates and personal treasure.[1]

In putting their skills in transferring funds and opening credits at the service of princes and popes, the European medieval bankers were concerned with percentages, not with power. Their first aim was to enrich themselves. The bankers of the Renaissance had perhaps a keener sense of the political potential of their financial instruments. The Medici family combination of bankers and rulers still symbolizes the moment of brilliance of the Italian republics before they perished under internecine strife and Spanish conquest. The Europe-wide acceptability of the *forint* depended on the favourable trading balance which replenished the Florentine mint with gold, and ultimately on the security of the city republic itself. The bankers were acutely conscious of the role wealth played in the intrigues between ecclesiastical and temporal rulers: they had to haggle over terms with the *condottieri*, whom they engaged to fight their battles: many of them had served in a *stato*, the staff of trained administrators which could be hired in the same way as professional soldiery by any ruler or council in need of competent men to run police, collect taxes, administer justice, conduct embassies, and test the weighing-machines. The *stato* had not yet acquired its legal, ethical, and even metaphysical connotation as the 'state': the Lombards knew it as an instrument of a ruler's power.

Description lags behind

Since the process has been one of flux and change in which circumstances often overtook the actors, the latter's own language of description and analysis has not infrequently been out of date and even misleading. The thinkers of the Renaissance and of the two succeeding centuries naturally enough tried to describe the world of commerce and finance in terms of number, weight, and measure, the basic elements of the merchant banker's skill. The most dangerous threat to wealth seemed the practice of debasement of the currency, the easiest and sorriest refuge of improvident governments. Treatises on coinage,

---

[1] The Fuggerbank, refounded in 1954 under the present Prince Fugger-Babenhausen, functions as a local Bavarian bank.

rent, and taxation by Tudor and Stuart writers, such as Sir William Pett, were concerned with 'just' rates, reflecting the grievances of merchants, tradesmen, and farmers. The standing armies and centralized bureaucracies of national rulers brought fresh burdens to classes and professions who in England and Holland had only begun to enjoy a tentative say in the running of the state. The wave of mid-seventeenth-century anti-monarchical rebellions, spreading from Naples to Portugal and northwards to Britain, reflected alliances, usually uneasy and short-lived, between nobles resentful of being despoiled of their older privileges and urban merchants and rural property-owners who had not fully secured their own.

The language of political revolt, couched in the borrowed vocabulary of theological discourse, attacked the inherited grievances—monopolies, 'unjust' levies, and unrepresentative tax burdens. John Locke, insisting that the laws of trade were 'akin to the facts of nature', advanced the concept of a natural rate of interest, and attempted to demonstrate valid equations between the volume of money and the need for it. Sir Dudley North extended the notion of supply and demand from money to rent and prices on the basic assumption that 'Trade is nothing but a commutation of superfluities'; he went on to sketch out how a natural equilibrium should regulate the movement of coins and treasure in a world of peace and freedom. Such a philosophy fitted in admirably with the aspirations of Amsterdam and London, which had assumed the role of active centres of finance once enjoyed by the Italian cities and the Hansa towns.

The resources of the Dutch bankers had been speedily organized in the service of political aims. Hardly had the Spanish yoke been thrown off by the United Provinces than a new threat to their independence loomed up from the centralized and expansionist French monarchy. Dutch courage and the English alliance were not the only two defensive weapons. The wealth of the Dutch Republics, the highest *per capita* in Europe, combined with the highest average rate of saving, enabled the Amsterdam bankers to raise loans—with interest guaranteed by the States-General—of up to 500,000 guilders for their foreign allies to cover the cost of campaigns now fought with paid soldiery. Raising this series of foreign loans, a task allotted to the Collector-General of the United Provinces, created a new mechanism for the speedy mobilization of funds, the issue of printed bonds on a basis of wide, popular participation, and paying arrangements for interest and principal. The scrupulous attention to the promises and undertakings of each issue made them a safe vehicle for savings drawn not only from the Netherlands but from England, Germany, and even

North America. The quoted list of authorized bonds with appropriate discount provided the basis for Amsterdam's great bourse, to which sound borrowers from all Europe could have access.

Amsterdam's organization was such that in 1693 only six weeks were required to raise a loan of 500,000 guilders for Spain, and, not unexpectedly, the Collector-General, who was paid $\frac{1}{2}\%$ commission on the amount of loans, had become one of Holland's richest citizens, with a fortune of 2,000,000 guilders, the present-day equivalent of £1,200,000. As a comparison, England's wealthiest men, the chief land-owners among the Lords Temporal, earned in twentieth-century terms an average of £16,800 per household per annum, while in one year the Dutch Collector-General's income rose to £63,000.[1] But on occasion England could also produce an impressive mobilization of funds. When in 1617 the East India Company invited the public to subscribe for £1,500,000 worth of stock, the list was soon closed with a thousand subscribers, among them thirteen dukes and earls, eighty-two privy councillors, justices, and knights, while the largest groups were 213 merchants and 314 tradesmen. Scotland's one great colonization effort, the ill-fated Darien scheme of 1698 in Central America, lost the country £450,000, half its realizable capital.

There was nothing self-regulating about the economic process which created or lost this wealth. The weakening of Spanish military power, the slackened vigour of Portugal, the exclusion of Venice from the high seas gave the new openings to the thrusting merchant companies of England, the Netherlands, and France. 'Peace', meaning the absence of civil strife at home, allowed the domestic credit basis to expand in an orderly way. But this did not mean peace on the high seas nor a 'natural equilibrium' in those overseas lands where the chartered companies set up their forts and raised private armies. This was conscious human purpose at work, and the increased wealth, whether from plantation, spice trade, or mine, was the result of planned endeavour. The backwardness of Spain, in spite of Peruvian gold and silver, demonstrated that bullion by itself was not wealth, not even—except in the appropriate political and economic context—an effective instrument for creating wealth. Among the commercial classes of the eighteenth century—the hey-day of the great merchant companies—the principal currency was neither bullion nor bank-notes but bills of exchange. Their circulation was directly related to the volume of trade, while coin was left for the expenses and daily needs of wage-earners.

---

[1] Figures and details from 'Private Life and Public Money: The Accounts of The Collector-General of the United Provinces, c.1700', B. E. de Muinck, *Progress*, The Unilever Quarterly, Vol. 51, No. 287 (1966).

So by the time Adam Smith had rightly diagnosed that the wealth of nations was the sum total of consumable goods, he, too, was out of date in his basic assumption that it was based on the annual production of grain. From this in turn he derived a logical series of corollaries on rents, wages, and prices. In fact, the profits of the joint stock companies blossoming out in every field of business were the new basis of economic expansion.

By the 1740s economic growth, particularly in Britain, France, and Bohemia, was accelerating, exports and imports were increasing in volume, and in England agriculture was bounding forward as a result of the technical improvements brought about by the enclosures. With their vast estates, their planned rotation of large-scale crops, the intensive use of fertilizers, their skilled breeding of pedigree herds, the English landed proprietors in their own mansions and elegant policies seemed outwardly as much the wielders of economic power as they were the dispensers of political patronage. But in practice wealth was again undergoing a significant qualitative change, which in 1803 could prompt the Duc de Richelieu to say: 'There are six great powers in Europe—England, France, Russia, Austria, and Prussia and the Baring Brothers.' The last had just completed, on behalf of the United States, the $15,000,000 Louisiana Purchase from France. 'Finance' had emerged as a major separate instrument of power.

There was another adjunct to the political armoury. Tom Paine, author of *The Rights of Man*, and of whom Baron de Cloetz had written in 1792 'A single journalist wields as much power as Brest, Toulon, and Rochefort', had still five years to live. It was one of the misfortunes of nineteenth-century Europe that it ascribed to both Man and Mammon an autonomy which neither had ever possessed, and ascribed to both rights based on natural or self-regulatory principles. In fact both Man and his Money were purposeful concepts whose validity was narrowly determined by their time and place of origin.

Rise of the merchant's bill

The rise of Meyer Amschel Rothschild, born in 1743 and founder of the modern house of Rothschild, epitomizes in one generation the evolution of the notion of wealth from coin-hoarding to conscious credit creation. Trained in boyhood with the Hanover bank of Oppenheim, he early found favour with an ardent numismatist at the local court, General von Estorff, on whom he called regularly with an attractive tray of specimens found in his daily exchange dealing. With an introduction from Estorff, Meyer Amschel became in 1769 Crown Agent to the Principality of Hesse-Hanau, with an estimated income of between 2,000–3,000 gulden.[1] By the end of the century his fortune was estimated at one million gulden, and he had built up an extensive trade in food, wines, and cloth, all of which had soared in price since the outbreak of the Revolutionary Wars. In 1797 one son, Nathan, had been sent to England with a working capital of 250,000 gulden and another to Paris to operate in the opposing camp. Trading in merchants' bills had become more profitable than handling goods, while with the growth of long-distance trade it was the movement of goods rather than their accumulation which created opportunities for massive profit.

So even in war-divided Europe a financial mechanism had come into being which served to bring interest and discount rates into equilibrium and apparently operated above and outside national jurisdictions. The Rothschild standing had been further enhanced by the appointment in 1800 of Meyer Amschel as Austrian Imperial Crown Agent. Although Napoleon's campaigns were at their height, the power of the Rothschilds' good name was such that they were able to raise seven large loans for the Austrian government.

Peace brought even greater gains. The House of Rothschild handled the transfers of French indemnities, totalling £120,000,000, to the victorious Allies. In 1818 the London branch raised its first big loan, £5,000,000 for Prussia. By 1848 some £200,000,000 had been raised through London for foreign borrowers, mostly governments, by Rothschilds. The Paris operations were on an equally large scale. All was not plain sailing. The Republic of Haiti borrowed 150,000,000 francs from Rothschilds and never repaid them—one of Europe's first essays at what is now called 'untied aid to developing countries'. In 1830, Rothschilds of Paris issued 80,000,000 francs worth of *rentes* for the government of Charles X, and the bank had to sustain them by massive purchases when the price fell by 20% to 30% at the time of the July Revolution. The much-publicized and risk-free purchase in 1876 on behalf of the British Government of the Khedive's £4,000,000 share in the Suez Canal seems small beer in comparison with such tasks.

Because war was a major stimulus to the creation of an international loan mechanism, the age of the great financiers has acquired its own myths and sinister connotations. Yet the appearance of a supranational freemasonry of private bankers and financiers wielding power

---

[1] At present purchasing power, approximately £7,500, while on the same basis one million gulden would be £3,000,000.

10

over peoples and governments proves on closer examination to be illusory. In the first place there was no tightly-knit conspiracy. While the bankers, particularly the London merchant banks, knew that success depended on a reputation for integrity and on observance of the canons of prudence and honesty, the competition among themselves was intense. The Rothschild family network, extending across Britain, France, Germany, the Austro-Hungarian Empire, and the Kingdom of the Two Sicilies, may seem to justify some of the accusations of an international Jewish financial solidarity at odds with national aims and welfare. But no quarter was shown by the Rothschilds in their battles to displace their Jewish competitors for *k und k* custom. The Viennese houses of Arnsteen and Eskeles, Frier, Geymüller and Steiner faded into international insignificance, particularly after the Rothschilds took over the financing operations for railway construction in Central Europe and the Balkans. A Hungarian conversion loan of some £50,000,000 was said to have brought the House of Rothschild a profit of £12–13,000,000.

The world standing and freedom of action of the bankers themselves depended on the free convertibility into gold of currencies of the major European powers and of the United States, and so ultimately on the ascendancy of free trade and the unchallenged right of individuals over the wealth acquired by their own efforts, irrespective of the effect of these on community aspirations and aims. This ascendancy in turn depended on the predominance of British power and on reasonable stability in the conduct and conventions of relationships between major states. The historical coincidence of these in the nineteenth century gave London its moment of concentrated political, commercial, and financial power, and as a market where everything could be traded it served the world well for half a century. The free convertibility of sterling meant that money and bills, commercial or governmental, could also be traded as commodities. In applying their skills the London bankers and bill-brokers were themselves creating credit, and so broadening the whole world process of manufacture and trade.

Central banks take over

By mid-nineteenth century the system was already under siege from national and political pressures. It had never been free from attack, not only from those who objected to being dismissed as 'unfit', and who in the forties were increasingly disposed to man barricades and challenge systems whose self-regulating virtues were mainly visible to the wealthier beneficiaries or to holders of professorial chairs.

In Britain's case it was the need to develop a coherent policy for the growing range of central banking operations which produced the main challenge. On the Continent, under both the uncertainly established democratic regimes or traditional authoritarian rulers, the new requirement was for conscious institutional rules to order and make the best use of national resources. Whatever the prevailing academic fashion in political or economic philosophy, the countries of the Western world were all embarking on a remarkably similar process of bringing national financial resources under the control of a central banking mechanism subordinated in turn to more or less coherently expressed political objectives.

In the first century after the Bank of England's foundation in 1694 its main task had been management of government debts and handling of state accounts. Revenue accumulated as government deposits on which no interest was paid. When payments exceeded revenue, the government was allowed to overdraw, but it had either to pay interest on the advances or have deficiency bills discounted. The Bank kept the books in which transfers of government stock and annuities were recorded, made dividend payments, and received a commission for its services. Bank and National Debt thus grew up together, the former's profit depending on the size of the latter. The Bank of England note issues, in practice circulating mainly in the London area, were but a small part of eighteenth-century currency, made up of the numerous issues of private and country banks and of bills of exchange.

Here again it was the Revolutionary Wars which forced a change in emphasis and a re-examination of the validity of ideas. During the eighteenth century, although theoretically the United Kingdom was on a silver standard, gold coin afforded the best practical measure of value for trade and exchange purposes, and enabled a reasonable tally to be kept on fluctuations of prices and wages. But as the country became more deeply committed in the wars against France, the gold coinage estimated at £20–40,000,000 virtually disappeared from circulation. In 1797 an Order in Council, later confirmed as the Restriction Act, suspended the obligation of the Bank of England to make payments *in specie*, while in 1811 its notes were declared to be legal tender. The object of this last measure was to protect tenants whose landlords had been demanding payment of rents either in gold—which was no longer available—or in notes to an amount which would enable them to buy gold on the market. Since notes were at a discount, debtors were having to pay higher rents. The Act of 1811 made it illegal to take a higher price in notes than in gold.

The motive behind the two measures was clear and sensible, but straightaway a debate was started which continues today. The increase in Bank of England note issues and the rise in prices and foreign exchange rates provoked alarm and public controversy, and with them the proliferation of monetary theories as a separate branch of political economy. The high level of foreign payments incurred by the war and not by domestic economic factors was the cause of the price fluctuations, but this did not prevent a flow of specialized studies on how the quantity of money affected prices and unemployment, and how discount and interest rates were determined by the marginal yield on capital.

The Bank of England itself held a straightforward view which the Medici would not have disputed. 'The real supply of cash can only be obtained by the effect of the general balance of trade in our favour,' said the Deputy Governor of the Bank to Parliament in 1797.[1] This remained an article of faith for some hundred and fifty years, and the nineteenth-century operation of the Gold Standard was based on this apparently simple and unambiguous belief. Under this, the selling and buying of gold between private dealers were presumed to have a direct effect on the domestic prices of countries with freely convertible currencies. Whenever exchange rates appreciated or depreciated beyond the point where the shipping of gold became profitable, bullion would be withdrawn from the central bank of the country whose currency exchange rate had fallen and be sold to the dealers and central bank of the country whose exchange had appreciated. The immediate effect of such transactions was buying pressure on the weak exchange and selling pressure on the firm exchange, and the movements continued until the shift in rates made the shipping of gold no longer profitable.

Where central authorities observed statutes or customs limiting their countries' credit basis, the direct effect of such transactions on their reserves was reinforced by secondary effects on the domestic volume of credit and eventually on interest rates. An outflow tended to raise interest rates by making credit scarce while an inflow reduced them. The result was a transfer of short-term funds from the country gaining gold to that losing it, thus bringing about more buying of the depreciated exchange. Finally the rise in interest rates and the contraction in credit caused prices to fall in the country with a depreciated exchange and thus reduced domestic demand, while the

---

[1] J. Raikes. Evidence to the Committee of Secrecy on Outstanding Demands on the Bank.

opposite phenomena were supposed to occur in the country with the appreciated exchange. The trade balance would therefore swing back and the exchange rates be corrected in due course, so that the process could begin all over again. This was orthodox financial theology until 1931, and it is not yet out of our system. There are still politicians who believe in it and professors who teach it to their students.

As a method it seemed ideally suited to the Bank of England's role of maintaining the reserves, and during the first decades of the nineteenth century when the world's stock of gold received only small annual additions, the system appeared to work, albeit at the price of recurrent social distress. After mid-century it *seemed* to be working magnificently, and the academic elaborations of the theory became more intellectually esoteric so that only other professors affected to understand them.

In practice the beautiful self-regulating system had ceased to operate. It maintained an appearance of still doing so, partly because of the increased flow of new gold through London from America, Australia, and eventually South Africa, but mainly because of the expanding basis of industry in all European countries and the open markets available to all those who could manufacture and sell. New forms of credit were being consciously created, even by the central banks themselves. The scale of government expenditure, for both peace and war, was making demands on the central banking system which could only be met by linking extensive revenue-raising and state-borrowing operations within new directive concepts. At the beginning of the nineteenth century, official dealings in securities were confined to Exchequer bills, mainly to give temporary support to the market at times of weakness. By mid-century large-scale Bank of England dealings in government stock had become the rule; as such securities became increasingly the backing for the note issue instead of commercial bills (as was the case in the eighteenth century), the Bank had set itself apart from the rest of the money market.

In setting a discount rate—the Bank Rate—above the market rate for bills, the Bank became a presiding authority available as a last resort in times of emergency, not just another rediscounting house. In 1877 the new Treasury Bill appeared on the advice of Walter Bagehot, changing a 'free' money market into one under central government influence: for weal or for woe the Treasury Bill has since been used as a major instrument of control over the cost and availability of credit to all sections of the community. From being a method of easing temporary government financial stringency arising from the irregular inflow of revenue, it had by the 1920s absorbed nearly half of the

14

short-term funds of the discount market, and by 1967 accounts for two-thirds of the assets of the discount houses.

The money market had thus been steadily subordinated to the needs of the state while the self-regulating theories could only have been valid if they had enjoyed universal application in a world where the predominating financial transactions between governments were those arising from normal trade. This was never so. The Crimean War caused a drain in bullion to the East, resulting in a City panic and a drop in reserves to £581,000. After the Franco-Prussian War the French indemnity to Germany was £200,000,000, requiring large-scale gold transfers of £6,000,000 a time through London by the Banque de France. The last year of this movement of gold saw twenty-four changes in Bank Rate.

In practice the United Kingdom was the only country which permitted complete free convertibility. The gold re-exported by London stayed in the reserves of other central banks or went into private hoards. Although by 1886 the world annual gold output had risen to 150 tons, the net imports of gold into the United Kingdom between 1871 and 1888 were only £4,700,000. When Bismarck put Germany on a gold standard and gave the death-blow to silver as a measure of monetary value, he drew away even more free market gold. The low interest rates in London stimulated large-scale foreign borrowing, and the financiers who arranged the loans drew their profit so long as the borrowers remained solvent. When they did not, as happened in 1890 in Latin America, the Bank of England had to step in to help Baring Brothers with liabilities of £28,000,000—a warning that in Europe at least the age of great financiers as operators independent of material power was coming to an end, and that central banking had consolidated its dominating position.

The basis on which it was consolidated was that of national authority, and it was with the willing co-operation of institutions and persons in Britain and its dependent and associated overseas territories that the Bank of England built up its controls. The Treasury and public bodies who had entrusted their funds to the Bank endeavoured not to embarrass it in times of stringency: neither they nor the commercial banks would have unloaded government bills and bonds on the market without prior consultation with the Bank. Because London was basically a creditor in the world, a rise in interest rates did not have to be so steep as to restrict or hurt home trade and industry, which in 1890 were carrying out their domestic operations by means of cheques. In 1833 the Bank of England had held £13,000,000 of deposits and the commercial banks £40,000,000; in the early seventies the proportion was £28,000,000 and £600,000,000, and from this last the money market derived its main liquid assets, not from short-term transfers from abroad.

By the beginning of the twentieth century commercial banks were expanding or contracting their advances, not automatically as the Bank Rate fell or rose, but on a basis of 'hints' from Bank officials. In 1905 for the first time the joint stock banks were 'invited' by the Bank of England to lend to it. None of them refused. The way was open for 'directive controls' and for the 'special deposits' which the clearing banks now have to make with the Bank of England whenever it is endeavouring to restrict internal credit. In essentials this was the same system which the Reichsbank, Banque de France, Banca d'Italia, and other European central banks had operated under statutory authority and was adopted by the United States Federal Reserve System set up in 1913 by President Woodrow Wilson.

Ideas hardly caught up with this important emphatic change in the methods of financial control. The nineteenth century had begun with a debate between Ricardo's view that interest was the marginal yield of capital and the City's daily belief that it was the price of money. The variants of quantity theories of money had drawn their apparent validity from the phenomenon that as an international creditor the City could bring in sufficient movement of funds to enable the Bank of England to replenish its reserves in the short term. So Britain appeared to finance its internal industrial expansion and its foreign trade with gold reserves which for over a century rarely rose above £22,000,000 and were frequently below £5,000,000.

But since the City was an international market, the flow of gold and paper was only a symptom, while from the end of the Napoleonic Wars until the Hungry Forties the symptoms were only alleviated by the gold standard itself at the price of stop-go. Hunger and distress were eventually cured and the prosperity of Britain and Western Europe renewed in the second half of the nineteenth century by the conscious invention of credit arrangements based on expectations of an increase of goods. The rate of interest had therefore never been a monetary phenomenon. The greatest need of the system—and one which the nineteenth century failed to meet—was to extend the conscious co-operation of the national agencies to the international field in order to stabilize interest rates, and protect domestic trade from the effects of temporary adverse balances.

Since the gold standard had been based on a myth, even a cherished one, it did not prove so difficult in practical terms to scrap it officially and go over to the so-called Gold Exchange Standard when world crisis hit Britain in 1931. This decision was the recognition that in monetary matters the role of gold was now that of a unit of account for clearing purposes between central banks. The short-lived British attempt at free convertibility between the wars had finally broken down because under almost universal tariff protectionism and large-scale Latin American and Central European default no 'self-correcting' element could operate to restore trade balances.

The substitution of 1931

For the gold standard the British Government in 1931 substituted control of exchange rates through systematic official intervention in foreign exchange markets, hoping that in practice the swings in the trade balance of the sterling area would not exceed £800,000,000. This did not diminish the risk of losing gold or foreign currency reserves as the result of a depreciating exchange nor prevent their acquisition from an appreciating exchange. But the risk no longer arose through the operations of private dealers who—except in special cases—are no longer entitled to draw gold from central banks, but as a result of official intervention by sale or purchase of foreign currencies for official central reserves. The successful operation of the system depended on the willingness of the participating governments to hold a major part of their reserves not in gold but in other currencies.

And this is the system to which formal lip-service is now paid by the central banks of countries which are members of, or associated with, the International Monetary Fund set up at Bretton Woods in 1944. The implication is clear. Participating governments are under a *de facto* international obligation as to the manner in which they conduct their financial policies.

The significance of the development is veiled by the apparent simplicity of the technical engagements freely entered into at Bretton Woods. The countries merely engaged their central banks and currency authorities to prevent an appreciation or depreciation of the United States dollar beyond 1% of the official exchange parity of their respective currencies. They agree to do this by selling or buying dollars to the extent required. This differs materially from any other system of money-changing. Nor is it rigid pegging which, since Roman times and even earlier, every government has tried at one time or another, and which at best has only been partially successful under wartime conditions when governments could enforce a monopoly of exchange dealings. It differs from the gold standard since it is based on official intervention and not on any automatic functioning. The authorities are entitled to convert into gold the dollars they acquire by support purchases at the official United States price of $35 per ounce and to replenish their dollar holdings by selling gold to the American authorities at the same price.

Paradoxically, the IMF system, by thus setting out the responsibility of national governments and so reinforcing their political authority in the domestic financial field, in another sense permitted an enlarged area of individual freedom. For the direct role of official exchange intervention was confined to limiting the fluctuation of IMF member currencies in terms of United States dollars. Within this framework the task of reducing the fluctuations of non-dollar currencies can be left to private dealers and commercial banks, which in this field now conduct a greater range of foreign exchange operations than ever before in history and can do so even more effectively in the interest of trade. Stability of non-dollar currencies can thus be ensured in dollar terms by official intervention.

At the same time there has been a renewal of international lending on a scale hardly seen since 1900. For under the general supervision and control of central banks and finance ministries, individual borrowers and lenders can enter into new forms of credit-creation. Profiting from their past experience of the gold standard, that whenever profit from interest differentials exceeded the maximum loss which could arise from depreciation, underwriters do not consider it necessary to cover the exchange risk in their loans. And because of the changed role of gold and foreign exchange reserves there is no automatic operation of reserve loss on the internal volume of credit.

It may seem hardly tenable to describe the Age of Great Financiers as having passed by the third quarter of the nineteenth century, when Goulds, Mellons, Vanderbilts, Rockefellers, Duponts, Carnegie, and Ford were still climbing to their pinnacles of wealth, buying up real estate, oil-rich lands, powder mills, and steel plants. Yet none of them played international roles comparable to the Barings, Rothschilds, or Morgans, and it was through their London connection that the last had been able to exert overseas influence. The power of American financiers was circumscribed by domestic political factors. The East India Company maintained its own armies while the great American financiers had to content themselves with hiring Pinkerton's strike-breaking experts. Like the Krupps, Schneiders, and others, they could, as members of an establishment, make their voices heard in political councils but their influence was no more than that of any other lobby. There was no higher appeal left to the House of Morgan when under a Federal banking measure they had to hive off their oldest type of business, that of company finance, and break their formal links with their erstwhile parent, Morgan Grenfell and Co. Ltd., of London.

Seen against the perspectives of history this whole process has since ancient times been one of finding fresh uses for old skills within new frameworks of institutionalized ideas. In the case of early human settlement and its direct exchanges of goods, gold, silver, and copper had served well enough as measures and storages of value. They represented tomorrow's demands for weapons, tools, and ornaments. But as merchants pushed further afield and brought new commodities to both markets and craftsmen, their promises to pay underwent a qualitative change into an institutionalized notion of trust or credit.

To the state this no doubt seemed an attractive new instrument of authority. But in trying to control the institution, governments also saddled themselves with the ancient myths and the time-lag of latter-day ideas.

2. Ideas lose their way

Expansion through privilege

Survivals and setbacks have also characterized the companion political process of the extension of civic privilege within its own institutionalized framework—the process called by the name 'liberty'. Although this evolution is usually described as deriving from a dualism of freedom and authority, both these appear in historical context as facets of the same growth of political power. But the problem of finding adequate contemporary descriptions has been no less difficult for political philosophers and orators than for economists, particularly given the recurrent paradox that apostles of freedom are frequently the advocates of causes which could utterly destroy civic liberty if they attained their objectives, while on the other hand demands for state action often come from those most reluctant to face the implications of strong public authority. Magna Carta, on which the British notion of liberty is proudly based, when read through appears less a charter of freedom than a safeguard for those whose handiest method of raising working capital was by persecuting and expropriating Jews.

However, in the liberal-humanitarian vocabulary of Tom Paine and his successors, the mind is supposed to advance through a process of emancipation from old thralls. To admit a need for authority is held to be a regression, and should be overcome by a love of freedom, or at least the need should be subordinated to some higher 'life-enhancing' principles. The latter turn out to be little more than tautologies for consciousness itself and bear an obvious kinship to the self-regulating virtues of economic liberalism. But when individual privilege, whether political or financial, is so firmly set within an institutional framework as to be inseparably linked with instruments of power, the practical issues of government which have still to be faced by those in charge generally depend on clarifying the nature of authority. This has not been easy to reconcile with the liberal preference for appearing right-minded rather than effective. Since the spur to the Western struggle for liberty was protest against arbitrariness, the practical requirement of privilege has been in essence a demand for more equitable authority. This conflict of concepts has not yet been resolved.

Because privilege has steadily extended under both authoritarian and democratic traditions, we have felt 'freer' and European institutions have generally fostered individual creative activity. Where they have acted negatively or oppressively, they have been overturned to the accompaniment of cries of freedom and of some therapeutic blood-letting, but were at once replaced by a new and usually more elaborate institutional superstructure. In this respect financial privilege was no different from the civic version. In the domestic framework, with all the inertia of tradition and environment, it was sometimes better to endure the irritating imposts; in new overseas settlements, if they infringed the privileged ways of planters and merchants, the cry of independence was not long in making itself heard.

The security of privilege, once attained, only released energies to seek new outlets, whether as soldier, merchant, or missionary. The phenomenon was neither metaphysical nor intellectual, but since it could be justified in terms of law and reasoning, it was natural enough in the seventeenth and eighteenth centuries to believe that an 'emancipation' in the whole field of human activity could be brought about by the growth and diffusion of knowledge, just as under their eyes they saw the physical extension of their universal notions by conquest and trade. They could hardly be expected to foresee all the consequences of both military and commercial endeavours.

'Man' sets a snare

Knowledge can oppress as well as emancipate, and even be as destructive as obscurantism. Human consciousness is liable to imprison itself when it gives a universal stamp to its objectified creations, and the intellectual mints of the Enlightenment were zealous in putting this on their medallions of 'Man'. It was perhaps gratifying that in a thousand years a human being should have been transmuted from a chattel—a unit of wealth—to becoming a universal measure of metaphysical value. But universal ideas stand in contradiction to the passage of time: conceptual reconstruction—Europe's special accomplishment—can thus become a hazardous process. The most thoroughly schooled people of Europe, the Germans, found themselves subjected to the greatest tyranny of all—that of ideas which had come to matter more than human beings. So in the end they turned men back into numbered objects in order to validate the ideas.

For 'emancipation' comes up against the same paradox as civic liberty. We may desperately feel the need to be detached and objective, but our mental detachment turns out to be only the recognition and rational description of our attachments, just as liberty has been only a rational description for privilege under authority.

For the philosophers, political and economic, had minimized— where they had not ignored—the possibility of there being different and valid categories of knowledge. Even where this was tentatively admitted, there was an immediate assumption that one type of knowledge was 'superior' to the others. Instinctive experience, if noted at all, was relegated to the savage past of 'Man' or left as a suitable subject for poetry. The passions were not to be put on an equal basis with reason.

But it was only in terms of the philosophers' verbal rationalizations that reason had been in conflict with instinct and had apparently pushed it to a lower position in the hierarchy of thought and experience. Here was their error. An idea does not become valid because it has taken on the appearance of an objective recreation of yesterday's action: submitted to today's test of action it is just as likely to be realized by skill or 'cunning', by our 'being able to', as by conscious knowing.

European economic thought provides the classic example of reasoning gone completely off the rails. There never was any 'Economic Man' any more than there had ever been 'Man'. It has never been possible to work out laws which could be submitted to tests of contemporary experience or prediction. One cannot rationalize the irrational or classify and predict the consequences of greed, short-sightedness, and illogicality. One can only look back on the wasted days of youth devoted to reading Marshall, Hawtrey, Beveridge, Pigou, Schumpeter, and countless others, and wonder why their much-lauded wisdom seems to have so little contemporary relevance.

Even though those concerned with the market-place have by rule of thumb evolved a cunning which prevents our economic affairs from being too chaotic, they too have to struggle with notions such as 'margin', 'excess', and 'growth': no doubt all these are admitted to be relative, but relative to what? Human purpose falsifies all the predictions, so that in the end economics proves to be nothing more than it was with its eighteenth-century founders—a study of human motives and institutions. Even if we make this rediscovery, we have to be certain that we are really dealing with 'human nature' and not with some imaginary creation of our own.

For in the process of conceptual recreation which is European history, there was another hazard to be taken. Once heightened human consciousness attains a certain intensity, it can take two courses: it can continue to fasten on external objects, or it can fasten on itself, on the subject. In fact it has done both. Indeed, it would have been surprising if it had not. As the discoveries—both geographical and scientific—opened up the prospect of understanding universal processes of nature and the restraints of organized superstition were removed, Europeans threw themselves into the analysis of creation. And since the eighteenth century had also apparently detached human nature from the rest of creation and made it a separate object of consciousness, it too came up for analysis. Here is 'Man'! Work out his universal process according to the same rules which are valid for external reality!

The implications were not immediately apparent. Described in the concepts of natural law, 'Man' was so useful. He provided elegant arguments for the French *noblesse de robe* in defence of their privileges and justified the subversive activities of Boston merchants and Virginia planters. At some point, however, human consciousness would start testing up to the edges of the concept of 'Man' to see whether it was a real object, whether it offered the individual as secure a sense of identity as had civic privilege, whether it could prove another useful instrument over one's fellow-men, or was simply a release for emotion. It appeared to promise all these. And human emotion was consciously turned full blast on to the idea of universal human nature. At first it was very bliss to be alive, even if the political corollary of equality—in its French version at least—tended to put all its heads in one basket, while in some of its financial applications the notion of Universal Man resulted in new forms of national insolvency; for it seemed that men still trusted gold more than pieces of paper issued in the name of liberty, equality, and fraternity.

It took a generation for the romantic notions of the fathers to be visited as intellectual concepts on the children. Not all the consequences were quite what had been expected. The sharper the surface clarity of the moral and political ideas about 'Man' and the higher the apparent motives of their exponents, the more uncertain became the prospect for 'Man' himself. If we all believed in ourselves as Universal Man, there was bound to be trouble the moment doubts arose. The clashes of identity were acerbated. The hitherto instinctive resentment of people with one language for administrators speaking another became a new, self-conscious nationalism, which before long had each nation proclaiming its own universality, making life as difficult for the Rothschilds as the assertions of independent princes had done for the

Fuggers. And again it fell hardest on the Hapsburgs, who had continued to follow the oldest tradition of European rule and for their *stato* had engaged competent men of any race or tongue.

Even without the social and economic issues raised by the Industrial Revolution and the advance of technology, this development would have ushered in a time of stress and strain. As the skill of using other men as instruments, power had to be wielded by much the same type of man, but in the new context of authority he had now to employ more elaborate arts of dissimulation. Given the numerous traditional-instinctive survivals in every European society, political compromise was not only a matter of reconciling material interests. For the new self-consciousness was in complete occupation of the intellectual stage, and with the development of communications the fashionable jargon was given rapid currency, even if the majority hardly grasped what the ideas were all about. If Schiller had sensed that there was a difference between naïve and sentimental poetry he could hardly have foreseen that one day we should also be enjoying naïve and sentimental politics, naïve and sentimental moralities, and even naïve and sentimental economics. But Sir Roy Harrod was on the way.

What happened to the British?

Ironically enough, at the end of a century and a half of self-consciousness heightened to an extreme, the British had undergone the widest divorce from external reality. To begin with, they had been less self-conscious than most. They had never taken 'Man' as seriously as the Continentals and the Americans. In their Bill of Rights they had led the van by defining 'privilege' in prosaic practical terms, their pioneering in economics took the form of Adam Smith's scepticism, and in creating the City as a working demonstration of a global financial skill they had headed the European commercial and imperial expansion. Where 'pure' external reality could be divorced from human purpose, as in the natural sciences, they had led the world.

So only wilful withdrawal from reality, an obsessive illusion with self, can explain the fall represented in 1961 by Vienna, leaving British governments as helpless as the Hapsburgs hanging on to the belief that their subjects were still *kaisertreu* while events careered off in another direction. And thereafter came years of growing confusion, sterling crises, the muddle of 1964, and the prospect of complete dependence on the goodwill or the self-interest of some other ten industrial countries. How had this come about?

The danger signals had functioned admirably. In mid-1964 sterling had reached its lowest rate in dollar terms for some three years. This was dismissed as seasonal commercial selling of pounds. In August 1964 the National Institute of Economic and Social Research forecast a growing trade deficit with no prospect of any automatic swing back into surplus, and pointed out that recent United Kingdom deficits had been financed by the reserves of the overseas sterling area which would soon have to be drawing on its balances. The Reserve Bank of Australia had already reported an appreciable deficit on current account, and from September onwards there was a continual drawing of reserves by Australia, Nigeria, Ghana, and India as well as selling pressure on sterling by non-sterling area countries. The old dilemma loomed up once more—either put right the balance of payments or restrict internal credit. But the then Chancellor of the Exchequer, Mr Reginald Maudling, mindful of the impending election, professed to see in the seasonal slowing-down of industrial production and retail sales a sound reason for doing nothing.

Even if the Chancellor's reasoning had been correct, it was based on a mythical premise, namely a steady 4% annual growth of the gross domestic product, estimated by the Government as the minimum requirement to create an export surplus as well as meeting home demand. In April 1964 the Treasury had warned that real annual growth was probably no more than 3%. After the General Election the cat was out of the bag! The new Chancellor of the Exchequer confessed on 7 December that the true rate was 2% per annum. There should have been greater suspicion when in February Sir Robert Shone, Director-General of the National Economic Development Council, had called for a 'new economic morality' to solve the nation's problems, for when 'morality' is on English lips, someone else is going to be asked to foot the bill.

The extent of the losses which led up to the end-of-year sterling crisis can be deduced from the $4,000 millions borrowed to enable the Bank of England to prevent devaluation by buying sterling in foreign exchange. The sums lent by other central banks and international institutions at the time of two previous major currency crises illustrate the accelerated deterioration of the British financial position—$1,300 millions at Suez, $2,000 millions in 1961—against a 'normal' gold and foreign exchange reserve of less than $3,000 millions.

The impressive speed of the Bank of England's action and the effectiveness of its subsequent foreign exchange operations were unquestioned. There was nothing wrong with the skills. But for this situation to have arisen—even allowing for the customary indecision, ambiguities, and outright lies of political life—there must have been either deficiencies in the functioning of institutions or incoherence in the framework of concepts.

There was no mistaking the consequences. When a country's borrowings exceed its reserves with no certain prospect that it can repay the former and restore the latter, it loses its financial sovereignty. If the aims of domestic policy, in so far as these are discernible, have to be subordinated for an indefinite number of years to international conditions for the maintenance of sterling parity, then Britain can at most urge or try and persuade in world councils: she cannot command. The period of 'full convertibility', and with it the assumption that sterling could be a reserve currency for other countries, had lasted less than six years, no longer than the interval between the restoration of the Gold Standard in 1925 and the cataclysm of 1931.

The great gold futility

A currency's acceptability for international trade and finance depends upon the prospects of maintaining its current value in terms of other currencies. If prospects are so uncertain that confidence is lost, the only recourse is to some more enduring measure of value, and 1964–5 saw the greatest gold-rush in history. The daily demand for gold, higher than at the time of the 1962 Cuban crisis, rose from an average $3,000,000 to $6,000,000, sometimes to double figures, and on one occasion to $30,000,000. De Gaulle's sale of dollars for gold was as much effect as cause, and the West Germans with less publicity raised the bullion proportion in their reserves from 54% to 60%. During 1965 China moved in with sterling and dollars to buy £40,000,000 worth of gold in the London bullion market. To maintain the gold convertibility of the dollar the United States Congress had to authorize the release of another $5,000 millions' worth of gold from the statutory Federal reserves, and there were sighs of relief in every capital when Russia restarted its sales, suspended in the spring of 1965, and which had provided half the last annual additions to the bullion stocks of Western central banks.

For though in theory civilization could have been possible without gold, nothing from mankind's past is ever lost completely from consciousness; 'gold' as a notion, as a metaphor, and as a description is deeply embedded in our daily thought and speech. The most powerful arguments in logic against its use are liable to be set at naught by the reminder that from mid-1964 to mid-1966 no fewer than eighty-one full or partial currency devaluations took place. In more than one hundred states, currency rates are determined by black markets which multiply as newly created states begin their nominally independent political existence by introducing foreign exchange controls: in some cases the turnover in such 'black' or free markets exceeds 10% of the gross national product of the individual country whose currency is being traded.[1]

Out of the 110 different monies of the world only the Lebanese pound and the Canadian dollar were in 1966 free of exchange restrictions. Since the key agricultural and industrial materials of the world, expressed in dollars or sterling, have risen 55% and 76% in price since 1939, neither governments nor individuals can be blamed for wishing to accumulate emergency bullion reserves. The logical case against devaluation may be indisputable, but:

> On ne dévalue jamais gratuitement pour le plaisir de dévaluer. On dévalue parce qu'on a commis préablement des bêtises qui rendent la dévaluation inéluctable.[2]

But the massive movements of gold arise today not as a result of the requirements of trade but because of its cheapness and availability in the London gold market, in its present form and functioning the most skilfully run futility in human history. Created on its existing basis in 1960 after the restoration of the 'full convertibility' of sterling, it represented the hopeful next step in re-establishing a stable system of exchange rates. A flight from the dollar into gold in the autumn of that year had raised the price to over $40 per ounce and dislocated the international arrangements for periodic dollar settlements between central banks. The nine chiefly involved in such settlements therefore agreed to ensure stability by forming a 'pool' to supply gold buyers. This would be replenished, first by purchases of newly mined gold from South African and Commonwealth producers—for whom the Bank of England acts as agent—second, from Russian sales through London bullion dealers, Zurich banks, or occasionally the Bank for International Settlements in Basle, and third—when required—by using the existing gold stocks of the United States Treasury and of the participating European central banks in the proportion of half-American and half-European.

[1] Figures from *Pick's Currency Yearbook* (1964–5 and 1965–6).
[2] *La Vie Française*, M. René Seillat (December 1964).

For the first two years of the pool, operations were fairly stable with matching demand and supply except for understandable upsets, as at the Cuban crisis. In 1963 the pool acquired over $600,000,000 worth of gold, and in the first half of 1964 at a time of substantial Russian gold sales to pay for foodstuffs, it gained even more. Since then there has been steady deterioration. South African supplies, the main source, have been coming in at $4,000,000 worth a day, i.e. $1,000 millions a year, while the daily offtake was $6,000,000. About half of this was taken by Asian hoarders or by international companies or groups with spare funds to hold. France not only acquired $300,000,000 worth of gold in 1964 but central banks of smaller countries increased their buying and the pool's previous gains were lost.

In 1965 the United States lost $1,664 millions' worth of gold, only slightly below the record of $1,689 millions of 1960. More than half the loss was due to French conversion of dollars, so that of France's $5,500 millions reserves, 85% was held in gold. The upshot was that world stocks of monetary gold remained at $43,000 millions while of the total of $1,900 millions of newly mined gold and Russian exports, some $1,600 millions had gone to private hoarding and to industry. By the end of 1966 the United States' monetary gold reserves had dropped by $575,000,000 to $13,159 millions, the lowest level since September 1938. The world's industrial requirement continued to rise, having already doubled between 1959 and 1965 to a total of $465,000,000. Asian hoards were estimated as having risen to $17,000 millions and, at the year's end, no gold had been added to the total of the world's special reserves.

What is the effect on trade of all this buying and selling of gold? Although bankers, economists, and politicians raise cries of alarm at the effect on world commerce of the gold losses of central reserves, the figures in fact do not bear this out. In 1913 Germany's gold reserves amounted to 9·9% of the annual value of her imports: in 1963 the figure was 51·9% and in 1965 the German authorities raised this to 60%. For the Netherlands the figures were 4% and 33% for 1913 and 1963 respectively, and for the United Kingdom 5·7% and 20·1%. Even in the two countries whose gold reserves were exceptionally large in 1913, France and the United States, the 1963 percentages were for France 40 as against 48·8, for the United States 68·1 as against 92·4. And over this fifty-year period the proportion of national reserves held in gold as against acceptable currencies has continued to decline, particularly since World War II. In 1938 the proportion was 93·8%, by 1953 it was 66·7%, and by 1963 61·6%, including the gold holdings of the International Monetary Fund and other international agencies.

An increasing proportion of gold has thus been going into private hands. Yet this has occurred against a background of an unprecedented growth of world trade and capital movements on a scale never before seen in history.

Logic—in so far as it can be applied to a subject where men's irrationality is involved—suggests two 'sensible' courses of policy for gold. Either the gold pool should be available only to central banks, treasuries, or official international agencies, and national authorities should then make their own arrangements with private interests for private purchases. Or gold should be freely traded as a commodity, allowing those who require it to pay their own price. The final outcome would probably be more stable prices for all commodities and a considerable disgorging of private hoards. The American objection to altering the present gold parity of the dollar, although based mainly on *amour propre*, is usually presented by Washington as a political question, since it would bring immediate profit to the two main challengers of the myths of 1776, the Soviet Union and the Republic of South Africa.

Yet if the immediate beneficiaries of the present system are the hoarders of Asia, the losers are the Americans themselves, for the fixed parity contributes to pressure on the dollar and to the fall in the United States' official gold stock. For the longer term, as the South African Minister of Finance pointed out:

> More than half of the free gold production outside South Africa is produced in countries which have already found it necessary to subsidise their gold mines and even here in South Africa the Government has had to come to the assistance of certain marginal mines. In the absence of revaluation there is little doubt that South African and other non-Communist gold production will within a few years begin to decline, and it is not beyond the bounds of possibility that within a couple of decades Russia—where economic considerations need not be the deciding factor—could become the dominant gold producer of the world.[1]

As if to underline his warning, the complete figures for South African gold output in 1965 at £350,000,000 showed a rise of only 5% over 1964, less than the average gains of recent years.

The official operations of the gold pool have thus not so far been demonstrated as standing in any causal relationship to growth or shrinkage of world commerce. For in human consciousness gold now plays a different role. In older recorded history it moved back and forward between centres of power, and where it accumulated over long

[1] Address to the Economic Society of South Africa, August 1965.

periods, as in the imperial Roman treasury, this was against the needs of war or political security. During London's century of ascendancy it served to prime the capital-raising machine but was not in itself capital, and traders showed confidence in the pound sterling by not changing it into gold. Even on the basis of the present dollar price for gold and the fall in monetary values, British reserves in 1914 were the equivalent of only $400,000,000 in present-day terms. But in the contemporary world the movement of gold between the world's major financial centres has again become determined by the political considerations of governments.

'Liquidity' debate begins

Similar uncertainty over the role of institutionalized forms of finance and credit characterized the growing international debate on the need for 'liquidity'. This should not mean anything more than the ready availability of assets which can be converted into media for payment. Are the assets to be ultimately convertible into goods by further exchanges or by the release of some productive process? But liquidity itself cannot be an end nor is it a sort of ectoplasm to be materialized by invoking the shades of the late Lord Keynes. Nor is liquidity to be equated with 'reserves' or 'credits'. The confusion has come in great part from trying to isolate quantitative symptoms and link them in some apparent objective cause and effect relationship—a hangover of the eighteenth-century fallacy of the existence of a 'superior' brand of rational knowledge separated from 'lower' human motivation.

The need for more 'liquidity' to finance trade is supported by the argument that world trade has expanded four times in money terms since 1938, while the credit base, by which is meant the sum total of the world's central reserves, is said only to have doubled. But if trade has quadrupled while the reserves have remained behind there is equally no direct causal relationship between trade and reserves. In 1964 when a 'world liquidity crisis' was reported to be reaching a head, the rate of increase in world exports, according to a United Nations Survey, was 12% compared with 5·9% and 9% in the two preceding years. In 1965 the overall increase proved to be under 8%, but once a breakdown had been made by countries no direct relationship could be shown between this percentage and national reserve situations.

Trade is financed by opening commercial credits provided it is possible to foresee with confidence the final stage of the transaction as an exchange of goods. Creation of more liquidity by the extension of credit on any other basis would result not in an increase in wealth but in the devaluation of the media of credit in terms of goods. The financing of long-term development projects is a problem of different order, where liquidity is a subordinate issue. In the general context of the financial situation of the major powers of the world, there can be no shortage of liquidity if the two so-called key currencies are in surplus and have to be held by other countries which do not want them. The confusion arises from attempting to draw a 'liquidity' analogy between national economies and individual overdrafts. An individual can do little more than call in his loans and/or cut down his spending to keep down his overdraft. A government can use powers to reallocate resources as between individuals and institutions, shift them from less productive to more productive sectors, and reduce one type of expenditure to increase another. Someone may have to go without, but there need be no overall reduction in resources.

The creation of a new framework within which instruments of finance can be purposefully operated is inseparable from the attendant issues of authority and privilege born of the evolution of self-conscious statehood. And these remained unresolved. Had United States' conduct of its own world policies been such as to inspire confidence in the American view of monetary 'universality'? Had Europe a common policy (as well as the economic capacity) to maintain a reserve currency of its own? How far could the United Kingdom still claim sovereignty over its own financial policy? Sterling appeared, like silver a century before, to be becoming a mere unit of account dependent for its acceptability as a medium of commerce and circulation on other currencies. Although in 1966 Western governments made much play with expressions such as 'a collective judgement of the reserve needs of the world as a whole' and 'long-term trends in global needs', by whom were these needs to be determined and under what authority would they be met? The authority of 'Man'?

Britain's downward financial course since the Vienna conference of 1961 seemed in part to result from a disregard of history's lessons. Even though each moment in history may be unique, human behaviour and relationships have their abiding patterns, so that old analogies are not irrelevant to new situations. If Commonwealth currencies were carrying faces and emblems as strange as those on the *solidus* of the provincial mints of disintegrating Rome, should we have been trying to maintain a sterling area at all? The acts of British governments towards their merchants and bankers seemed as arbitrary as those suffered by Jacques Coeur at the hands of Charles VII. The acceptability of a currency, as with the products of the Florentine mint, depends on a favourable trade balance and a healthy society. National credit depends as much as in the days of the Collector-General of the Netherlands, on the belief of the domestic financial community that authority is being exercised in the national and not a sectional interest. There can be no ignoring the nineteenth-century lesson that reserves are rebuilt and exchange weakness ultimately overcome not by elaborate manipulations of gold and credit mechanisms, but by an increase in goods.

Meanwhile, men can go on acting out old skills, many of them inherited—even in finance—from pre-rational and pre-verbal modes of conduct and communication. But the human make-up also includes a need for mastery: power is freedom for those who exercise it and freedom is lost by those who fail in its exercise. And the political and legal framework of the modern state has created a field where economic, technical, and scientific developments are brought together in one process, creative or destructive, while we are only in the first phase of the era of application of scientific discovery. Lenin found power in the gutter ready to be picked up and used, and if we, too, cannot direct it into a new and valid path of ideas it will once more be taken over by those who have at least retained their cunning and have a sense of action.

3. The English sickness

The West still thrusts forward

It is attractive, this temptation to believe that we can do without the ideas, carry on with the skills, and that in a setting of general trade expansion the power issues will eventually take care of themselves. Although there may have been some percentual ups and downs in world trade in latter years, for the period 1954–64 it has doubled—outside the Soviet bloc. Each year GATT reports sounded a note of warning but each new annual figure belied the pessimism, and in 1965 even those backward countries (euphemistically described as 'developing') increased their gross domestic product by more than 5%: in 1963 and 1964 they may have shown a net trade deficit, but this was not due to an adverse balance with the industrial West but to an excess of imports from the Communist countries. The less developed countries even showed a small 1965 surplus with the rest of the world. The growth-laggards were to be found in the centrally planned economies of the Soviet bloc.

In this setting the West keeps up its economic pace, with the internal trade of both EEC and EFTA consistently growing at higher rates than overall world trade. Manufactures rise faster than the output of raw materials, making 57% of the 1965 total world trade figure of $169,000 millions and giving better value to the buyers, since, on an average, the price of manufactures rises only 1% per annum. The great increase in world trade is accounted for by exchanges between industrial areas —from 37·1% in 1953 to 65% in 1965, while as a world percentage the exports of less developed areas have fallen from 27% in 1953 to 20·2% in 1964. The United States' share of exports, excluding intra-Common Market, has grown fastest, representing 14% in 1964, a total of $22,000 millions. Even gloomy forecasts for world trade in 1966 and 1967 did not suggest recession but only a slightly slower growth rate. Leaving aside the rising Japanese contribution, the continual extension of Western economic power is indisputable.

If the United Kingdom is playing a major part in this forward surge how can one then talk of an 'English sickness'? Against such a background can sterling exchange difficulties not be treated as a minor dislocation? And what is the 'sickness' which other Western countries are so fearful of catching? It is generally described as a form of cost inflation arising from low productivity per head of worker in comparison with Western Europe and North America. The outward manifestation of the inner weakness is that from 1958, when currency convertibility was reintroduced, up to 1964 United Kingdom exports increased by only 31% against a 74% rise of world manufactures, while the British share of total world exports fell from 17% to 13%. Although in the late 1950s and early 1960s, according to the IMF, Britain managed to keep its domestic price levels in line with other industrialized countries, its export prices rose by 9%, almost double those of most of her competitors. Germany and the Netherlands, after revaluing their currencies upwards by 5%, have not reached this figure in real terms. In the rather obsessive context of 'growth' (the annual increase of gross national product) the critical state of the patient is fully revealed.[1] In 1965 Canada headed the 'growth league' with 7%, followed by the United States, Australia, and Russia at 6%, Germany at 4%, the various other European countries between 4 and 3% and Britain remained at the bottom with a 2% growth.[2]

Yet Britain has not been a stagnant country. Even in the crisis year of 1964, its exports increased by £184,000,000 over 1963. Pressure on supplies may have been a main factor preventing an even greater rise, while in strict annual bookkeeping terms a £150,000,000 build-up of industrial stocks and an unusually heavy overseas investment of £251,000,000 may have caused the immediate critical trade deficit (leaving aside the net debit on government overseas account): but these were not evidence of stagnation. Nor is a gross national product of £28,691 millions. A net 1964 income from 'invisibles' of £610,000,000 showed that the £3,600 millions foreign investment built up by the United Kingdom since the end of World War II had been soundly placed. It can be argued that it might have been more profitably invested in Britain itself, where foreign capital takes a return of 10% per annum as against the 8·7% on the book value of British overseas investment. But this is also evidence that the British economy does yield a good return, and in practice the British capital account was not the cause of strain on sterling. Over the five years 1958–63 the main

---

[1] Gross national product (GNP) may be defined as the money value of goods and services made available to a national economy during one year.
[2] UN Economic and Social Council Report. Summary of Salient Features Of The World Economy (June 1966).

export of British capital was to the sterling area, and the United Kingdom itself was a net importer of capital from the non-sterling area— some £600,000,000. Over the same period the overseas sterling area was a net importer of £1,200 millions of long-term capital. The capital deficit of 1964 was exceptional, and has not recurred. The crisis arising in 1964 from Britain's short-term liabilities had nothing to do with its growth of overseas capital assets.

Of what, then, does the English sickness consist? If the general symptoms have been read aright, some powerful inflationary factor or factors are at work preventing it from holding its own in a competitive world. But after this point diagnosis falters and the doctors' dilemma begins. For where all is relative, as in financial and commercial matters, the isolation of a virus—if that is the correct analogy—may prove impossible, and the specialists will argue for ever over the significance of each symptom. Relatively some change in Britain's position was bound to happen, and through no fault of its people.

Similarly the declining British share of the main industrial exports of the world from 33·2% in 1899 to 21·3% in 1939 and 13·4% in 1966 means little as an isolated percentage in view of the expansion of the world total. The export of components to wholly-owned overseas subsidiaries of British companies, their assembly abroad, and repatriation of profits as 'invisibles' makes straight percentage comparisons odious. If one takes *per capita* export figures, Britain was in 1966 exporting $274 per head of population—80% more than the United States, and 25% more than France, although 40% less than Germany. If the British were in 1966 the biggest importers at $296 per head (with the Germans following at $288), their invisibles were at least sufficient to pay for this, and they had met the seemingly impossible post-war target set by the Attlee Government of increasing exports by 75%.

And the basis of confidence on which capital once flowed to London for rechannelling to the whole world has been destroyed by default and wars. If in 1850 our overseas investments at £500,000,000 were in real terms higher than today's £3,600 millions total, that, too, cannot be solely laid at Britain's door. The effect of war and instability was such that direct long-term British investment abroad which before 1914 was running at a yearly rate of £200,000,000 had dropped to £150,000,000 in the twenties and £34,000,000 in the thirties. New countries try to run their own insurance arrangements, by-passing Lloyds and investing the premiums to meet domestic needs. Commodity dealings gradually follow the same pattern. Although the City still contributes some £200,000,000 without any import content to our invisible earnings, the influence it once exercised through the whole globe has been dispersed and has not been recentred round any other national capital.

The residual importance of London is still significant: its international trading and financing activity is greater statistically than that of New York, even though the latter's domestic business may be larger than London's combined international and domestic total. But there is no one central font of capital creation as in the nineteenth century, when the world provided Britain with reserves by borrowing short and paying interest. The international mechanism of the City, while still impressive, exercises no outward power over other economies, and debt collection can no longer be backed up by gunboat. Talk of the restoration of London as the 'financial centre of the world' seems akin to the British claim to 'moral leadership'.

Sterling illusions

A belief that sterling is 'essential' for world trade has also been part of the illusion. By 1962 non-sterling area holdings of pounds at £605,000,000 had dropped below those of international organizations such as the International Monetary Fund and the World Bank. When the balances of payments of both the United Kingdom and major members of the sterling area, such as Australia, weaken at the same time, this additional liability to international organizations adds to the mass of unwanted or unusable sterling. Under such circumstances the pound ceases to be a world currency and becomes a global menace.

At the time of its creation in the 1930s, the basic philosophy of the sterling area was the assumption that Britain was the workshop and the overseas sterling territories were its suppliers of raw materials. Over a period of years, the see-saw of prices should therefore function as a self-regulating system; the loss in one country's portion of the central reserves would be restored in subsequent years and, allowing generously for an overall swing of £800,000,000, the reserve total kept in London by the Bank of England would eventually balance out. In 1964 this proved to be the deficit figure which the United Kingdom could no longer absorb, even against annual inward and outward trade and financial payments totalling some £14,000 millions. Here fully displayed was the statistical margin of financial power—or weakness.

In any case the pattern of trade had changed. The sterling area concept was defensive, designed for the depression of the thirties, and its inner disintegration began when in the fifties world trade expansion was resumed and the British economy failed to produce a continuously satisfactory balance of payments. Our chief raw material import—oil —has to be paid in part with United States dollars, which are spent elsewhere. Although higher prices of raw materials have gone far to increase the incomes of backward societies, these have been used only to a small extent to buy more British goods. Although between 1964 and 1965 imports by the overseas sterling area rose by 8%, those from the United Kingdom increased only by 3%, while intra-sterling trade was down by 3%. Even attachments of sentiment and loyalty did not offset the trend, since in 1964 Australia's total imports rose 12% above 1962, and New Zealand's, 30%; yet their imports from the United Kingdom rose only 6% and 9% respectively. In 1966 the trend was continuing: a decrease of 1% in the first quarter's sterling area imports compared with the same period of 1965 masked a 5% drop from the United Kingdom and from each other, while those from North America had risen.

The export pattern of the sterling area tells the same story. Over the first quarter of 1966 sterling area exports to the United Kingdom were rising by 4% over the previous year but those to the non-sterling area by 9%, while exports to each other by overseas sterling area countries decreased by 8%. The pre-war global commodity-workshop pattern was likewise altered. In 1964–5 a large increase in the prices of copper, tin, and rubber was offset by a fall in those for wool, sugar, coffee, and wheat, so that Commonwealth exports rose by 4% compared with the world's 13%, and at the same time Commonwealth imports rose by only 1%. The former workshop of the world has become heavily dependent on Europe for machine tools and on the United States for sophisticated electronic equipment. The changed world situation is not of Britain's making, but one feature of the English sickness was unwillingness to recognize or at least admit the change.

The only free movement of capital within the sterling area has in recent years been from the United Kingdom to the other members. The non-Commonwealth members—Burma, Iceland, Eire, Jordan, Kuwait, Libya, and South Africa—have kept increasing proportions of their own reserves in gold and currencies other than sterling: the abuse of this privilege led to Burma's expulsion in 1966. When the margin of balance has become so narrow, major damage can be caused by misjudgements such as the upset in copper supplies and the forced switch to American tobacco resulting from arbitrary United Kingdom action against the Rhodesians. If for the year 1966–7 a small surplus for the sterling area seemed likely[1] Commonwealth finance officials meeting in London in July 1966 admitted that over the past twelve years the trend was for the current deficits of most sterling area countries to increase, and that these would have to be offset by greater capital inflows.

And when we turn to possible domestic reasons for Britain's economic difficulties, the debate—usually launched round the theme of wages and prices—invariably becomes an argument over what is cause and what is mere symptom. At best a consensus can be reached that in the United Kingdom higher rates of productivity have not kept pace with the advance in money wages, while on the Continent and in the United States increased productivity has absorbed the increases. Britain also appears at the bottom of the list for the proportion of national savings devoted to productive investment and to the essential structure of public services such as railways, highways, ports, fuel, and power.[2]

What, then, has deterred British enterprise from investing as much net new productive capital as its competitors? Has it been the protection of comparatively high tariffs and would it thus be better to be a low tariff economy such as the West German one and be exposed to the full blast of competition? Is the low investment rating the result of a 'real' shortage of savings or of their misapplication? If labour has been hoarded and underemployed, was the initial fault that of the employers or of the trade unions? They both seem equally responsible for the later stages of the situation. The English sickness cannot be caused by the *per capita* cost of the 'Welfare State', since the total cost of social services as they fall on taxpayer, employers, and employed is approximately the same as with most of our successful European competitors.

The doctors' dilemma

In the end, then, the English sickness appears traceable to a failure of

[1] The surplus of the overseas sterling area with the rest of the world for the first nine months of 1966 was in January 1967 provisionally estimated at £450,000,000.

[2] Comparative figures given in *The Times* of 20 October 1966 for investment as a percentage of gross national product were:

	%
Japan	28·8
West Germany	23·7
Italy	21·6
Sweden	22·8
France	19·2
Denmark	18·7
Belgium	18·4
USA	17·1
UK	15·8

will or recognition rather than to some quantitative first cause. And the failure of recognition seems to begin among the diagnosticians themselves. Economists, both academic and those in government service, have succumbed too easily to the temptation to isolate the surface phenomena of inflation, present them as a basis for their favourite theory of cause and effect, and thus demonstrate another intellectually satisfying and self-regulating system. According to the theories, either 'demand' or 'rising costs' must be the cause: governmental remedies should therefore be either restriction of money in the hands of potential spenders by means of credit policy, taxation, or legislation, thus dampening their demand or the restoration of a missing competitive factor to bring down costs, such as the creation of 'spare' labour or 'spare' capacity.

Even in a field of study necessarily lacking in current data for definite proof or refutation, the irrelevancy of such general lines of thinking can be only too easily illustrated. In November 1961, for example, the OECD Ministerial Council proposed a growth rate for its member countries of 4·1% per annum between 1961 and 1970. The British representatives accepted this as both feasible and probable, although such a rate would have required a doubling of fixed capital investment at home over the next ten years. Two months later, Treasury figures showed that British manufacturers who had originally estimated that they would be spending 1% *less* in new plant and equipment in 1962 than in the preceding year had made a fresh calculation that they were, in practice, spending 5% *less*, and for 1963 considered that they would spend 10% *less*.

Yet over the same period the British Government continued to follow a deflationary policy (allegedly under the influence of the theories of demand inflation by Professor F. W. Paish of London University) when, judging by the rising costs on the production side of the economy, our troubles probably arose from cost inflation. In his writings Professor Paish continued to preach the existence of an 'excess demand for labour' when the statistics for the years 1952–61 indicated that there was no excess demand at all. In the years when unemployment did go up there was no slackening in price rises.[1] But by 1966 Professor Paish had moved on from explanations of why his theories did not seem to be valid to the advocacy of courses of action which would validate them—and that is more than professors have a right to demand.[2]

---

[1] Professor Paish's ideas are set out in 'Studies In An Inflationary Economy': *The U.K. 1948–61* (Macmillan, London 1962).

[2] Articles in *Daily Telegraph* of 16 February 1966 and *Financial Times* of 27 April 1966.

There is an 'unused margin' in existence, such as Professor Paish requires to help to reduce inflationary pressure, namely the 30% average unemployed capacity of modern plants in Britain and the fact that production per man is only half that of identical machines in the United States.[1] In addition, British maintenance engineers are employed 30% to 60% of their time as against 85% in most industrialized countries.[2]

In all fairness to the Professor—who is a stimulating writer—his definitions were not the only ones in fashion at the Treasury where officials are quick to seize on any catchword which looks like finding Ministerial favour. But 'demand inflation' and the 'creation of spare capacity' seemed to be the sort of factors which could be made to operate through traditional money-market manipulation. There are, however, so many methods of creating credit or speeding up the circulation of monetary substitutes which elude central control that government measures based on the assumption that to control the money supply is to control inflation proved to be little more than the treatment of minor symptoms without attacking the malady of a too slowly growing economy.

Economists who have probed into the problems of increasing productivity, such as Dr Nicholas Kaldor (now installed in the Treasury as special adviser to the Chancellor of the Exchequer), have rightly seen that the theoretical answer must be an increase of resources rather than a restriction of demand, and that full employment should theoretically create more growth than creating unemployment. High rates of investment and a rapid return on new investment should bring a faster rate of growth because technical innovation and the rate of accumulation will continually increase capacity. Since Kaldor's system makes profits depend upon the propensity to invest and desire to consume, the injection of new minds, new ideas, and new techniques is seen as the motive power of the system. The distribution of income is consequence rather than cause of the rate of growth, and Kaldor's 'mature' economy is a state of affairs where real income per head has reached broadly the same level in the different sectors, extractive, manufacturing, and servicing.

But the politicians whom Professor Kaldor has chosen to serve, whether in Britain or overseas, have, alas, fastened on to his ideas on taxation as a means of 'rectifying' the 'inequities' of distribution in favour of wage-earners. Doubtless in backward communities where inequalities of wealth seem most blatant, taxation may theoretically

---

[1] 'Making Good Use of Inflation', Harold Wincott, *Financial Times* (26 July 1966).
[2] 'Britain in Blinkers', William W. Allen, *The Sunday Times* (12 June 1966).

40

take the place of saving. But capital gains taxes, property taxes, and profit taxes, however effective as instruments for exacting levies from those who manipulate balance sheets, fail to provide the incentives without which there will be no new ideas and no new techniques.

Sadder still, but not surprising, is the collapse of the Keynesian succession. For the late Lord Keynes was never a very consistent person. His 'General Theory' was a very generalized explanation of a hypothetical relationship. Total income, he suggested, was composed of investment and consumption, and alterations in these two factors determine the level of economic activity, employment, and interest rates. The propensity to save (i.e. not consume) and to invest is the determinant of consumption. Since human expectations as to the relative attraction of goods, securities, or cash is the major influence on both private and industrial investment, changes in interest rates are by themselves insufficient to alter the level of confidence, and only changes in output levels can hope to succeed. The way out of depression was for Keynes to spend, not to retrench or deflate further. The notion of public works in times of distress was not new. It had preceded Keynes by some four thousand years under the Pharaohs. But re-enunciated in modern terms and backed by Keynes' personality and dialectical skill, 'deficit spending' became the new orthodoxy. And having restated Pharaonic skills Keynes took his own wisdom to the grave.

The economists' preferences, even their moral ones, are natural enough in view of the eighteenth-century origins of their vocabulary. While this has kept it a lively rather than a dismal science it has played havoc with their capacity for disentangling cause and effect. The reaction has been the emergence of other schools trying to make their science mathematical and abstract, concerned with what is, rather than what should be, and seeking methods of excluding 'normative' elements from what should be 'positive' judgements. So the models and parameters now in vogue among planners are attempts to reduce the complex economic process to abstractions lending themselves to mathematical symbolization, and believed to be capable of demonstrating ideal functional relationships.[1]

But even mathematical and mechanical notions of self-regulation suggest a perfect state hinting equally at eighteenth-century ancestry. Theories of cycles, whether of investment, production, or demand, tend to suffer from this a-historical approach. For each moment of

---

[1] In the sense used by statistical economists, a parameter is a quantity which is constant in a particular case considered, but which varies in different cases. Perhaps its astronomical usage is equally apposite: 'The data necessary to determine the orbit of a heavenly body.'

history may introduce a new factor and even the economist's own theory, by affecting men's ideas, influences subsequent actions. Action knows no model situations, only imperfect recognitions and approximations, and follows single precedents. 'Why not?' says experience. If something has once worked, it will probably work again. And except within extremely limited fields of offer, 'free' preference exists as little with abundance—the prevailing economic phenomenon in the West—as with scarcity. Human beings cannot express preferences which are isolated from the material factors of environment while the whole trend of European economic activity has been one of conscious interference in men's lives through manufacturing, marketing, and financial processes.

The one proposition to which Paishites, neo-Keynesians, and parameter experts all subscribe, is that 'spare' or 'surplus' productive capacity must be created by one means or another, whether by disinflation or growth, if Britain is to escape from its recurrent dilemma of choosing between currency stability or economic advance. Yet in the 1930s the consensus of economic opinion, including Keynes himself, was that the capitalist world had become a 'mature economy' (the expression was even then in vogue) in which growth had outstripped consumption, where capital surfeit and surplus productive capacity made for stagnation and depression, and where the mule, stubbornly refusing to drag the plough through the growing corn so that the American farmer could qualify for a Federal grant for ploughed-back crops, symbolized out-of-date moral notions about God's bounty. The moral argument is always the most short-lived. Although today the eighteenth-century enclosures still cannot be 'morally' justified, without them there would have been no profitable large-scale farming and the growing working population of the Industrial Revolution could not have been adequately fed. Revolution and political instability might also have been Britain's lot in the nineteenth century.

So the clamour of voices—reflation or devaluation, liquidity or discipline, parameters or models—indicates that economics is suffering from the same fate as theology after mankind had ceased to be regarded as a separate order of creation. In spite of the dialectical skill of the theologians their subject took on the character of verbal narcissism, and this may also be happening when financial realities fail to correspond to the basic propositions of economists. Capital does not flow from surplus to deficit countries but piles up in Germany and Switzerland. In credit squeezes the weak survive and the strong are held back, from which it would appear that 'disinflationary measures' are in practice pushing up the cost of production per unit and preventing industry from benefiting from large-scale productive innovation. Holding down consumer demand cannot cure cost-inflation, while large sections of society have found effective ways of defending themselves against both deflation and inflation. The expansion of profits and liquidity of funds which follows the relaxation of a credit squeeze thus results not in increased production but in inflation, so that each 'go' has bred its future 'stop'. With sterling facing a basic situation of a ratio of international liabilities to liquid assets of four to one, the national financial position must remain one of weakness, not strength.[1]

Was Whitehall innocent?

With such inconsequentiality in the language of economic description, successive Chancellors of the Exchequer seem almost innocents although, given the milieu of sophistication in which they function, innocence can hardly be regarded as the appropriate attribute. If their Treasury advisers entered their profession before government departments were expected to have competence in such matters, both politicians and civil servants do nevertheless make some attempt to re-educate and re-equip themselves as do members of other callings. Most of them acquire a nodding acquaintanceship with the fashionable jargon by reading a selection of the books and articles on what is wrong with the British economy, while all pay lip-service to the notion of deficit spending. Until the great 'freeze' of 1966–7 the Treasury routine of implementing this as 'financial policy' was well established, proposing to Ministers an easement of credit, marginal tax reductions,

[1] On the eve of the 1964 sterling crisis, UK sterling claims on other countries totalled £1,069 millions while its liabilities were: foreign governments £2,444 millions, international organizations £619,000,000, private holders £1,290 millions. The series of loans, stand-by credits, and government security transactions since then have obscured the basic liability situation although in the first quarter of 1966 official statistics showed external liabilities to all countries as having fallen by £37,000,000. But by the end of the year liabilities to North America and Western Europe had risen again by £336,000,000 and sterling liabilities to international organizations totalled £1,656 millions. Total sterling liabilities were given as £5,145 millions at the end of 1966. The United Kingdom's gold and convertible currency reserves stood nominally at £1,118 millions in January 1967. The £11,000 millions of British overseas assets, made much of by Mr Harold Wilson, would not lend themselves to liquidation within any time-scale which would prevent crises of the 1964 order. Nor would this be possible without permission of national governments who would have to cope with domestic market reactions. Capital and current accounts represent different types of claims.

and extensions of public-authority borrowing whenever the Ministry of Labour reported a more than seasonal increase in unemployment, or the Board of Trade foresaw a falling-off in industrial orders. If prices had been rising sharply and Britain seemed to be importing 'too much', the procedure was reversed.

A similar rule-of-thumb is followed by most Western European governments and their central banks. So what is the British sin? Wrong timing is the usual accusation—that deficit spending was launched when recovery had started, so that boom became inflation, or that the brakes were applied when the boom was really over. Government statistics are so incomplete that anticipation of economic trends is little more than intelligent guessing, and even retrospective analysis fails to verify how near the mark were the financial suppositions. The Treasury, it is usually suggested by financial journalists, works in too rarefied an atmosphere, if not in a vacuum, and if Chancellors brought in better-informed outsiders such as financial journalists, all would be well.

But the 'booms' and 'slumps' only seem marginal to the basic weakness of an economy suffering from inflation and from an inability to bring about rapid increases in productivity. And the greatest single factor making for inflation or deflation, namely government expenditure, continues to rise, irrespective of 'stop' or 'go'. If one set of taxes is marginally reduced, another is increased, and government borrowing merely changes labels—from gilt-edged issues to Treasury Bill operations or to debt increases by nationalized industries.

The prevailing ethos among Treasury officials is a sort of playful scepticism which finds reinforcement from the clash of contradictions among academic economists. The one situation they have all feared— mass unemployment—appeared to have been averted by World War II and its aftermath, bringing massive investment and diversification to what in pre-war days had been an overspecialized and under-capitalized industrial system inherited from the age of coal and cotton. The choice of verbal adornment on economic memoranda for the Cabinet has been a secondary issue, and Treasury officers concerned with planning from 1947 onwards—Sir Roger Makins, Sir Edwin Plowden, Sir Leslie Rowan, and Sir Denis Rickett—felt no need to probe deeper. When other persons put up embarrassing arguments or proposals, they could call on their expert advisers, first Sir Robert Hall and then Professor Cairncross, to pick holes in them without requiring them to put up positive alternatives. The main task of the Treasury was still the Budget and the control of departmental expenditure. Its other responsibilities—money, credit, and government borrowing—

were increasingly handled for them by the Bank of England after its nationalization in 1948: the detailed skills for these were gradually lost to Whitehall and the officials' sense of involvement in the outcome of the operations steadily weakened.

The responsibility for economic co-ordination was only transferred to the Treasury in 1947, when Cripps took over at short notice as Chancellor from Dalton and brought across his functions and staff from the Ministry of Economic Affairs. Since the Budget remained the Treasury's annual exercise, it was simple to erect it as the totem round which all would dance. Cripps enunciated the doctrine in 1950: 'Indeed the Budget itself can be described as the most important control and the most important instrument for influencing economic policy that is available to the Government.' That may have been so. But what was the economic policy itself? This was never agreed, and the upshot was that economic surveys and forecasts were written with a view to budget policy and departmental considerations, and not the other way round.

The risk is less one of misjudgement than that judgement is never brought to bear. The unthinking approach was revealed in the excessive devaluation of sterling in 1949 instead of the choice of a narrower rate which could have been subjected to later adjustment. The aim had been to improve Britain's competitive position, but the size of the sterling drop (from \$4·00 to \$2·80) provoked devaluation by other countries and added to inflation at home, fostering an almost obsessive desire on the part of subsequent British governments to avoid further devaluation. As it turned out, the government statistics on which the decision was made to devalue, based on customs returns and reported foreign exchange transactions and authorizations, were inaccurate. The aggregate balance of payments deficit from 1946 to 1948 was thought in 1949 to be £1,100 millions. It later proved to have been only £694,000,000, and by 1948 the trade gap had almost been closed.

A second error of this nature was the failure of Mr R. A. Butler, as Chancellor of the Exchequer, to challenge his Cabinet colleagues on the issue of wages outrunning output by some 5% per annum. This first became apparent in 1953 and continued uninterruptedly during his Chancellorship. In a purely political context the appeasement of trade unions can be justified but, as then practised, was incompatible with a policy of controlling inflation through monetary and credit instruments. This was the 'wrong turning', since when Britain has had to take the low road. The deterioration of the quality of government, first under Eden but mainly under Macmillan, caused a general spread of cynicism, indifference, and personal irresponsibility, which has probably corrupted a whole generation of politicians and civil servants.

The decade 1955–65 illustrated the widening gap between political motivation and financial realities. The 1955 April Budget policy offering £135,000,000 in tax reliefs was announced by Butler when wage increases had caused domestic demand to expand and imports to soar. In the summer it had to be abruptly reversed and the reliefs cancelled out by an autumn budget. The need for a longer-term policy of encouraging industrial investment had not in any case been met by the piecemeal allowances of Butler's spring Budget. Macmillan, succeeding as Chancellor in 1956, talked of expansion but introduced further restrictions, which left business uncertain and stagnant during the year. After the Suez crisis Thorneycroft took over, and in accordance with the Tory need to prove that all was now well began with tax reductions and confident reassurances. By the autumn he was raising the Bank Rate from 5% to 7% and cutting private and public investment to cope with what proved to be Britain's biggest loss of gold since the war, largely precipitated by a spate of rumours of pending currency changes following the devaluation of the French franc. By then Thorneycroft and his Treasury Ministers had seen the necessity to hold down the uninterrupted rise in government expenditure. Their attempt ended in resignation.

So Heathcoat Amory reigned in their stead, and although as a result of Thorneycroft's measures the balance of payments seemed to be in order and production was declining, he played a mouse-like game. By the time he was ready to give the economy a boost by easing hire-purchase controls it had already started to pick up by itself, so that a special pre-election give-away Budget in 1959 pushed the United Kingdom into an 'investment boom', over-employment, spectacular wage rises, record imports, and a large trade deficit. Selwyn Lloyd was given the task of putting on the brakes. In 1961 an increase in Bank Rate, an emergency Budget, and an IMF drawing had all to be arranged simultaneously: this was at least more expertly executed than in 1965, when the Bank Rate was raised and its psychological effects allowed to evaporate before a patently inadequate IMF facility had been negotiated. But since 1962 confusion has reigned whoever has been Chancellor. Both monetary and prices-and-incomes policies are said to be applicable, deflation is the cry but inflation persists, money is said to be taken out of circulation by the introduction of new taxes and by increases in existing ones but soaring government expenditure puts it back.

In honesty it must be recalled that the formal acceptance of economic stability as a chief responsibility of government dates only from the 1944 White Paper on Employment Policy. The men who had to carry this out could only use the language of their time, and the notion which was most appealing was the control of the aggregate spending of the whole community. But 'national income' in one fiscal year is still only the sum total of all individual incomes, and the elements of delay even over a twelve months' period are such that accurate estimates require statistical services which no British government has yet possessed. Manufacturing expansion decided on during a recession may result in an excess in demand in some other sector of the economy as much as two years later. It is only when customs-house returns point unambiguously over a long period to dangers to the balance of payments from some particular demand for goods, or if unemployment is visibly growing in specific industries, that a British government can tentatively select the appropriate category of taxation to control demand. Timing is not easy.

But the Treasury and Bank of England insistence on the Bank Rate weapon and their underestimation of the growing hire purchase credit sector are less excusable. The failure at an early post-war stage to produce a working hypothesis of relationships between government expenditure, private investment, and gross national product and make this a basis for forward budgeting cannot be justified. Nor have the longer-term trading factors ever been carefully assessed by government. Is our long-term export position really deteriorating, and should Britain therefore not plan a long-term import policy to offset this? At home under the conditions of a sellers' market and rising wages, the increased interest rates rising from the Bank Rate weapon have an inflationary and not a deflationary effect, as they are passed on to consumers, while a $2\frac{1}{2}\%$ rise in the Bank Rate adds a considerable burden to the interest payable abroad on Treasury Bills and short-term sterling liabilities.

A national conspiracy

Within this confusion of general ideas and fumbling action by central authority, the performance of the British economy is remarkable for its steadiness, whatever its other alleged shortcomings. It is as if its practitioners—industrialists, bankers, investors, managers, and workers —had among themselves reached a sort of equilibrium of effort or balanced pace which met their needs from year to year. The pace is perforce a slow one. Britain's 3% industrial growth rate remained behind that of Western Europe and the United States of America. For manufacturing industry as a whole productivity per worker rose 2·3% annually from the end of the war up to 1961 compared with 3% in the United States, 5·7% in France, 6·6% in Italy, and 9·2% in Japan: these are also countries enjoying annual growth rates two to three times higher than Britain. By 1964 output per man in the United States was about three times above that in the United Kingdom, and in France twice as high.

Public ownership made no difference. Comparison between British and North American productivity shows the former in its most unfavourable light in the case of coal, gas, and railway transportation— all nationalized in the United Kingdom. The United States' productivity per worker for these sectors is 4% and higher, and for Britain under 1%. For electricity the figure for both countries was the same at 4% plus, understandable enough, since the basic equipment, layout, and staffing of a power station is much the same the whole world over.

Before we damn the worker, we had better look at the capitalist. Statistically speaking, he is cast in the same mould. As a proportion of the national product, annual new private investment in manufacturing reached 5% in 1961, fell to 4% in 1963, rose by 9% in 1963–4 to just above the 1961 total (£1,219 millions), and evened out at 5% for 1965–6, the bare level required to keep fixed plant and equipment up to date, while there was actually a fall in engineering and steel. Board of Trade estimates in January 1966 considered that the real rise was then no more than 2·5% and by mid-1966, investment was still at the same level as in the last quarter of 1965. After this came the 'squeeze', when the capitalist could do no more and the only argument about the prospect for 1967 was whether the consequent *drop* in manufacturing investment would be 8% or 20% from the existing level.

The comparison with European countries is saddening. West Germany has on an average invested 9%, France 6%, and Italy 7% of national resources measured as a proportion of gross national product. If between 1957–9 and again between 1961–3 British investment in manufacturing had actually fallen, this was at least a tribute to the effectiveness of the 'credit squeeze' of Messrs Thorneycroft and Selwyn Lloyd. But in Germany there were no falls over the same period, at worst a *rallentando* in the rate of increase. The best British achievement was a 10% investment rate released for some months by the 1964 pre-election 'boom', a somewhat misleading figure since it came mainly from the chemical industry, which accounts for 20% of all industrial investment.

The outcome has been that the prices of all company assets have since 1958 grown by little more than 2·3% a year, which represents little change in real terms. Nearly one third of some 2,000 companies reviewed by the Board of Trade in 1963 showed less than this rise.[1] The inflated prices paid in take-over bids between 1958 and 1961 cannot have helped here, although the resultant concentration may have brought other gains. The state of Britain's industrial equipment is best illustrated by comparison with the annual growth of its overseas assets, i.e. some £700,000,000, the rough equivalent of a 7% growth. Since 1964 the effect of Callaghan's reduction—by use of a Corporation Tax—of the value of Butler's investment allowances has begun to make itself felt, while his substitutes have still to prove their effectiveness.

These overall figures and percentages may obscure the advances in technology and efficiency in many sectors of British industry. But they do help to explain the growth of imports of machinery and semi-finished products. This had reasons other than limitations of capacity or straight price competitiveness.[2] An economy characterized by active investment is one where design and delivery of capital goods and equipment enjoy a high priority. As far as the quality of British investment is concerned, it was considered by Sir Robert Hall (emerging after retirement from his shell of discretion) that much of this had taken the form of straightforward additions to existing productive capacity and not to complete rationalization or modernization.[3] As a result there was a shortage of labour to man the new plants, thus adding to the apparent paradox of overfull employment and unutilized capacity. If this is not a final diagnosis of the English sickness it is at least evidence of a conspiracy between employers and workers to try to conceal that they had both caught a doze.

And not only they. In 1950 official estimates of the country's fuel requirements were also a projection of the past into the future. The Ridley Committee,[4] miscalculating the future demand for coal, over-

---

[1] *Company Assets, Income, and Finance in 1963* (HMSO, London, August 1965).

[2] According to the London and Cambridge Economic Bulletin of October 1966, the import of machinery and equipment rose in value between 1963 and first quarter of 1966 (the period of the Maudling investment 'boom') by 75%—about £260,000,000 per year. Over this period the volume of investment in plant and machinery increased by 33% and the import ratio of this in the field of private investment was about 50%.

[3] Articles in *The Economist* (16 September and 23 September 1961).

[4] The Ridley Committee sat under Viscount Ridley in 1951–2 to work out a national policy for the use of fuel and power resources.

optimistic about nuclear power, dismissing gas, and underestimating thermal energy, only reflected the British Government's current preoccupation with the coal industry. For some fifteen years official fuel policy was thus more concerned with persuasive argument about the past than in genuinely attempting to forecast the future. Taxes to hold back oil consumption and encourage the use of coal became the rule, while the growth of primary energy consumption in the United Kingdom was considerably slower over the last decade than in the majority of industrialized countries.

A relative drop in the British share of an expanding world demand for exports is therefore not to be wondered at, for in manufactures alone our growth rate in 1964 was 5% compared with the 14·6% average of all industrialized countries, Japan leading the field at 23·4% and the United States and Germany following with 18·3% and 14·5% respectively. Even worse, the engineering exports of the former workshop of the world rose no more than 1% in 1964 over the previous year compared with the 14% in aggregate of the main manufacturing nations (Japan, Netherlands, Canada, Italy, Belgium/Luxembourg, the United States, Sweden, Germany, France, Italy, and the United Kingdom). Even when British exports are 'buoyant', this background must be borne in mind. But it is also good to recall the background of government muddlement against which this plodding advance was conducted, like the stubborn hang-dog British infantryman, loaded with the most useless ironmongery produced since the Hallstatt Age, moving to final triumph in spite of the confusion and mistakes of his generals.

And like the soldiery, those involved in the present muddle even manage to make themselves reasonably comfortable, especially when there is a chance to do some swift scrounging. If we cannot invest, let us at least build up stocks. They may come in useful if there is another credit squeeze or import cut. The deterioration in the visible balance of payments between 1955 and 1960 was in great part due to higher stockbuilding. When import duties are suddenly imposed, as with the 15% surcharge at the end of 1964, the stocks did come in useful and, unlike currency, had not depreciated. When domestic demand remains buoyant the extra cost of machinery and materials is quickly absorbed. Not surprisingly, Britain's imports show sharper rises and fluctuations than exports, which increase in their own slow way. If British industrialists, as soon as credit is available, prefer to buy foreign machinery rather than place long-term orders at home, this, too, is in part the result of their sad experience that 'stops' or 'freezes' are liable to be applied half-way through their re-equipment programmes.

Maudling's gamble that if industrialists could make investment plans on the assumption of a faster growth rate the investment itself would provide the accelerated rate and fresh export surplus, was a gamble against the habits of two decades. It failed.

When called upon to put fresh effort into the less profitable export trade, British industry merely calls on the government for help and in producing the necessary credit insurance the government in turn connives in the conspiracy. By the end of 1965 United Kingdom exporters were in consequence owed some £1,300 millions by their customers, while British importers owed only some £370,000,000 to their overseas suppliers. The outstanding credit balance of £900,000,000 almost exactly matched the United Kingdom liability to the International Monetary Fund. The very success of an export drive conducted on the basis of medium- and long-term credit had proved to be yet another factor in putting sterling in pawn. Yet overseas investment, which could bring a 100% return over a quarter of the period allowed for export credits, was by 1966 either discouraged or completely banned.

A too narrow investment base, a general excess of home monetary demand over productive capacity, an ever-growing demand for imports, and ever-rising prices would have been problems enough. But, to cap them all, the state—while calling for restraint in spending—has steadily increased its own expenditure on non-productive supply services. Extra taxation imposed as part of a 'stop' phase does not take money out of circulation, and by reducing private saving may even encourage resort to consumer credit and instalment buying. Under Maudling's White Paper On Public Expenditure 1964–68 (December 1963) it was assumed that the economy would grow by 4% per annum and the share taken off this by the public sector would grow by 4·1% per annum, thus increasing from 40% to 41·5% by 1968: the lowest post-war proportion of the gross national product taken in any one year had been 30% in 1956. But if growth had never been more than 3% per annum and most of the time probably less, the increasing proportion of gross national product taken by public expenditure will result in a steady *shrinkage* of resources for the private sector. And Maudling's forecast did not even take into account losses in nationalized industries or the pressures and bottlenecks which might be caused in specific sectors because of public spending.

Throughout the post-war era, British taxes on expenditure have become proportionately less important while the tax burden on incomes and the contributions for national and health insurance have risen. During the years of expansion between 1951 and 1956 the recovery of personal savings coincided with smaller proportions of personal income and of gross national product being taken in taxation. Since 60% of all taxes are paid by taxpayers earning under £1,500 per annum, who in turn are the main beneficiaries of public expenditure and services, taxation as a deflationary instrument has become meaningless. Even in the face of the exchange crisis and severe internal inflation of 1965–6, the British Government increased taxation by close on £1,000 millions and expenditure by £1,178 millions to a total of £10,000 millions. As demand was pushed still higher imports also soared, yet government supply estimates for 1966–7 were £660,000,000 higher at 8·5%. 'Cuts' announced up to the end of 1966 had all been in public investment not in current expenditure. If 1967 promised more public investment, private investment was falling and output was at best stationary. The outlook was still inflationary.

In a general way the City professes to worry about all this and its spokesmen prophesy national bankruptcy unless government expenditure is reduced. But City finance houses have developed the same schizophrenia as the rest of the nation. Although cynical about fixed interest issues in an inflationary era, they found no difficulty in 1965 and 1966 in raising debentures, unsecured loan stocks, and preference issues on a larger scale than ever previously undertaken for British companies. For most of them, too, international banking and financial business has become divorced from the fate of the domestic economy, something which was not the case in the nineteenth century. In lending their skills to international transactions—loans, promissory-note placings, and bond issues—conducted outside the United Kingdom with non-British funds, the City becomes less emotionally concerned with domestic affairs.

The workers share in this split mentality. Some 12,000,000 are members of occupational pension schemes and another 2,000,000 are already in receipt of similar pensions. Including their dependents, this probably covers 26,000,000 persons, or almost half the population. Calls by working-class spokesmen to penalize profits are consequently threats to labour's own security provisions and industrial disputes harm their own nest-egg schemes. The unions may be blamed for 'restrictive practices', but only one-third of the British working population belongs to unions affiliated to the Trades Union Congress while wages account for less than 40% of personal incomes; and until the shipping strikes of 1966 what employer seriously tried to call union bluff? The introduction of a shorter working week meant that many workers decided to imitate their 'betters' and enjoy more leisure. In spite of so-called deflationary measures the supply of labour contracted at much the same rate as demand fell.

Planning for incoherence

Since in the later years of the Tory administration neither monetary policy, nor general credit measures, nor budgetary control could apparently offer a cure for the English sickness there was a slow shift in fashion, first in academic and professional circles, then in the Press, and finally in the political parties, towards the notion of 'planning', meaning the setting of economic priorities, allocation of resources, and control over incomes and prices with 'growth' as the ultimate objective. Tory appeasement of trade unions at any price called for some action over the unchecked rise in money wages while between Budgets some form of regulator over consumption seemed advisable. *Something* had to be seen to be done about encouraging industrial investment where lags were creating manufacturing bottlenecks. What began as insincere Tory gimmickry gradually blossomed into Labour's 1965 plan.

First hesitantly, then more confidently, and eventually in his steady, pedestrian way, Selwyn Lloyd introduced, if not exactly planning concepts—that would have been beyond his capacity or that of his Treasury advisers—at least a series of individual measures which semantic ingenuity could present in the semblance of a new directive system. Government expenditure was to be assessed in a perspective of years and not of months, there were to be 'norms' for incomes related to the growth of productivity (this last to be planned by a National Economic Development Council), and the presentation of Budget accounts was to be changed. Between Budgets, powers to vary taxes—the so-called regulators—were acquired.

For British policy as a whole it was not a time of great coherence. A departmental appraisal conducted under Cabinet auspices in autumn 1959 of the United Kingdom's future over the next decade, concluded that the sooner the country joined the Common Market the better for the economy, but that pending such an outcome nothing should be done to upset the Anglo-American 'special relationship', that government overseas expenditure in excess of £200,000,000 per annum would mean cut-backs in home investment, and that the Commonwealth could be progressively disregarded as a significant factor in policy calculations, political, military, or economic. Having agreed with these conclusions, Macmillan then set off on a Commonwealth tour whose outcome was to precipitate a series of African crises, during his Premiership permitted defence and overseas aid expenditure to soar to an annual figure of £400,000,000, offended the American President by dragging him unwillingly to Paris to be personally humiliated by

Kruschchev, and for two years firmly discouraged any British approach to the Common Market.

Occasional suggestions by Treasury and NEDC officials for the introduction of new categories of taxation which would fit in with an incomes policy came to nothing. The deterioration of the balance of payments was concealed by an inflow of short-term funds to profit by high interest rates intended to have precisely the opposite effect and reduce money in circulation! When the upward revaluation of the German mark in March 1961 was thought to herald a general change in currency parities, the 'hot money' vanished and the thin state of the reserves was revealed.

When by mid-1961 the European central banks, which had given temporary help to sterling by increasing their holdings to £300,000,000, indicated that they had had enough, Selwyn Lloyd unhappily introduced an emergency Budget, applied the regulator in the form of a 10% rise in consumer taxes, cut government expenditure, and called for a 'pay pause'. Wages had risen by 6·5% in the second half of 1960 and retail prices by only half this percentage. The trade unions complained that they had not been accorded the courtesy of prior consultation and Selwyn Lloyd's Cabinet colleagues blandly ignored the pay pause in their departmental decisions. For the Prime Minister, government had by then become an amusing game of playing one Minister off against another. In spite of the Hofburg warnings, successive British Government acts failed to establish a firm stance from which to influence the economy in any general direction. 'Guiding light',[1] National Incomes Committee, the 1962 NEDC announcement of a 4% annual growth target—each emerged in an atmosphere of uncertainty accentuated by a panicky and abortive British attempt to join the Common Market; for all practical purposes all were ignored by finance, industry, commerce, and labour. No great premium was in any case placed on loyalty during the last phase of the Tory period of office.

The change of government brought no greater coherence in the shorter term. The renewed crisis of confidence in sterling precipitated by inept Ministerial speeches and an irrelevant 'emergency' budget struck severely—like the March crisis of 1961—because of the underlying trade deficit. Although a Prices and Incomes Board was set up, planning brought inside the departmental machinery, and regional development became 'regional planning', balance of payments con-

---

[1] A Conservative Government Income Policy Statement of February 1962, which proposed that money incomes should not rise by more than an annual average of 2·5%.

siderations still dominated, while neither monetary nor budgetary measures halted consumption or brought down prices. Labour could hardly have been expected in two or three years to reverse the itinerary along Butler's low road but they mistakenly persisted in the belief that there was a third way which would enable them to avoid severe retrenchment. Although the first British Five Year Plan published in September 1965 called for a highly desirable 25% increase in national output over the period, it was doomed at birth, because of the inconsistent short-term crisis expediencies. And as a projection based on replies by individual enterprises to a standard questionnaire, it was yet another attempt to turn the past into the future. While it was perhaps legitimate to forecast overall electricity requirements in 1970, it was fatuous to prophesy the output of consumer goods in fields where fashions change from year to year and even try to lay down in general terms what foreigners might wish to buy from the United Kingdom in five years' time. But some form of working hypothesis was doubtless better than none at all and, given their record, there was little that the parliamentary opposition could say against it.

In 1965 the effect of higher taxation was counteracted by a further increase in total personal income and consumption was maintained by a fall in savings. As industry coped with higher wages against an almost static output, there was a general pressure on profit margins. The final achievement of a 40-hour week, a 9-point rise in wages and salaries over twelve months had to be met from an estimated 1·5% rise in gross national product. It was not that Britain had been engaged on reckless consumption compared with other countries, for the increase in national consumption had been very much in line with that of gross national product. But since 1955 the income per head of employment had risen three times faster than output. The year 1966 was the end of the road, whatever the semantics of policy papers. The Labour party is to be criticized, not for introducing a Draconian prices, incomes, and dividends freeze (for something of this nature was psychologically necessary for continued solvency), but that for two years Wilson produced reasons for indecision which were as specious as those of the Macmillan era, although couched in less patrician language.

Although the balance sheet of Labour stewardship has still to be struck, there have so far been important negative gains, the chief of which is the explosion of the planning fallacy that to draw up a directive is the same as getting things done. Under the original Labour plan half of the average annual growth of gross national product of 3·8% (rising from £32,000 millions in 1964 to £40,000 millions in 1970 on a basis of 1964 prices) was to have gone to public spending, while the increase in personal incomes was to be determined by an incomes policy norm of an annual 3·5% increase. Since the growth over this period so far from being 25% would not have been more than 13% even under favourable conditions, the government would have been left with the alternative of taxing income by some £2,000 millions, the likely shortfall. This would have wrecked the basis on which personal savings were forecast, while industry could certainly not have fulfilled its investment and technical innovation programmes if consumption had been cut by this amount. Persistence in the planning illusion would only have presented the electorate with greater disappointment in a few years' time.

The second major gain was the re-opening of dialogue on forbidden and forgotten subjects. Mr Frank Cousins, who for almost two decades had huffed and puffed at government and industry, was himself blown over in two days' debate at Blackpool. With his discomfiture went the assumption of 'collective bargaining' between employers and unions, a concept without meaning when full employment had undermined the authority of both and where small key-worker groups under unofficial local leadership could act from positions of unchallenged strength. Even if the new concept of 'productivity agreements' had still to establish itself, an old chapter had closed. Employers were also forced to abandon one dearly held shibboleth—that whatever authority might do, it could never tell them how to run their own businesses. Now government proposed to do just that and even found compliant helpers in City and industry. Sense of duty? Collaboration? Betrayal? Or merely the hope of knighthoods? Whatever the motives ascribed, this was a situation which would have to be argued out, and not acted out.

Capital too had to re-examine its assumptions. The taxation changes introduced in 1964 and 1965 by Callaghan appeared to reverse—although probably only temporarily—the whole evolution from the eighteenth century onwards of the share-issuing market.[1] Finally the combination of sterling exchange crisis, falling production and investment, and sharply rising public expenditure forced a basic appraisal

---

[1] The incidence of Callaghan's Corporation Tax, assessed after deducting loan interest but before deduction of preference or ordinary dividends (to be charged gross instead of net), made it cheaper for a company to raise loans instead of issuing shares to the public. As industry finds ways of meeting this situation, there may be a swing back to the previous situation, but an increasing proportion of new loans and debentures were placed with big institutional investors, such as insurance companies and pension funds who must of course put their money to work. The Capital Gains Tax, inherited from the Tories, but increased in severity under Labour, means that that with inflation at over 3% per annum compound, 76% of an investor's earnings are taken in taxation. This is probably the chief obstacle to any acceleration of the rate of investment in the United Kingdom.

of the case for the annually mounting overseas government disbursements which had put the whole British balance of payments in such disastrous deficit. The issue of *either–or* which Macmillan had failed to face and Wilson sought to sidestep under his catch-phrase of 'keeping options open' could now no longer be evaded.

Britain's immediate problem is that of discharging the debt incurred to save sterling. This will require an aggregate surplus over 1967–70 of £900,000,000 while present trends indicate a cumulative deficit of £440,000,000, so a total shortfall of over £1,340 millions. Is this surplus realizable, and if not can British financial sovereignty in any form survive another major international loss of confidence? Here the balance sheet must be drawn up in the next two years for the creditors are already standing by. Although the 1965 British trade deficit of £265,000,000 was approximately half that of 1964 and largely offset by net invisible private earnings of £129,000,000, overseas government expenditure put the overall balance of payments deficit back to £354,000,000. For 1966 the promise was still of deficit with 1967 holding out the hope of a surplus at the price of an almost static economy.

Can Labour really offer the incentives for the sharp rise in productivity which would rebuild the reserves? At this point a Labour administration comes up against its own inner contradictions. Can the egalitarian implications of an incomes policy be reconciled with a need to replace restrictive practices by incentives and create a national surge forward in an atmosphere where private investment is discouraged, high profitability frowned upon, and forced loans levied after the manner of the Selective Employment Tax? There is a limit to the extent to which investors are prepared to put money in enterprises where profits are ploughed back while ploughed-back profits in turn are liable to be used less effectively than funds acquired in the open market.

The economic views of Messrs Wilson, Callaghan, and Jay, derived less from a coherent socialist philosophy than from personal and social resentments, inherited or acquired, add up to a general and rather vague notion of substituting private savings by taxation and channelling investment funds through official agencies. Less from conscious guidance than as the reflex actions of men taking it out on someone else, the weight of Labour's financial measures has moved steadily in this direction, largely using Tory instruments and regulations introduced as gestures of appeasement, such as the Capital Gains Tax. 'Selfish minorities' was a slogan much employed by Labour Treasury Ministers, as they gradually extended these measures over the whole of the country's savers. On the top of this the government chose to nationalize a steel industry badly in need of rationalization just when it promised to become the biggest money-loser in the economy.

While these measures may create conditions morally satisfying to the Labour leaders and rank and file, they cannot in themselves increase wealth or strengthen the country's financial position. A surplus is still something to be earned by the private sector, a productivity agreement will only be implemented if in the end it brings profits to those who enter into it. And while a purely statistical planning solution to Britain's economic troubles is not too difficult to set out in terms of its likely trading situation over the next decade, it can only work in an atmosphere of coherence, discrimination, and open dialogue. The present prospect of the extension of nationalization to steel, docks, and freight is that incoherence will spread to these sectors as well.

But standstill offers its own opportunity. Even with incomplete data, a controlled release may start the steady advance which hasty braking and jerking resumption could never bring about. In a framework of confidence created by ideas seen to be valid, an economy can regain momentum soon enough. An overall capital requirement can be estimated and broken down into general investment priorities for the main sectors of the economy not on the basis of some ideal rate of saving but rather in terms of cost reduction and labour economy: the incentives, fiscal and other, which would assist in achieving this can be agreed if the debate between government, industry, and labour is open and uninhibited. Treasury and central bank can then apply their rules and their skills to stimulate and control marginal demand. A financial, trading, and manufacturing community which has accomplished so much in terms of practical skills and imaginative invention over so long a period of history does not so easily disintegrate. But can our central banking organs rise to this task? Or is our national financial sovereignty now so diminished that only in some larger alignment of central credit institutions can we find a cure?

4. Where lies the cure?

The deaf dowager of Threadneedle Street

The central banks of the Western world are as much the creation of European rivalries, antagonisms, and differences as our political institutions. Habits of consultation and confidence built up on common professional skills may have created their own bonds. The contingencies of history as well as other alchemies of change have nevertheless allotted to the institutions different roles in the policies of their countries. Perhaps the persistence of the differences is their most remarkable feature.

The Bank of England, for example, affects a two-hundred-year-old tradition of reluctance at being obliged to undertake tasks beyond the capacity of yesteryear. The now ageing leading lady finds it difficult to learn a new part and the Bank of England, from its foundation in 1694, while accepting that it was the government's bank and the bankers' bank as well, had never held to any particular general theory covering its note issues and the state of the exchanges.

The directors of the Bank applied their traditional standards of immediate credit-worthiness to all clients, whether governments, banks or individuals, and when their judgement over raising or lowering rates and calling in credits was challenged in or out of Parliament by the classical economists of the early nineteenth century, they yielded to what they accepted as unavoidable pressures. When the 'atomatism' of the gold standard was political fashion they followed it. As crises and distress followed in the twenties and thirties of the nineteenth century they yielded afresh to the latest notion of a managed note issue and credit system. 'Your ladyship's carriage has arrived,' they were told, and were helped off the stage to rest until the next act.

The appointment of a new Governor every two years, the routine mass of work involved in handling state borrowing, paying interest on government stock and annuities, international settlements and payments, the business of money and bills in the comfortable professional exclusiveness of Victorian England, made for unflurried pragmatism in daily operations and required no great consistency from the officials in describing what they were up to. But one virtue of the system was that it was constantly under attack from both Parliament and informed members of the public so that Governors had always to be ready to offer at least some explanation of their actions and decisions. Paradoxically enough, as the Bank of England's working relationships with national authority grew closer it became increasingly immune to criticism. The consequence of being nationalized for the public good is that even the right of the people's elected representatives to question or criticize it has been denied.[1]

A further paradox is that the rules of silence and discretion nowadays invoked over the Bank's operations to the evident satisfaction of Labour Ministers are the outcome of the long Governorship of that Socialist bogeyman, Montagu Norman. Lasting from 1920 to 1944, this broke the two-centuries' tradition of two-year governorships.

There is evidence enough that Norman fully realized the social consequences of deflation but, like the majority of his generation, believed that the choices facing a British government in the twenties left no option but to accept them. His task was to maintain order in currency matters. Keynes on the other hand while opposing the return to gold was equally concerned at the social consequences of *inflation*. Neither, in fact, could know all the answers. But the detrimental long-term consequence was that Norman's own passion for secrecy and delight in autocratic power became the philosophy of the Bank itself. And in the City the corollary has been an exaggerated deference to the views of Bank officials still immured in their Norman keep.

After World War II the nationalization had predictable consequences. In the first two or three years its officials were resentful and touchy at the suggestion of a new subordination, even though the Governor preserved 'the right of direct access' to the Chancellor and Downing Street—an old Establishment trick for softening Whitehall take-overs. Before ten years had passed, the Bank officials had found that Whitehall was a sympathetic conspiracy akin to their own and as the top-level executives became enmeshed in the maze of policy-making committees and interdepartmental steering groups and working parties, the empathy was complete. The Bank even conceded a little of its formal etiquette and introduced a touch of the tweedy friendliness Whitehall affects with outsiders.

[1] On 3 November 1965, in reply to a general question by Sir Cyril Osborne on future high-rate policy, the Chancellor of the Exchequer told the Commons: 'It is never the custom to make statements about Bank Rate and I do not propose to break that custom.' Such was the ignorance of British legislators that not one challenged this outrageous untruth. In November 1966, however, the Government said it would consider printing the Bank's annual report as a White Paper.

The outlook of the Executive Directors—from whom the present Governor and Deputy-Governor have risen—as well as the assistants and departmental heads, has been determined by a long apprenticeship in the day-to-day business of the bank. This is not inconsiderable, covering the transfer and payment business of overseas central and British commercial banks, note-issuing, registering and paying out government stocks, and control of the discount market. Outsiders are brought in as advisers and on occasion given accelerated promotion to executive directorships. But in the parlance of the Bank 'brilliance' stands for a nimble rather than a profound mind, while 'profundity' implies less a reflective nature than a pompous manner.

The Norman doctrine—in so far as there was one—ended with Britain's abandonment of the Gold Standard, the collapse of the Austrian Creditanstalt and the German Darmstädter Bank, and the introduction of a managed currency. But it was still his Bank. Norman did his best to cope with the new order and co-operated with Dr Schacht to maintain a semblance of tidiness in an increasingly chaotic world of inter-state finance. Just as the Cunliffe Report of 1918 considered that pre-1914 co-operation between central banks in operating the self-regulating Gold Standard left nothing to be desired, so the prevalent feeling in Threadneedle Street is that if only central banks and the international clearing bodies they have created could have the technical freedom to operate on the widest possible scale, all questions could be resolved.

The chief political obstacle to this is seen as the inability of British politicians to argue out an electorally safe fractional margin of unemployment. But since—until 1966 at least—politicians seemed to shirk this obstacle, the Bank officials do their best with an imperfect world. This is much the same tale as in the post-World War I era, where the lack of competitiveness of the older staple British industries was regarded as the chief factor in ensuring that the Gold Standard of the twenties failed to 'work': Norman produced a financial scheme for closing them down but a new positive policy was not within the Bank's range of skills. Lord Cromer in his time complained of rising government expenditure, but his officials went on finding means of financing it. On taking over as Governor, Mr (now Sir) Leslie O'Brien said that the Bank would not hesitate to take up the cudgels on the City's behalf if it saw its interests likely to be harmed. He could hardly have said that the Bank would not! An open dialogue between Westminster and Threadneedle Street, as it existed in the nineteenth century, no longer takes place.

Indeed, the existence of a City mechanism born of a past which has now acquired mythical overtones is a barrier to the sort of self-examination which would bring about new attitudes to changing circumstances and suggest fresh descriptions of reality. The existing organization and hierarchy of the Bank depend on preserving the institutions of a past order, while the institutions in turn—the discount and accepting houses and the great brokerage community of the City—depend for their profitability on their privileges with the Bank. Traditional methods of control work excellently over traditional methods of credit creation. The catch about it all is that other countries appear to prosper without them, and in the City there has been something of a breakdown in the traditional divisions between its institutions. The outcome is that the City is by-passed and the Bank finds that it has overrated its capacity to direct domestic credit and even keep itself informed about sterling transactions by foreigners.

For when the value of funds in 'unofficial' and secondary money markets, such as local authority borrowing, hire purchase finance, inter-institutional lending, and Euro-currency transactions exceeds that in the discount market, this becomes the determining factor in the movement of international short-term funds, particularly since the abandonment of 'cheap money' in 1951. At the end of 1965 the total of funds involved in such secondary markets was some £4,000 millions, while the total resources of the discount houses were £1,400 millions. High official interest rates thus raise levels in unofficial markets, draw funds away from the discount market, and add to general price inflation. Where a superbly executed obsolete skill fails, authority has to step in.

The City's very pride—its 'world' character, with 170 international banking offices holding deposits greater than the combined assets of accepting and discount houses and its foreign exchange market of 350 skilled dealers—means that critical pressures are operating against sterling before the Bank of England and Treasury are able to make a statistical analysis of their significance. The cry even rises among Labour back-benchers that the City is a menace, holding back Britain's growth, and that there are disadvantages far outweighing its £200,000,000 annual earnings.

Sterling crisis of 1964

In practice it is less a question of the City putting the pound first and growth second than of the warnings registered by its financial mechanism being misread so that remedial action is no longer possible by British authority alone. On 23 November 1964 the Chancellor of the Exchequer told Parliament that the 2% rise in Bank Rate was to place beyond any doubt the Government's determination to maintain sterling and bring to an end the outflow of funds. Forty-eight hours later the Governor of the Bank of England was making his famous series of telephone calls to borrow $3,000 millions and 'save sterling'. For the non-resident holders of sterling—including the head offices of the 170 international banks represented in London—were selling their sterling at any rate they could obtain. Since British trade and industry had no corresponding requirement, the Bank of England had to expend the equivalent of £320,000,000 in foreign currencies to buy in sterling.

With undoubted skill the Bank went on operating on this scale until the late autumn of 1965. By August of that year, $750,000,000 borrowed against sterling from the Federal Reserve Bank of New York was exhausted and a further 'standby' operation by central banks excluding the Banque de France, put the equivalent of £500,000,000 in foreign currencies at Britain's disposal. With a passing change of sentiment in September, the selling stopped, and by October the Federal Reserve was being repaid and by the end of the year repayments of short-term debts to central banks were being made at the rate of £50–60,000,000 per month. The old skill seemed to have worked.

But only *seemed* to have worked. For it was a one-time operation, and later it leaked out that the Federal 'swap' had been largely offset by a part sale of £316,000,000 worth of British Government-owned securities taken over under wartime regulations from private British owners and since kept in New York. And this was the first sterling crisis in which a large part of the pressure had been in the 'forward market', and where the Bank had supported the pound by using this market on a large scale. 'Forward commitments' are a guarantee to buy a currency at some future date at an agreed price. By large-scale forward purchases the Bank can create a temporary scarcity and thus reduce the forward discount on sterling. But it has the disadvantage of making it cheaper for those who mistrust sterling to maintain a 'bear' position, i.e. sell out at spot rates in the hope of buying back at lower rates. Against this, the Bank's commitments are not, until they mature, a charge on its reserves of foreign exchange. And if bear positions are speculative they will be closed out at a profit to the Bank *if* confidence picks up, and if they are commercial they anticipate charges which would have to be borne anyhow, either when imports arrive or exports are paid for.

The scale of the operation can be gauged from the estimate made by the Bank for International Settlements that at the end of March 1965

British liabilities for Euro-currencies were almost $1,000 millions more than assets. Since almost the only seller of forward dollars was the Bank of England or other central banks acting on its behalf, this measures the extent of its forward position. Indeed in September 1965 two of the leading British commercial banks had forward commitments to buy foreign currencies for their clients or on their own account of £1,370 millions: the total for all British banks may have reached some £2,000 millions at its peak. The Bank of England was probably using up some £15,000,000 of foreign exchange weekly to support the sterling exchange rate, and in the last three months of 1965 this had doubled.

A year later, as credit became generally tighter in Europe and the United States, with forward exchange contracts still at the same level, pressure on sterling increased. Since London banks have to buy a certain quantity of currencies in the spot market to cover legitimate forward positions, switching out of sterling into dollars had even more severe repercussions. The lower the forward rate for sterling the more a dealer can earn by selling spot sterling for dollars on which he could earn interest in the meantime and then in due course buy back the sterling cheaply. By August the Bank of England belatedly reduced the dealing limits of London's authorized exchange dealers, but foreigners still went on selling. With a basic balance of payments deficit and no recovery of confidence in the British Government's ability to put its financial affairs in order, this type of operation had reached its limits of effectiveness. The Lombard skill could do no more.

Yet while this exchange crisis continued without interruption during the first half of 1966 there was a strange alternation of optimistic statements and dire warnings. In a pre-election speech the Chancellor claimed: 'During the last 16 months the nation has made a substantial breakthrough in the post-war handling of the balance of payments problem.' And lacking adequate information Press and Parliament took up the euphoric chorus. So when the July 1966 crisis broke, the emergency measures announced were utterly inadequate if not irrelevant to the problem of restoring the exchanges.[1] Was truth either disregarded or perhaps no longer recognized? Had Labour Ministers a deep-seated plot to wreck the private investment sector and replace it by their own system? Or were they so carried away by their resentments as neither to care nor foresee the outcome of their actions?

[1] These included corporation taxes, subsidies to out-of-date industries, an unemployment tax drawing an arbitrary distinction between manufacturing and distribution, rent restrictions which would tend to reduce labour mobility, and an egalitarian incomes policy which could only encourage or freeze factory-floor divisions and practices.

64

Under interrogation the Treasury officials would probably turn out to be no less confused. For if the Bank of England fashions executants without ideas, the administrative institutions which find their top embodiment in the Treasury produce assortments of notions which can be only too easily reconciled in committees where consensus means banality and whose members have no responsibility for execution. The business of administration is to keep administrative arrangements moving as smoothly as possible. A concept means something quite different to the Treasury official than it does to the outside executant. What is 'revenue' for the government is 'taxation' to the citizen. The planner's 'growth' is the businessman's 'profit'. The consequences of a Capital Gains Tax (introduced allegedly against speculation and tax evasion) can be discussed in two different economic contexts, that of the choice facing savers or that of the fall in monetary values. Within Treasury walls the reconciliation of arguments made in both contexts may appear satisfactory, but outside, this is not necessarily the case. In foreign affairs the high dialectical skill of Treasury knights, so often described as 'penetrating intellect', may even be our undoing, notably when American leaders and officials are left with the feeling that matters are under control when they are nothing of the sort.

These shortcomings are not removed by the introduction of outside experts and academic advisers, since 'option' for one school of thought is 'necessity' for the other. No agreed objective estimate is likely to be produced on how far the disincentive of high marginal rates of interest will offset the benefits of the redistribution of revenue as social expenditure, nor on how devaluation would operate as against deflation. They may succeed in agreeing on how to limit men's freedom of action by legislation, taxation, government borrowing, and expenditure even to the extent of robbing them of freedom of choice altogether. But that is as far as Treasury and Bank can be expected to take their Ministers: positive acts of execution depend on consistency of purpose by authority, on shared aims and assumptions.

Lord Cromer, Macmillan's choice of Governor of the Bank, launched his periodic salvoes at government. The effect was apt to be lost during the process of reloading and reswivelling. Sir Leslie O'Brien follows the Bank's older tradition of coping with problems after they arise. As Deputy-Governor defending the Bank against accusations of lack of foresight in countering currency speculation, he complained that his critics did not realize 'how much it is the form in which the problem presents itself that determines the shape of the solution'.[1]

[1] Speech to International Banking Summer School, 20 July 1964.

This is an old story. When the exchanges turned against Britain in the autumn of 1824, the country had been stretching its export credits so far that payments were not being received in time to rectify the pressures. The trouble arose in great part from the Bank of England's refusal to regulate its credit policy by reference to the exchange situation and to distinguish between external and internal money drains. Imports, too, were booming, and since gold could be obtained cheaply and exchanged for foreign purchases, the Bank began to run out of bullion, so that when its reserves had been reduced to just over £1,000,000 on Christmas Eve, Rothschilds had to buy some millions in gold for the Bank through their French connections.

Under the Bank Act of 1844, the Directors were put under an obligation to maintain an adequate reserve in their banking department. The use of a rise in Bank Rate as an instrument for attracting money from country banks and foreign lenders and so helping the balance of payments was fully accepted, to the delight of the classical economists who had campaigned for the Bank to undertake this responsibility. Referring to a current bullion drain, *The Economist* of 2 January 1864 stated: 'We need not be alarmed at it after the recent and most wonderful proofs of the effective nature of the remedy in our hands; the Bank of England has only to raise its rate of discount and supplies flow into it from all quarters.'[1]

The classical theories had, alas, only been reluctantly accepted by the Bank when the circumstances under which they had been adumbrated had ceased to be valid—namely a stable society and primarily agricultural economy with a note-circulation of £22,000,000 and bullion and reserves of £15,000,000, to which was added some £20,000,000 of issued securities in the country. The great domestic boom in industrial investment and railway construction in the nineteenth century meant a loss of money for banks when shares were called up. Action to tighten up the London money market by raising rates had disastrous reactions in the country, precipitating the crisis of 1847. The new need, in fact, was for the Bank of England to function as a lender of last resort, a role which it resisted strongly until forced into it by the 1866 crisis brought about by the failure of Overend, Gurney, and Co., a discount house which controlled half the business of the market. High rates of interest had failed to stem the loss of confidence at home and abroad.

In the second half of the nineteenth century, although in control of interest rates and ready to act as lender of last resort, the Bank faced

---

[1] Quoted in *The Theory and Practice of Central Banking* 1797–1913, E. Victor Morgan (Cass, London), p. 173.

a new problem of keeping gold in its reserves without embarrassing trade. Its officials had not yet grasped that the great loans made by London to foreigners were now the disturbing factor in the international movement of funds. It is easy to apply hindsight. But seen historically, the Bank learned its reluctant lessons because it was under sharp attack during the nineteenth century from City, Press, and Parliament. In an age when government domination of credit systems is here to stay, Sir Leslie O'Brien's discreet philosophy of trying to appear the servant of two masters, provokes the comment: 'H'm'.

The Treasury and Bank officials sent to discussions on international monetary reform can produce useful pragmatic compromises, but political confusion and financial muddle at home rob them of the power to bargain and the right to insist. And their European opposite numbers at such discussions not only enjoy the ascendancy of men controlling the resources which now underwrite sterling. The institutions which they represent or serve, in spite of varying national traditions, have all one thing in common, a well-defined role of direction and control. There has never been—as with the Bank of England and even the British Treasury at critical moments of history—any diffidence about assuming authority and exercising executive powers.

France's system of command

The above applies particularly to one of the most venerable, the Banque de France. Founded in 1800, it has preserved something of the ethos of command of the Napoleonic system. Its survival through the revolutions, *coups d'état*, defeats, and triumphs of France have re-inforced it with an authority at least equal to the country's centralized system of administration. Since 1946 there has no longer been any question of the Banque being at the service of the 'two hundred families' of the legendary French oligarchy. It is an instrument of power at the disposal of the French Government, which after World War II, took up its share capital, appoints the Governor for an indefinite period and also a Board of Direction, made up of four *ex officio* heads of the principal state financial bodies, a further seven to represent the main institutions and sectors of the country's economy, and one as representative of the bank's own staff. There is no ambiguous formula as agreed between British Treasury and the Bank of England, by which the former is allowed 'from time to time to give such direction to the bank as after consultations with the Governor of the bank, they think necessary in the public interest'. The prior consultations and gentlemanly agreements of the English conspiratorial system are unknown.

The French Government controls central bank and monetary policy through a Conseil National du Crédit, made up of seventeen members representing government departments and public financial bodies, the remainder appointed by the Minister of Finance from nominations by economic interest groups including employers and unions. The Minister presides over the Conseil and his Vice-Chairman is Governor of the bank. Since the shares of the four leading commercial banks were in 1946 also transferred to the state and their reserve and liquidity policies brought under a Banking Control Commission acting on the advice of the Conseil National du Crédit, the chain of command is complete.

In 1966 the process of formal concentration of banks and of the branch systems of all credit institutions was even accelerated. In France there has been no self-contained 'City' money market and discount mechanism playing its own role within the national financial system and acting as a somewhat distracting satellite of the central bank. The Banque de France has always discounted a large part of the bill portfolio of commercial banks, and this remains—rather than overdrafts—its preferred method for financing production and short-term trade.

The subordination to the general intentions of the state does not in practice mean that the French banking hierarchy plays a minor role. The Plans drafted by the Commissariat-Général receive their first outline and their final synthesis in a General Economic and Financing Commission composed of the Commissaire-Général himself and sixty-eight members appointed individually by Prime Ministerial decree. These include the two Deputy-Governors of the Banque de France, heads of other state credit institutions, the Delegate-General of the Bankers' Association, and seven senior managers from the nationalized, commercial, and private banks. The working groups of the Commission each contain a Banque de France representative. Even on the regional aspects of the Plan, the heads of the Banque de France's branches are called in by the *préfets*, while the Governor is a member of the National Commission for Territorial Settlement.[1]

For the execution of the Plan, the Banque de France controls the

---

[1] A useful summary is given in *France's Plan And The Part Of The Banking System In Its Drafting And Execution*, Pierre Fradault, *Banca Nazionale Del Lavoro Quarterly Review* (December 1965).

detailed functioning of the agreed credit policy by being both the rediscount bank and the executive agent of the Conseil National du Crédit. The credits for the equipment of industry are related to the bank's estimate of overall resources. In the case of building, for example, the total authorization of loans each year is agreed between the Minister of Finance, the Governor of the Banque de France, and the Governor of the Crédit Foncier, the largest mortgage bank, founded in 1852 under state sponsorship although with private capital. Files of all enterprises seeking credits are centrally examined and their ceilings for every category of borrowing must have the prior approval of the central bank. The red thread of the Banque de France control runs through the whole administration.

As one might expect, the presiding officers of such a system are men whose training and experience have been primarily the drafting and enforcement of regulations derived from laws and decrees. The logical dogmatism of their language of analysis may often be cover for a certain drabness of thought, and even for its absence, but it supports the transmission of the edicts of authority. When government is weak, as in the Fourth Republic, they have wide powers of administrative discretion on which to draw. This does not exclude clashes, as in 1960 between President de Gaulle and the then Governor, M. Wilfred Baumgartner. But personal temperament plays a minor part; if M. Baumgartner's successor, M. Jacques Brunet, appears to foreign negotiators or observers as relaxed and humanly approachable, he will not depart from the limits within which he must conduct Gaullist policy.

Given the combination of a constant expansion of demand and the heavy cartelization of French industry, the banking system requires continual decisions on the rapid and effective steering of savings into investment and carefully timed authorizations for capital raising. The limitations of such a system are illustrated by its failure in 1965 to start off a revived investment programme by the reduction of profit taxes. Self-financing, which had provided 80% of industrial investment in 1960, had dropped to 60% five years later, and the blockage of industrial prices under M. Giscard d'Estaing's stabilization plan had evidently cut profit margins too far. Since efficient administration cannot by itself create resources, the state had to resort to a loan to prime the investment pump.

But no *inspecteur des finances* could quite forget that between 1945 and 1958 France was the sick man of Europe in financial terms, underwent seven devaluations during which the franc lost 90% of its value in relation to the dollar, and exhausted the reserves. The brave talk in

Paris during early 1965 of 'a year's grace for the dollar', the campaign against the reserve currency notion launched by M. Giscard d'Estaing, the cold reception in August extended to the United States Secretary of the Treasury, Mr Henry Fowler, when he visited Paris to urge international monetary reform, can now be seen as the uncertain and at times unconvincing bluff of officials whose Presidential instructions, crudely put, were to attack the predominant position of the dollar. The head of the External Department of the Ministry of Finance, M. André Delattre, reported to have little sympathy with his government's line, had his department removed from under him and was left without any visible function.

But, in the meantime, France had certainly extended its limits of independent action. By accumulating official gold reserves of $5,000 millions—one-eighth of the world's official gold holdings—and assuming the position of the world's fourth trading nation, with the domestic money market isolated from international dealings, it was able to press its own views of trade and tariff adjustments and hold up the offers of others until its own had been satisfied, even with Common Market partners. The 'liberalization' measures of November 1966 were a controlled extension of French capital resources to other economies and a regulated method of permitting foreign enterprise to share in its internal economy, in the hope of remedying investment and technological deficiencies. The prolonged posture of opposition to monetary reform had also set some limits to United States financial freedom. Even though the network of central bank 'swaps' arranged in the summer of 1966 more than offset the risk to United States reserves of French gold purchases of $30,000,000 per month, these had forced the United States to demonstrate through both foreign and domestic credit policy, that she was trying to maintain the value of the dollar both in terms of currency exchange and of goods. A country which wishes to see that its currency continues as an acceptable element in the reserves of others, submits itself to an obligation. In scoring this point alone, the French President could feel that a Bonapartist system of financial control fully justified itself.

Banca d'Italia and national unity

The contrast with France's Latin sister is thus even more marked. Italy, emerging from twenty years of Fascist rule and in which parliamentary democracy had barely put down popular roots, might have been expected to follow the precedents of formal centralization. Yet outwardly the Italian reins of financial control appear loosely held. There is no great hierarchy of central bank controllers operating through a monolithic economic administrative machine, but, on the contrary, a flexible and at times apparently unco-ordinated mass of banking and credit institutions while wealthy families—Agnelli, Pirelli, Pesenti, Falck—seem to lord it over powerful industrial principalities.

But when financial crisis loomed up in 1963 and the will of national politicians disintegrated in squabbles and intrigue, the Governor of the Banca d'Italia, Dr Guido Carli, emerged as the embodiment of central authority. Credits were firmly called in, interest rates raised, foreign exchange transactions taken over from commercial banks and efficiently centralized under the state foreign exchange office, national provincial and local authorities submitted themselves to a severe financial discipline, and an American support loan for the lira was obtained without delay. A threatening balance of payments situation was rectified, domestic inflation slowed down, and by 1965 Italy was out of its crisis and the politicians re-emerged from their back lobbies and took up their old intrigues. And Europe recalled that it was from the Lombards and Florentines that the arts of state finance had been learned.

It was a pre-war, indeed a pre-Fascist, generation which guided post-war Italy through the first steps of reconstruction. The Banca d'Italia itself had only assumed the full powers of a central bank in 1926 and it was ten years later before the collection of savings and the granting of credit were placed under complete government supervision. If this was entrusted in theory to an Inter-Ministerial Committee for General Monetary Policy, the execution itself was vested in the Banca d'Italia. The Ministry of Finance concerns itself in practice with running of the state household and formal international financial negotiations, but the power of action, which has become the right of control, rests with the central bank. The ornate salon kept ready in the head offices of Italian banks for the use of the Banca d'Italia's inspector symbolizes this right.

Even a unified Italy is of recent date. How has this central system acquired its effectiveness in such a short space of time? Largely because it has been built up on the oldest extant banking skills in the world. It may be something of a patchwork, since it covers Europe's oldest banks, such as the Banco di Napoli, Banco di Sicilia, Istituto Bancario San Paolo of Turin, the Monte dei Paschi di Siena (with their origins in medieval municipal pawnshops and their parchments and ledgers recording the passage of armies and conquerors from all Europe), houses dating from the days of Austrian rule, and finally the main commercial banks established on French and German models between the *risorgimento* and the first great industrial development of the twentieth century. While the Ministry of Finance of united Italy gathered in a superabundance of poorly trained administrators and clerks nominated by patronage, nepotism, and plain bribery, and has remained chiefly concerned with unravelling its own mass of documentation and regulation, the Banca d'Italia has drawn from a tradition of high professional standards among the Northern Italian banks: the relative homogeneity of its hierarchy has been an important element in maintaining its ascendancy.

The system of control adopted is that of the United States Federal Reserve, namely fixing a ratio between commercial bank deposits and the proportion of reserves held by them at the central bank. The required Italian reserve ratio has since its introduction remained constant at 25% and the funds thus held by the Banca d'Italia on behalf of other banks earn interest at a rate slightly above that of one-year Italian treasury bonds. There is no competition from a free money market. The Mussolini era bequeathed an additional instrument of control in the form of the IRI state holding company, which includes three main commercial banks (Banca Commerciale Italiana, Credito Italiano, and Banco di Roma) and of a strong medium-term credit institution, Istituto Mobiliare Italiano (IMI).

Set up in 1933 as an emergency measure to overcome the difficulties of industries which had overborrowed and banks which had overlent as a result of underestimating the capital resources available to Italy and also of having to meet demands for loans to further Mussolini's grandiose schemes, IRI became the main instrument by which Marshall Aid was transmitted through the whole Italian economy under the central credit direction of the Banca d'Italia. Since 1953 it enjoys sufficient credit-worthiness to dispense with government guarantees for its bond issues, and during the five years 1953–7 the IRI group's entire capital requirement was financed by direct recourse to the capital market. During the next five years, of a total investment of the equivalent of $2,000 millions, 86% was raised in the market and 14% contributed by the Italian Government.

By 1965 IRI's annual capital investment had risen to $976,000,000 and its capital assets totalled $6,000 millions, making it the fifth largest enterprise in Europe. Its 150 subsidiaries, still formally enjoying the status of joint stock companies and with much of their share capital still in private hands, include the bulk of Italy's steel-producers, the major mechanical and electrical engineering firms, motor manufacture, shipping and air lines, toll motorways, radio, and television. IRI bond issues determine the state of the bourses while the main Italian share-issuing house, Mediobanca, is part of the group. When the state oil company, ENI, and the state electricity generating group, ENEL, are added, the complex of state economic interests with the Banca d'Italia as their direct financial controller are the dominant factor in financial life. But all enjoy legal autonomy and within the very wide criterion of 'public interest', efficiency and solvency are the tests applied in how they are run.

The share capital of the Banca d'Italia itself rests on a wide popular base, 60% owned by savings banks and the remainder by banks, financial institutions, provident societies, and insurance companies. The Governor and the main executives are appointed by the outgoing Governor and the twelve elected directors of the twelve regional boards, although the appointments must be formally approved by the Minister of Finance. If the bank has established its own initiatives in general financial policy, it is not only because of the high calibre of post-war governors but also because the Ministry of Finance has not been in a position to offer a counter-policy. And the policy itself has been what passes in British academic and political circles as 'old-fashioned orthodoxy', namely, control of inflation by credit measures directly affecting the balance of payments and the rate of industrial investment.

The basic philosophy of Dr Carli and his leading executives is that governments and governed have a number of basically irreconcilable objectives, and it is at the counter of the central bank that the contradictions emerge.[1] The sharpest and least reconcilable of the differences is between the motives of savers and those who wish to employ the savings. The role of the bank is to bring home to government, employers, and trade unions at what point and why their objectives are irreconcilable, and that dangerous inflation will be the only consequence of pushing further the irreconcilable arguments. The Banca d'Italia sees this as the historical development of nineteenth-century policy of a central bank maintaining its own prerogatives in the financial and business community while nevertheless adhering to customary rules. The Carli philosophy accepts as a feature of our time in Europe, that savers have an unshakeable preference for liquid resources and that this places limits on the development of capital markets.

If this central banking role has been accepted by successive Italian governments, it is because they have been persuaded by Carli that

[1] Leconfield Lecture in House of Commons, 28 June 1966.

Italy's economic problems must be settled in an international and not a national economic framework. By seeking international solutions Carli has—so far at least—created his instruments for reconciling national sectional objectives. Consumption was never cut back, savings were not interfered with. This required the courage to make decisions too soon rather than too late. The swing in the visible balance of payments from a $1,859 million deficit in 1963 to a $666,000,000 surplus in 1965 was the result of a decision by the Banca d'Italia to cut back imports when it noticed that their emphasis was shifting from investment to consumers' goods. Thanks to the broadened industrial base created by the years of capital inflow, domestic demand was sustained and a fresh expansion of exports launched.

The Italian surplus, unlike the French one, is put to work internationally: official statistics carefully record even the massive smuggling abroad of $1,500 millions in 1963. In a nation which throughout history has so often felt the hot rake of war, the constants of human motivation are not dismissed as impurities in economic prognosis and the smuggled bank notes did, after all, return while deposits credited to 'foreign residents' had mysteriously risen by approximately the same amount.

In his annual report of May 1965 the Governor had issued his challenge to France:

> We believe in the merits of slow evolution and in discussion and reciprocal agreements shaded from the glare of publicity which so upsets the delicate mechanism of the exchange and gold markets. But we oppose the proposal to return to a pure gold standard. We do so not only because it runs counter to modern theory and experience (the gold standard never was an automatic system but one consciously managed, at least to a large extent, and experience contradicts the existence of any mechanical link between the balance of payments and domestic liquidity): we oppose it also because the manifold needs of the modern world and the complex objectives of economic policy preclude the application of mechanical rules.

In short, Italy's financial leaders believe in skills and sophisticated management. A superficial fondness for rhetoric (with which Dr Carli's own annual reports are richly and obscurely adorned) and a sort of moral innocence with a *quintocento* quality enable Italians to indulge in interludes such as Fascism and emerge apparently unscathed spiritually. Fortunately, the capital requirements of modern industry and the necessity of satisfying international underwriters and investors limit the extent to which Italians can indulge in self-expression through material aggrandizement. The family industrial principalities, such as the Olivetti group, found that they too had to be submitted to central financial scrutiny when their ambitions outran their capacity. Even the Agnelli of FIAT, for all their international spread of wealth, come up against the firm though sympathetic rule of the *stato* as run in twentieth-century fashion by the Banca d'Italia.

German finance regains independence

If in Italy the amalgam of individual skill and the institutional heritage of Fascism have brought about a fruitful balance of freedom and authority, even more paradoxically has Hitlerism resulted in a re-assertion of German financial ideas which seem to derive their original from nineteenth-century liberalism. Perhaps the facility with which they have been produced since 1945 indicates a certain superficiality since no human experience, least of all Nazism, fails to leave an imprint on consciousness. But in the endeavour to reappear as good Europeans there has been an understandable reinterpretation of what happened back in 1848, when militarism and chauvinism on the West bank of the Rhine worried all Europe, while across the river was a peaceful land of respectable burghers, rather pedantic professors, and a romantically minded ruling class whose relaxation was *hausmusik* or taking the waters at their innumerable spas.

The illusion that all this could be recreated also existed among the victors. Prussia, pioneer in the emancipation and enfranchisement of Jewry, birthplace of legally protected trade unionism and enlightened industrialism, with its ethos of Protestant decency, was broken up by Inter-Allied agreement, while the home states of Hitler, Himmler, Goebbels, and Streicher were hastily reconstituted as forcing-beds for democracy. The Germans were made to go through the formal exercise of dispersing power, breaking up cartels, setting up 'strong' provincial governments and institutions, and establishing the outward forms of separate Federal and local financial jurisdiction.

There seemed a plausible historical basis for this, since the German credit institutions also claim a disparity of origins. Like the Italian banks of the Middle Ages and the British merchant banks in the hey-day of Empire, individual German merchants had to cope with a confusing assortment of coinages in Central Europe, and from the special skill thus gained in money-changing had progressed to being acceptors of trade bills, thence to founding the network of private banks of Hohenzollern Germany and their present-day successors. As modern industrial development brought new financial demands, it was the French Crédit Mobilier which became the model for the predecessors of today's German joint stock credit banks. And born of that powerful strain of idealism in the German nature, municipal savings banks formed for the thrifty poor and co-operative credit banks to further collective self-help among farmers, craftsmen, and economically weaker social groups have brought into being a third credit system, whose clearing and giro mechanism has a call on assets three times greater than the existing 'Big Three' credit banks.

Under both Imperial and Weimar systems, the Reichsbank, essentially the Prussian central state bank renamed after the foundation of the Second Reich, could theoretically exercise only a loose formal control over these three disparate banking sectors. Some of the other state banks, such as those of Bavaria and Württemberg, were permitted to continue a restricted issue of notes bearing the heads of their monarchs, much as the Scottish banks today print their own till money. But the homogeneity of German society and the gradual blurring of distinctions between all fields of banking offered the central authorities practical possibilities for much closer supervision and direction than were indicated in the formal charter of the Reichsbank. When the 1931 crisis and looming clouds of uncertainty over the Weimar Republic required emergency financial controls, this was a straightforward formalization of existing central credit arrangements which Hitler in turn found only too well suited to his purposes.

The post-World War II emotional reaction to this particular *endlösung* was predictable. When the central bank, now the Bundesbank, was re-incorporated in 1948, it was to be by law—although 100 per cent government owned—'independent of the instructions of the Federal Government', even if required to give 'due consideration to the general economic policy of the Federal Government and to support such policy within the scope of its tasks'. A Central Bank Council consisting of the Board (Direktorium) of the Bundesbank and the Heads of the Provincial Central Banks (now reduced in function to being the local administration of the Bundesbank in each *land*), determines monetary and credit policy. The members of the Council are chosen on the recommendation of the Federal Government, the heads of the Provincial Central Banks by the Federal President on the advice of the Federal Upper Chamber. The Central Bank Council itself is presided over by the Governor (President) and Vice-Governor of the Bundesbank.

But since it may buy and sell Federal bonds and bills without limit in the open market, the Bundesbank is unambiguously both adviser and executant to the Federal Government. Ministry of Finance and Bundesbank officials are men cast in the same mould and with the same scholastic background, so that there is no fundamental clash of philosophies, only differences in temperament. The 'economic miracle' of the fifties meant that Federal revenue requirements were met without recourse to the credit system, while the growth in real wealth and savings was such that there were minimal causes for tension between the commercial banks required to keep reserves in the form of deposits with the Bundesbank and the latter's general policy.

The personalities, however, were not entirely without significance. The first Governor appointed by the President of the Republic after consultation with the Board of the Bundesbank, was Geheimrat Dr Wilhelm Vocke, who although already advanced in years was strongly determined to maintain the independence in both judgement and action of the whole German banking system. A Bavarian by origin, he had as a pre-Nazi member of the Reichsbank temperamentally disliked the Prussian ascendancy. Although a personal friend of Dr Schacht, he had sadly seen how the latter had been drawn into being the instrument of Nazi policy. The priority Vocke gave to the encouragement of domestic savings as the basis of investment and the best safeguard against consumer price inflation also fitted in well with the mood of the times, while the Federal Government was building up a revenue surplus and reducing public debt.

When Vocke retired in 1957, his successor, Dr Karl Blessing, may have in manner appeared more pliant towards government—too pliant for the commercial banks. But in practice not only Blessing but all leaders of the German economy were faced by a new situation—a marked recession, from which the Germans extracted themselves by extensive spending of the accumulated revenue surplus, mainly through increases in social welfare payments, by cutting taxes or delaying their collection, and by accepting budgetary deficits. In latter years, Germany has had to cope with the same problem as the rest of Europe: how under conditions of full employment to keep a nice balance between factors of real growth and those of price inflation, and judging when the balance of payments situation—whether in deficit or surplus—is acceptable or menacing.

German economists, bankers, and businessmen are often criticized in the Anglo-Saxon world for their ignorance of Keynes, not only making no pretence of having studied his works, but even refusing to read them. In fact by following the basic tenets of *staatswirtschaft* and using common-sense judgements such as assuming that if the rainy day has come, savings should be spent and no longer hoarded, the Germans have been Keynesians for as long as the British. The Nazi leaders had even anticipated the notion of deficit spending and 'increased revenue projections'. 'The Proposals of Business Cycle Control', a paper issued in 1966 by the German Ministries of Economics and Finance with the help of the Bundesbank set out doctrines which were the practice of Roosevelt's 'New Deal' and of the Hitler-Schacht era. The use of public finance, either by grants or tax discrimination, to direct economic activity into one path rather than another had been Prussian practice for one hundred years or more.

And in public debate self-conscious attitudes and personal ambition rather than clashes of institutional interest have been the spur to acrimony, particularly since German pride in expert knowledge and sense of personal commitment are transmuted too readily into an overweening desire for power and ascendancy. The argument between Dr Blessing and Mr Hermann J. Abs, a managing director of the Deutsche Bank, Germany's largest commercial bank, may at times appear to reflect personal issues rather than professional differences. But the underlying homogeneity of the German administrative and professional establishment, intensified by the virtual disappearance of a Jewish upper middle class, produces compensating habits of intuitive understanding, so that apparently fundamental contradictions are left unresolved in theory but solve themselves in practice.

Yet all these inherent contradictory situations which in Germany's case are anxiously scrutinized abroad lest they give rise to social conflict and the re-emergence of authoritarianism, are resolved largely thanks to intelligent co-operation between industry and labour. Trade union demands for wage increases, at times up to 9%, are taken on the top of the general inflation without German prices ceasing to be competitive. The trade union leaders, supported by professional economic research staffs at their headquarters, join with employers in the search for labour-saving ideas and methods, and urge their followers to save and invest. The increase in real wages since 1953, although double that in Britain, has been 36% set against a 107% rise in production: Britain only matched the wage rise.

Behind the sectional interests of the German banks lurk no grey eminences such as allegedly plotted against the ill-fated Weimar regime. The names of the great German industrial dynasties, Krupp, Thyssen, Flick, von Haniel, Wolff von Amerongen, and Henkel still figure on boards and shareholder lists of the enterprises which, in spite of Allied anti-cartel measures, seem to be grouped much as before the war. But the directionis under a managerial bureaucracy and credit control is in banking hands. In theory the families could join together to make their influence felt politically: but the *herrenklub* is no longer the fashionable venue in German cities, and this would in any case be only one expression of view in a complex Federal government machine where other politically conscious elements now share power and influence: and in the confrontation the administrative establishments of Ministry of Finance, Bundesbank, and commercial banks would drop their sham dialectics (often little more than the Germans' habit of shouting at each other) and close ranks.

The Bundesbank method of control over domestic credit has been mainly to act as a sort of gyroscope, calling in one quota or category of deposit and releasing another with specified conditions as to its employment. Coupled with high domestic borrowing rates, this does enable equilibrium to be maintained. Against that the bank has permitted borrowing abroad at lower rates by first-class German enterprises, particularly if engaged in export or overseas operations. The general aim has always been to offset short-term invisible imports by encouraging industry to produce a visible export surplus to which end Federal tax concessions are also designed. The outcome may have meant that in recent years approximately DM 15,000 millions has been lost in book values of bonds and securities at home but it also meant that in 1966 home demand increased by 2·5% over 1965, while exports were 13·6% higher. If partial unemployment seemed to be rising, the future German growth rate was still 3·6% per annum. With gold and foreign exchange reserves at the end of 1966 totalling DM 30,000 millions and the overall short-term balance of payments deficit of DM 5,000 millions only half of the anticipated 1967 visible trade surplus, there was time for reflection, as Dr Kiesinger and his new government considered how to cope with a Federal budget deficit and the need for credit relaxation. At least Federal government and Bundesbank could shout at each other in public and as equals.

And in support of whatever course of action was chosen, Germany receives the full backing of foreign central banking authorities. For while she may be in no greater hurry than some of the other EEC partners to take decisive steps towards a European capital market, she has been one of the most co-operative in trying to create a new international monetary order. Germany's relative freedom from exchange controls and lack of restriction on short-term lending and borrowing abroad have given the financial institutions of other countries an important stake in her solvency. The European international currency market flourishes largely because German industry is allowed free access to it. Indeed in basic monetary thinking Germany has become the linchpin of the European position. Having joined the Reichsbank in 1920, a departmental head in the BIS in 1930, and assistant to Dr Schacht until dismissed by the Nazis in 1939, Blessing talks from long experience: 'In the last analysis what counts is not so much the technical aspects of the monetary system but the spirit and determination of the leading countries.'[1]

The Dutch mind their own business . . .

These are sentiments which find a strong echo from the fourth European monetary 'power', the Netherlands, which has had to face the problem put by Adam Smith as: 'The currency of a small state, such as Genoa or Hamburgh, can seldom consist altogether in its own coin but must be made up in great measure of the coins of all the neighbouring states with which its inhabitants have a continual intercourse'.[2] The solution, as the Dutch established soon enough in their history as international traders, is that their notes be issued by a bank 'established upon the credit and under the protection of the state: this bank being always obliged to pay in good and true money, exactly according to the standard of the state'.[3] This may have an old-fashioned ring about it, but it is still the foundation of trust upon which depends the wealth of the Netherlands. The country's first great credit institution, the Amsterdamsche Wisselbank, began with such a promise to pay.

> Each new set of burgomasters visits the treasure, compares it with the books, receives it upon oath and delivers it over, with the same awful solemnity to the set which succeeds, and in that sober and religious country oaths are not yet disregarded! [4]

Presiding over the finances of a country which exports 37% of its gross national product, which is the home of three of the world's largest international manufacturing and commercial concerns, Royal-Dutch Shell, Unilever, and Philips, and the hub of a world-wide range of shipping and trading firms, the Dutch central bank, De Nederlandsche Bank, bases its philosophy of control on the careful calculation of a

---

[1] 'International Monetary Problems'. Article in *Progress*, The Unilever Quarterly, Vol. 51, No. 288 (1966).
[2] *The Wealth of Nations*. Digression Concerning Banks of Deposit, Particularly Concerning that of Amsterdam.
[3] Ibid.   [4] Ibid.

liquidity ratio which indicates the proportion between domestic liquid assets and the value of the gross national product. This philosophy, as set out by Dr Marius Holtrop, Governor up to 1967, is basically a restatement of Adam Smith's proposition:

> '... in small countries with an open economy, central bank policy can in the last resort usefully defend the external value of the currency, i.e. its parity, but can influence its internal value, i.e. the purchasing power of money, only within the limits which are set by the maintenance of its external value.'[1]

The method by which the Netherlands Bank conducts this policy is to concentrate on the priority task of controlling other banks. It affects to be neither a font of original thinking on general economics nor an active proselytizer of new concepts of monetary theory, nor an agency of policy-making. Under the Bank Law of 1948, the Netherlands Bank is charged with the supervision of all credit institutions with the exception of the Post Office giro. A further law of 1952 on the Supervision of Credit lays down detailed rules and powers for the central bank. Some of them have been held in reserve under a gentleman's agreement with all institutions involved, and these extend down to stockbrokers. The commercial banks can be required to hold a non-interest-bearing reserve in the Netherlands Bank up to 15% of their liabilities, and the actual percentage requested is fixed by the central bank according to the quantitative changes in their gold and foreign currency reserves, and according to its estimate of the reasons for the changes, whether from trade, overseas investment, bank loans, or foreign currency operations. The same obligation falls on the Post Office giro.

The process of control has been helped by the amalgamation of banking houses, so that nearly 70% of deposit, loan, and overdraft business is now concentrated in the two principal commercial banks, Algemene Bank and Amsterdamsche-Rotterdamsche Bank. The great network of agricultural co-operative and local savings banks is linked by their own central institutions operating under central bank supervision. Although in any great international bond issue the order of battle of participating Dutch banks is impressive, most of them possess some element of ownership and control by the two main banks, and the truly independent banking houses, some of them bearing names famous for 250 years, are few in number. Apart from receiving detailed monthly statements from all these banks, the Netherlands Bank also requires a list of all advances of 500,000 guilders and upwards, so that

---

[1] *Report for the Year 1964*, 27 April 1965.

by a request (not to be ignored) it can slow down or speed up lending activity in any economic sector.

By concentrating on doing its main job thoroughly, the central bank is only following the basic custom of the whole Dutch nation. The international giants concentrate on their tasks. Employers and unions alike take on the duty of how to improve productivity. The government governs. Although the Netherlands Bank is 100 per cent state-owned and the Governor and his boards of commissaries (i.e. supervisors) and directors are appointed by the Crown and the Minister of Finance, the Governor's term of office is for seven years. He can disagree with the Minister's directives and appeal to the Crown, which would mean a full inquiry and eventually political debate. But in a country where in Adam Smith's words, 'it is unfashionable not to be a man of business', there is unlikely to be any disagreement on fundamentals. The system still allows for competition, for although there are none on interest rates, either debit or credit, and active bidding for business by Dutch banks is the order of the day.

The threat to the system can come from one of the parties failing to live up to its responsibilities: and it was government which failed. The restrictive credit policy maintained since 1960 by the Netherlands Bank in one sector or another and designed to keep as constant a ratio as possible between bearer money, bank money, 'near money' (e.g. bills), and national income breaks down if politicians evade decision. In 1964 and 1965 negotiated wage increases rose above what had hitherto been regarded as the permissible maximum of 7%, so that household spending rose 10% and the required export rise of 12·5% to maintain balance of payments equilibrium was threatened by soaring home demand. Government expenditure on social consumption went on rising in spite of warnings from Dr Holtrop, while Ministers hesitated and argued over cuts. By the time the state stepped in and took over wage negotiations, a crisis of political confidence had blown up, and the government fell to be replaced by a stop-gap Cabinet under Dr Holtrop's nominated successor, Professor Jelle Zijlstra, who as Minister of Finance had been responsible for the upward revaluation of the guilder in 1961. Although imposing a wage and price freeze and advancing a 20% turnover tax increase by six months and postponing income and wage tax reductions, Professor Zijlstra had hardly finished wielding the hatchet before a general election descended on him in February 1967.

But firm decision rather than panic measures seemed called for, where against gold and foreign exchange reserves of 8,000 million guilders, the immediate balance of payments deficit was estimated at 400,000,000 guilders, economic growth was still continuing at 5·5% per annum and investment at 7%. 'There is ever reason to adhere to our country's rule worked out in the fifties,' said Dr Holtrop, 'that the current balance of payments of the Netherlands, as a developed industrial country, ought to show on the average for a number of years a surplus which—even apart from trend growth of foreign exchange reserves and from any increase in development assistance—is at least equal to net outgoings on structural capital movements at the rate of one per cent of the national income.' It works so well that in November 1964 the Netherlands Bank contributed $75,000,000 to the support of sterling.

. . . And Belgium takes the strain

The Netherlands' neighbour, Belgium, may envy the social homogeneity and national cohesion which are at the basis of Dutch success. Belgium has other assets but not these two. Under his charter, the Governor of the Belgian National Bank is given wide powers of jurisdiction on the country's behalf in international financial affairs, even the right to negotiate agreements which in other states would be the task of governments. But the lack of national solidarity has weakened his power and influence. The dominance of Belgian finance and industry by an internationally-minded oligarchy (of which the £100,000,000 Société Generale holding and investment group is the strongest element), the freedom given to both Belgians and foreign nationals to export capital, the role played in international bond issues by Belgian banks and finance houses present the appearance of a strong outward financial thrust. In addition, Belgium's nominally strong trade position, its gold reserves of up to 44% of the note issue as against the 33% legal requirement, form strong defences against short-term pressures on the Belgian franc, so that it, too, could play its part in 'saving the pound'.

Yet the internal political tensions, whether between Fleming and Walloon, Catholic and Socialist, or Monarchist and Republican, at times prevent the government from bringing its full influence to bear at critical moments in world politics. The constitution of the National Bank, with 50% of its equity state-owned and the other 50% privately held and freely traded on the bourse, symbolically enough reflects the division. Although the Governor, at present M. Hubert Ansiaux, is appointed by the Crown for five years and his managers for six-year terms, there is a further 'College des Censeurs' of industrialists, professors, and trade union and other national leaders, to supervise their activities. The first dividend of 6% is paid to shareholders, the remainder—apart from a second dividend fixed by the *censeurs*—to the reserves.

And, apart from fixing the maximum discount rate for drafts covering exports or imports eligible for rediscount at the National Bank, the central monetary authorities do not normally intervene directly in the affairs of the commercial banks. But an official body, the Commission Bancaire, with members chosen from outside banking circles and confirmed by the Crown, supervises the application of laws relating to banks, fixes the proportions of assets to be maintained by commercial banks against liabilities, and follows a general policy of opposing the extension of big banks in favour of small and medium-term credit institutions. In practice events prove stronger than policy intentions, since there has been in Belgium an unbroken series of banking amalgamations and mergers and a proliferation of new branches of the large banks.

Even though in theory the National Bank has the same power over liquidity as the Nederlandsche Bank by the requirement laid on commercial banks to hold some 60% of their Belgian franc liabilities in the form of government securities,[1] it must also make funds available to the Belgian Treasury up to a limit equivalent to $200,000,000, a sizeable figure when set against gold and foreign currency reserves of the equivalent of $500,000,000 and bank deposits of just over $3,000 millions. Crisis, which breaks so often in Belgium, inevitably results in Minister of Finance, Royal Banking Commissary, and Governor of National Bank being summoned in succession to the Palace, while politicians balance the risks of inflation against the temptations of office.

Where pluralism succeeds

That pluralism of authority, division of powers, and even linguistic diversity are not in themselves necessarily a cause of political and financial weakness is borne out by the examples of Switzerland and Sweden. Neither the federal system and the three linguistic groups of

---

[1] A measure introduced to control the floating debt with which the Belgian Government found itself faced at the end of the war. Originally 65%, the figure has been progressively falling with debt consolidation and rising bank deposits.

the former nor the careful formal separation of legislature and executive of the latter detract from the effectiveness of their central systems of credit control. While the Swiss Federal Government appoints a majority of the Council of the National Bank which in turn selects its Board of Directors, the bank itself still remains a joint stock company with 57% of its capital owned by cantons and cantonal banks and the remainder by private shareholders. In respect to profits and reserves it conducts its affairs like any prudent company, and its sole legal federal power is to issue notes and fix the official discount rate. It was only in the summer of 1966 that discussions began between federal and cantonal authorities, commercial banks, and business organizations on a proposal to give the National Bank the formal right to demand minimum reserves and extend its opportunities for open market operations.

So far, it has maintained its authority over more than 450 banks (to a population of 5,500,000), each with autonomy in fixing rates and no legal reserve requirements. The minimum ratio between commercial banks' deposits with the National Bank and their own liabilities depends, not on decree nor on law, but on a 'gentleman's agreement'. This also applies to the arrangements for sterilizing the influx of foreign money. The stored currency wealth of this nature in Switzerland was demonstrated at the beginning of the sixties by the total equivalent of $11,800 millions banking deposits compared to the sterling equivalent in England and Wales of $28,000 millions. Since the outbreak of World War II the deposits of main Swiss banks have increased more than five-fold.

This may be a tribute to the advantages provided by Swiss laws to those whose main object is to find a way round the regulations of their own countries; and where the bulk of income and capital taxes is levied by twenty-five cantons and more than 3,000 autonomous communities there exists the prerequisite for the ideal tax-haven. The fear of internal inflation which could be caused by this accumulation of funds has induced such a policy of caution by the National Bank that foreign loans floated on the Swiss capital market have dropped from 1,012 million francs in 1961 to 381,000,000 in 1964, and 160,000,000 in the first half of 1965, while the investment of foreign funds in Swiss loans has been forbidden. Switzerland's share in the total of foreign loans issued in Europe had thus shrunk from 90% to 11% in 1964, and since Swiss bankers had begun to worry lest they should lose their foreign clients and the Federal Government became concerned lest public investment needs could not be met, plans for easement were afoot in 1966, albeit under many safeguards.

In spite of these complications and fears, the Swiss economy is not a stagnant one; price-inflation is not rampant, confidence in the currency remains complete, and Switzerland performs a complex pivoting role in the international network of official 'swaps'. The moral is perhaps the same as that to be drawn from the example of the Netherlands— that if the banking system concentrates on controlling other bankers, the outcome will not be unhappy. The apparently unimaginative approach of Swiss bankers, from Herr Walter Schwegler, Chairman of the National Bank Board of Directors, down to the directors and managers of the smallest banking houses, illustrates that high professional skill may be more important than originality of ideas— at least in a Swiss context. 'Neutrality' even extends to preventing the use of currency in certain types of international settlements or as a unit of account in loans. Indeed Switzerland's main monetary worry is that others will persist in treating it as a reserve currency when it is still basically the medium of exchange for a small but modern economy where credit is predominantly a matter for cantonal banks. Too much confidence by the outside world at times seems an infringement of neutrality.

On the other hand Sweden's main financial problem is an internal one—how to find an acceptable way of living with continual price inflation under full employment conditions and still keep Swedish products competitive in world markets. This result is somehow achieved, although official credit measures seem at times contradictory. Since 1963 a restrictive credit programme has been followed theoretically by the central bank, the Riksbank, with little dampening effect on the rate of increase of commercial bank credits, although it may appear to reduce the quantity of funds in the money market. National budget forecasts are often far off the mark, revenue estimates prove to be inaccurate, private consumption and consumer prices rise faster than expectation, while rising imports indicate increasing domestic demand.

The Riksbank, founded in 1668 and Europe's oldest central bank, possesses ill-defined means of control and maintains an ambiguous official position. Although 100 per cent state-owned and supervised by Parliament, it remains formally independent of the executive branch of government. The Chairman of the Board of Directors is a Cabinet appointee, but his six colleagues are chosen by Parliament, and among themselves they elect the Governor—in practice the managing director who can and does act independently of the Minister of Finance, even in such matters as altering the Bank Rate.

Yet Riksbank itself and the commercial banking system are over-shadowed by the operations of the National Debt Office, which directs government borrowing, in accordance with the needs of the national budget, through the central bank. And since the Riksbank acts as government banker and since Sweden is the most advanced welfare state in Europe, the overriding task of the central bank has been to support government bonds at attractive market prices. In spite of shortfalls in revenue income, the government continues to follow a budgetary deficit policy and encourages a large-scale building programme. To reduce the resulting liquidity the National Debt Office carries out large-scale borrowing operations outside the banking system and makes funds available to the market on a day-to-day basis. In 1965, tactics required that the National Debt Office reduce loans from the Riksbank so that banking liquidity rose 5% at the same time as deposits were increased by contributions from a number of bond and debenture issues. But because of the high liquidity ratios, the need to provide building finance, and the tight money market, the banks had to borrow at the penal rate of 11% and the Riksbank had to act in the market to maintain high rates on government stocks. Meanwhile the Central Pension Funds (which grow by the equivalent of $600,000,000 annually) and the insurance companies moved in to profit by the high rates. Inflation thus seems to spiral upwards without a halt.

Yet it has not brought Sweden to the same crisis in exchange rates as the United Kingdom. The moral appears to be that monetary measures affect only a small part of total demand.[1] For gross national product has risen by 60% over the past fifteen years, and over the same period exports have almost quadrupled to more than the equivalent of $4,000 millions. Over the ten years 1955–66 gold and foreign exchange reserves have risen from $150,000,000 to $890,000,000. The apparent paradox of rising reserves and deficits on current account is partly explained by the use made by Swedish exporters and importers of foreign credits so that in 1966 for example an export expansion of 6·5% can be planned while home demand is kept down. By the most stringent controls over capital movements and international security dealings the domestic capital and money market is kept insulated.

Sweden plays no costly 'world role' akin to Britain. But the major domestic factor of economic success is the co-operation of Swedish manufacturers and unions in offsetting lower profit margins in industry by bringing down costs; there is continuous labour and industrial specialization, fresh investment and innovation as workers are transferred from low to high productivity tasks. The Wallenberg banking family, whose Enskilda Bank was founded in 1856, and

---

[1] Estimated at 15% to 20% by L. Thunholm, Managing Director of the Skandinaviska Banken, in an address to the London Lombard Association, 24 November 1965.

financed the original development of Sweden's major industries, maintains all-pervasive influence today on the boards of industry by still being innovators and pioneers in modern processes. They possess no majority control in any enterprise, and the great mass of wealth created by a century of banking and industry is now owned by a Wallenberg Foundation for the advancement of science and education. Social democracy has made its peace with the Wallenbergs and their ascendancy is that of merit not money.

Sweden has no incomes policy such as Britain has endeavoured to formulate in recent years. The basis of wage negotiation between employers' and workers' federations are the forecasts prepared by industry and trade unions on future production and commercial activity. A tax-free element of profits paid by industry into a special government fund for release as capital expenditure in slack periods maintains a steady industrial growth without there being a defined 'growth policy' as such. A high standard of education among Swedes of all classes ensures that ideas and data can be intelligently exchanged and understood. Swedish pluralism teaches the same lesson as Western European centralism or dualism, that consistency of purpose and sustained action and not elaborations of theory are essential elements to health in national finance.

5. Limits of independence

The open American debate

If in Europe authority's historical task of protecting society against the usurer's greed and enforcing the rights of the lender has combined with other functions of the state to form a power of ultimate financial command, the issue still remains open in the United States. Here a whole *diapason* of moral overtones dominates financial argument and monetary and credit policy-making.

The debate had, to all intents and purposes, begun among Americans even before the peace treaty had been concluded after the War of Independence. The Founding Fathers, notably James Madison, doubted whether the new federal state had the strength to sustain a central banking system, and the first Bank of the United States, based on a charter drawn up by Alexander Hamilton, was less a central or government bank than a national joint stock bank. While the controversy between British Parliament and Bank of England in the early nineteenth century centred round the correct policy for controlling credit and maintaining the reserves, the American debate developed in the context of a clash of political and moral philosophies, of federalism versus state power, of the honesty of planter and merchant as against the subtle skill of the banker, the virtues of community banking contrasted with the suspicious anonymity of finance.

The already influential banks of Philadelphia, Boston, and New York were not unnaturally on the side of small-town virtue! By vetoing in 1832 a Bill passed by Congress to recharter a second Bank of the United States after the first charter had expired, President Andrew Jackson put paid not only to prospects for a central bank on European lines but also to nation-wide branch banking. The United States Treasury became the agency for managing central finances, for issuing and controlling the currency of a continent which in the process of being opened up and settled, changed the fundamental character of its economy at least three times over a century.

In historical retrospect the United States has not been on balance a loser from Jackson's decision. During American history there may have been major failures of state and city banks. But it is doubtful whether a central bank would have been able, under conditions of vast distances and slow communications, to arrange the technical means of preventing them and controlling all the opportunities for negligence or plain dishonesty. In practice it was the City of London which provided the United States with its central credit and money market services, and through the agency of the old-established banking houses of the Eastern seaboard—many of them linked to British merchant banks—financed American exports and imports and found the funds for the railroads and factories which were to form the basis of American economic and military power.

The prolongation of the moral–mythological controversy meant, however, that insufficient attention was given to improving the shortcomings of the workings of the American banking system. Congressional orators preferred instead to conjure up spectres of sinister Wall Street influences, while monetary cranks of every kind vied with popular preachers and moral crusaders in trying to hold the allegiance of the American lunatic fringe. Meanwhile in the face of the growing complexity of the North American economy in the second half of last century even the most ingenious correspondence arrangements of local and state banks supported by Treasury bill operations were inadequate to cope with reserve problems at critical moments. Eventually in 1913 a Federal Reserve Board was set up to provide for the discounting of commercial paper, supervise banking, and improve the currency system. Even then the institutional arrangements reflected the deep-seated American distrust of concentrated financial power, for the system was devised in the form of twelve regional reserve banks rather than as a single central bank. The Board and its regional banks were initially empowered to supervise federally-chartered or national banks only, while state-chartered banks could come into the system on a voluntary basis.

So while the Federal Reserve Board has the right to conduct examinations of the affairs of member banks of the Federal Reserve System, the official audit is carried out by the Comptroller of the Currency who can independently charter new banks, and grant new authorizations for the issue of debt capital, financing, leasing, and for buying new categories of bonds. Similar powers are exercised by state banking superintendents and examiners over banks chartered under state laws.

The wave of bank failures after the Stock Exchange slump of 1929 and the depression of the early thirties led to the setting up of a Federal Deposit Insurance Corporation with the right to conduct examinations of all banks whose deposits it insures. In 1965, of the nation's 13,600 commercial banks the Federal Deposit Insurance Corporation and state authorities examine 7,200 insured members, while less than 300 uninsured banks are examined by the states alone. The New York Clearing Houses Association has also a privileged role since it, too, can examine the books of all its members, including the leading United States banks. In practice normally only one examination is conducted, and the results are made available by courtesy and custom to the other authorities. The political pluralism which Americans regard as one of the chief safeguards of their liberties is paralleled in their banking system.

In the Banking Act of 1935, which reaffirmed the Federal Reserve System, it is described as a public institution, neither as a governmental one nor as a Presidential agency, although its governors are appointed by the President of the United States. Ambiguity begins at the top, for, if the Federal Reserve Board is entrusted with powers over the supply of credit and the structure of interest rates, the Employment Act passed by Congress in 1946 gives the President a mandate to keep unemployment low, prices reasonably stable, and promote an adequate rate of economic growth. This unique legislative formulation of para-Keynesian economics accords the Federal government a wide interpretative discretion in its power to tax and spend, to finance Federal debt, and give grants in aid to individual sectors of the economy.

But to reach his decisions the President has to reconcile the views of three separate and high-powered groups of official advisers. First, his Council of Economic Advisers, headed at present by Mr Gardner Ackley; second, the Secretary of the Treasury supported by a department of well-informed officials; and third, an influential Director of Budget operating his own agency.[1] If the debate still has occasional mythical overtones, the success of United States financial policy is due in no small part to the fact that there is a debate at all and not a well-bred backstairs compromise. Even the subjects of discussion at the President's monthly lunch with these top three experts appear to be known to the Press in advance and the views expressed round the table are never secret for long.

The time-honoured right to examine banking affairs is not excluded

[1] At the time of writing Mr Henry Fowler was Secretary of the Treasury and Mr Charles Schultze, Budget Director.

from debate, as in April 1965, when Senate investigations into bank failures and defalcations prompted the Chairman of the Federal Reserve Board, Mr William McChesney Martin, to say that the reports of the then Comptroller of the Currency, Mr James J. Saxon, had deteriorated in quality, that he was failing to observe the tradition of consulting the Federal Reserve before granting charters to new banks, and was making rulings on deposit conditions and borrowing limits which conflicted with reserve liability requirements. Playing the role of the independent banker's champion against the Federal system, Mr Saxon appointed a committee of national bankers, which advanced the suggestion that the Treasury should be the sole regulatory credit power. The President's Council of Economic Advisers produced a compromise call for closer co-operation between Comptroller and Federal Reserve. The President bided his time, announced a year later that Mr Saxon would not be reappointed, and in November 1966 appointed a Treasury career official, Mr William B. Camp, then First Deputy Comptroller, as his successor.

How the 'Fed' operates

The debate extends throughout the Federal Reserve System itself, by the process through which a policy is agreed for open market operations, i.e. the purchases and sales of United States Government securities as a means of influencing bank reserve positions and the availability of bank credit. By crediting or debiting the accounts at the Federal Reserve Banks of the banks handling the purchases or sales, their reserves are increased or diminished. The amounts transferred to the accounts of the dealers, some of whom are banks themselves, are rapidly telegraphed throughout the country. Since reserve requirements average about 15% of demand deposits for all banks in the Federal Reserve System, open market purchases can create a six-fold expansion of bank credit.

The directives for these operations are drawn up every three weeks in Washington by the Federal Open Market Committee, composed of the seven members of the Board of Governors and five of the twelve regional bank presidents, one of whom (the President of the Federal Reserve Bank of New York, the centre of the financial market) serves by law as a continuing member, while the presidents of four other Reserve banks serve one-year terms in rotation. Because of the

Committee's importance for financial policy formulation, each Reserve bank president, or his alternate, attends each meeting and participates in the discussion, even if he cannot vote. The Manager of the System's Open Market Account, a senior officer of the Federal Reserve Bank of New York, who at any one time carries the responsibility for dealing in some $30,000 millions out of the $200,000 millions of marketable United States Government Securities, presents a report on developments since the last meeting.

Each regional Federal Reserve Bank president, drawing on his own board's expertise in banking, business, industry, and agriculture in his district, gives his report on the current economic situation and the monetary requirement. The international developments are reviewed, the Chairman presents his appraisal and formulates the consensus for future credit policy and the need for easement or tightening. A directive is crafted, voted on, and issued to the Federal Reserve Bank of New York as valid until the next meeting. Without such a regular national review and debate based on first-class financial intelligence gathered systematically through the United States, the present sensitive and successful timings of American financial direction would not be possible. The debate is real, not sham. In August 1966—as a report submitted to the Joint Economic Committee of Congress revealed—Board members and regional presidents had disagreed vigorously over the pros and cons of tightening credit, recorded dissenting votes, and overruled the recommendations of the permanent officials.

Since membership of the Federal Reserve Board of Governors is for fourteen years, staggered so that one term expires every two years, its personnel develop a sense of independence. The system is not closed against the pressures and intrusions of political expediency. Federal Reserve Board appointments, like those to the Supreme Court, have other uses. The appointment to the Board of Mr Andrew Brimmer, an Assistant Secretary of Commerce and academic economist, was presumably prompted as much by the President's need to demonstrate that negroes were being accorded their due share of high office as by his desire to reduce the business element on the Board. For the first time, in fact, it includes a majority of professional economists, most of them affecting the 'liberal' views of President Kennedy's selection of advisers. However, although Presidential nominees must have their appointments confirmed by a Senate alert to any threatened increase in Executive power, the Chairman of the Governors once in office, enjoys the strength of continuity.

White House is challenged

It was not, therefore, surprising that McChesney Martin, a man of decided views, challenged President Johnson's cheap money policy in December 1965 by his—largely symbolical—decision to raise the discount rate from 4% to $4\frac{1}{2}\%$. The American need was to sustain a boom without its degenerating into a scramble for limited credit. Selective measures, not general monetary deflation, was obviously the appropriate course and the Board faced the task of maintaining moderately tight monetary conditions and at the same time persuading the President of the virtues of some increase in taxation. The debate turned round an estimate of whether existing taxes and levies could 'take out' $5,000–$8,000 millions, which McChesney Martin considered would inflate the economy dangerously if left in the hands of consumer and industry. The banking system itself, he felt, had played its part in reducing loans to foreigners, holding down domestic lending, but still meeting legitimate needs by moderate selling of state and municipal securities. It was an argument not of doctrine but of judgement on figures and trends.

The controversy derived from the very nature of the American banking and credit system. Although both Federal and state authorities may fix different maximum rates of interest for various types of loan facilities and borrowers, United States banks are prohibited under both federal and state laws from paying interest on demand deposits. But they may quote fixed rates on time deposits, and to this end have introduced negotiable deposit certificates. These may not exceed the legal maximum laid down by the Federal Reserve Board. The traditional basis of regulation by the Federal Reserve has been that all member banks must keep a percentage of demand and time deposits with their regional Federal Reserve Bank. These are at present for city banks $16\frac{1}{2}\%$ against net demand deposits and 4% against time deposits, and for country banks 12% and 4% respectively. With total deposits running at nearly $300,000 millions, the Federal Reserve requirement has been a powerful instrument of liquidity control.

But as the American economy continues to expand and gross national product rises to $800,000 millions at an annual 'real' rate (i.e. allowing for price increases) of 4% to 5% per annum, the question arises whether the liquidity base is broad enough. In bidding for time-deposits the banks have also had to seek higher yields, and invest increasingly in bonds and mortgages. Credit restraint brought about by a rise in interest rates could mean large-scale liquidation of deposit

94

certificates to obtain higher yields elsewhere. The possibility of a fall in the market price for bonds could cause embarrassment in a banking system which in a few months had increased negotiable time-certificates of deposit from zero to eight figures. The loan to deposit ratio of commercial banks over the last ten years has grown from 43% to 64%, most of the growth taking place in 1965. The 'free reserves' of banks, i.e. those over and above the Federal Reserve requirement, were at the beginning of 1966 $180,000,000 less than outside loans.

For the Federal Reserve this was a dangerously over-extended situation, and for the President and his advisers there was a dangerously short money supply, particularly as, to meet the cost of the Vietnam war, large United States corporations were being asked to pay their taxes on a current basis instead of under a delayed arrangement. The requirement for tax payments and for additional stock to finance the nation's $200,000 millions capital investment programme came at a time when banks needed higher rates to bring in funds. The President, on the other hand, needed cheap money to ensure that further gross national product increases would provide additional revenue to pay for both the Great Society and the Vietnam war.

One easy way out, advocated by Mr Alfred Hayes, President of the Federal Reserve Bank of New York, would have been the elimination of reserve requirements on time-deposits and a transition to monetary policy governed by interest rates without ceilings. The credit supply would be determined by the depositing public's preference for cash and demand deposits rather than interest-bearing alternatives outside the banking system. But since this would have involved the reversal of the whole evolution of the Federal Reserve System and given it an undue increase of influence *vis-à-vis* that of the Federal government, this was not the type of solution which a Chief Executive who expresses a preference for consensus cared to face. The raising of the Federal Reserve discount rate still left it one of the lowest in the Western world, and was not likely to have a major adverse effect on the rising gross national product.

Since United States Presidents have become decreasingly disposed to see their authority challenged and Secretaries of the Treasury are only human, the issue still rankled. In July 1966 Mr Henry Fowler requested Congress to enact a temporary statutory ceiling on commercial bank interest rates—then $5\frac{1}{2}$% per annum—on time-deposits of $100,000 or less and on similar savings and loan dividend rates. The Presidential search, as put by Mr Henry Fowler, was to find 'a better way to limit credit than by simply raising its price'. Lower interest rates and 'fair' allocation of existing supplies of credit was the new doctrine supported by an announcement in September that Federal borrowings in the long-term money market would be severely curtailed for the rest of the year, covering the great range of loans to mortgage associations, home and banks, small businesses, etc. This implied that the Treasury would have to intervene in both bond and money markets to take over refunding arrangements for all the agencies involved. Directive credit controls determined in a political context? Or monetary measures operated through the banking system on its own estimate of the economy's needs? The old debate took on fresh colouring.

But it still retained its rather mythical quality largely because it took place in an atmosphere of booming prosperity. And by the end of the year the proper balance seemed to have been struck: whether this was the result of Federal Reserve action or merely as a result of the adjustments of supply and demand, of investment and consumption can doubtless be argued over indefinitely. By the third quarter of the year the rate of annual rise in GNP had dropped from $16,800 millions to $12,000 millions on average. The Department of Commerce predicted an annual rise in investment in new plant and equipment for 1967 of 8% as against 16·5% in 1966. Since under 3% would have been regarded as recession and over 8% as risking inflation, the President could weigh up the question of tax increases and adjustments in terms of his Budget needs not as an uncertain instrument of financial policy. Even if price increases would account for 2·9% of the predicted rise in GNP, the hoped-for real increase of 5% would be met, and although profits were said to be declining more than seasonally towards the end of the year, they were still 10% higher than 1965. Although the Federal Reserve gave no indication that it was changing its policy, the easing of credit conditions was reflected in Treasury bill rates, dropping in December below 5% for the first time since August. The year 1967 opened with interest rates visibly falling and bank deposits rising.

So, unlike the United Kingdom, where over-optimism has been endemic, warnings of ill-omen tend to be disproved in the United States. The main threat to further advance was an impending shortage of skilled labour which employers, acting in the unhesitating American fashion when faced by a problem reducible to quantitative terms, met by crash recruitment and retraining, so that the United States looked like maintaining the 15% lead in labour costs which it has held over comparable industrial countries since 1958. Given the capacity of American society—whatever the sharpening of internal conflicts arising from its lack of racial homogeneity—to pass through major political and economic change with only a shifting and vaguely defined idealistic goal ahead of it, the President had correctly enough gauged the factor of confidence—at least for another year.

The scale of the governmental effort which such an economy can finance was demonstrated by the 'guns and butter' Budget of January 1966, envisaging expenditure of $112,800 millions compared with 1965's $106,400 millions. Tax receipts of $110,000 millions against $100,000 millions for the previous year were described, and accepted by Congress and public as 'a modest measure of fiscal restraint'. The cost of the Vietnam war was raised by $5,700 millions to a total of $11,500 millions. A year later the President forecast a 1968 Budget of between $125,000 and $140,000 millions with the total cost of the war rising to $22,400 millions. Defence spending as a whole was expected in 1968 to rise to an annual rate of $75,000 millions and even in 1966 a quarter of the increase in the nation's plant and equipment outlay had related to military purchases, according to the Department of Commerce. Consumer spending reached a new peak, and unemployment at 2,600,000 was the lowest since 1953. Budget deficits, although abhorrent to older American as well as European financial orthodoxy, have in theory to be set against the two-year budgeting forecast procedure introduced for all Federal agencies in 1962.

The dollar abroad

So what had been the basis for Federal Reserve Board anxiety that there were financial limits to United States Government policy which could be overstepped only at risk? Apart from the possibility that the President and his advisers might have underrated inflationary pressures, there were two potential threats. One was the *cumulative* budget deficits, which by 1966 required $12,000 millions in interest payments and single Treasury debt refunding operations of over $9,000 millions. The second was the continuing balance of payments deficit, with consequences not only for the gold and foreign exchange reserves but also for the countries which, by holding on to their dollars, were helping to finance it. While the ability of United States industry to raise finance by bonds and loans continued unimpaired, low yielding Treasury bonds had dropped, particularly the $4\frac{1}{2}\%$ Treasury bills, the stand-by of the American money market. An erosion of government credit at a time of rising interest rates is not a comforting prospect. The President's curtailment of government-held loans—which had been expected to bring in $4,200 millions to the Treasury—thus had sinister undertones.

As far as the reserves were concerned, the Vietnam escalation was by 1966 costing the United States an annual $700,000,000 in gold and convertible currency reserves, even with a drop in the balance of payments deficit from $2,800 millions in 1964 to $1,300 millions in 1965. And this trend looked like being reversed in 1966 with the rise in the cost of the war. 'Equilibrium', according to the Secretary of the Treasury, lay in a swing between an annual $250,000,000 deficit or surplus. But set against a prospective GNP of $740,000 millions, why should even such deficits be a source of worry? The answer lies in the Federal Reserve System's belief in the interdependence of its three main functions, to foster a flow of credit which will facilitate orderly economic growth, maintain a stable dollar, and in the long run preserve a balance in international payments.

In this belief, in 1962 the United States Government had passed Kennedy's Interest Equalization Act, a vigorous effort to restrict the outflow of capital, halt overseas lending activities of American banks and firms, which dropped from $2,500 millions in 1964 to a slight inflow in 1965 while some $1,200 millions of funds were repatriated. The immediate consequences were not all welcome to Treasury officials, for the very success of this change in the flow created a stringency of dollars abroad which caused European-owned funds to move out while the possibility of further dollar-shortages hastened conversions into gold. Hopes of seeing European interest rates come down and preventing further outflows were dashed. The decision of the British Government to 'liquefy' some $500,000,000 worth of its $1,250 millions of United States' securities meant an additional potential liability. One way or another, United States' money liquidity had been theoretically reduced by $900,000,000.[1] Since in February 1965 the 'swap' network of the Federal Reserve had already reached $2,350 millions, thus more than the annual payments deficit, the vulnerability of even a marginal situation was evident. So the 'pros' of a reduction in interest rates to maintain industrial advance as against the 'cons' of further outflows of liquid funds in search of higher rates elsewhere could not be weighed up by President and Treasury in a purely national context. The delicate factors of balance at work were illustrated in October 1966 when, although France had stopped buying United States gold, Treasury stocks still dropped by $45,000,000 worth.

The United States has reached a point where the satisfaction of

---

[1] Statement to United States Senate Banking and Currency Committee by Henry H. Fowler on 18 August 1965.

internal credit requirements and of external liabilities can hardly be maintained under a system of free exchanges controlled by traditional credit and monetary methods. The international stability of currencies has become enmeshed with the internal purchasing power of the dollar, something that in the fifties the Americans had put at the back of their consciousness on the assumption that the dollar was impregnable. Foreign exchange operations, whether initiated by the Treasury or the New York Federal Reserve Bank, had at that time only the limited aim of evening-out exchanges or facilitating transfers of funds at the best rates.

In 1961, however, operations had to be extended in scope 'to create a first line of defence against disorderly speculation'. By 1962 these had been extended into the 'swap credit system', by which countries can boost each others' reserves by the simple exchange of credits denominated in their respective currencies: at the end of the year such facilities negotiated by Mr Charles Coombs of the New York Federal Reserve Bank had risen to over $1,050 millions. The motive was not merely to maintain a stable dollar rate but to provide assistance to other countries in exchange difficulties and even help to feed the Euro-dollar market as American funds were withdrawn. The operations often ran through several stages, buying German marks from the Bundesbank, swapping them for Swiss francs at the Bank for International Settlements or using them to buy Dutch currency to replenish the United States' reserves with guilders previously swapped against sterling.

The elaboration of the procedure was mainly to ensure the disposal of the embarrassing accumulation of any one currency in any one central bank as a result of Bank of England purchases of sterling to maintain the rate. Whenever confidence in sterling sags, the merry-go-round of buying and selling is accelerated, and as part of the process the Federal Reserve played the biggest single role in the swaps. The greater the hope of keeping the swap credits moving, the less likely it seemed that the gold exchange standard would or could be abandoned.

The process came to a grand climax in September 1966 with the announcement between eleven of the world's central banks and the New York Federal Reserve Bank that the network of regular swaps had been raised in total from $2,800 millions to $4,500 millions. Although much play was made of this as being part of international actions to support sterling (and as part of the operation the Bank of England did receive a gain of $100,000,000), it was the United States that obtained immediate relief. It also set a new limitation to American freedom of action. In return for other countries accepting such large dollar credits as part of their reserves (in most cases for periods of a year), the United States accepted the obligation to protect the purchasing power of its currency from undue erosion by domestic inflation.

The ripples from the decision to slow down American overseas investment and bank-lending went on extending. It seemed at the time an obvious short-term method of easing the situation. And the restriction of new bank loans abroad to a 5% ceiling above $11,000 millions outstanding on 31 December 1965 still meant that some $550,000,000 would be made available. In any case, German and French bankers were launching somewhat obscure diatribes against Americans for 'exporting inflation', i.e. making funds available to their clients at rates which challenged their protected little profitable worlds or giving American enterprises credit facilities to acquire European subsidiaries. So effective was the President's appeal to American business to slow down the export of capital and find it abroad instead, that investment funds to Western Europe alone dropped from $535,000,000 in the first quarter of 1965 to $110,000,000 in the third. By November of the same year, American borrowers in Europe had raised $162,000,000 in long-term funds and the 1966 prospect for United States' corporate borrowing in Europe was nearly $700,000,000, so that the Euro-dollar rate rose from 5% to $6\frac{1}{2}\%$. The same French and German bankers, still led by Mr Hermann J. Abs, were now complaining that Americans were mopping up Europe's liquid funds.

But the New York short-term rates were still rising, and American measures could no longer operate in isolation, while the English sickness was much worse than anyone had imagined. On 10 February 1966 President Johnson sent a special message to Congress calling for studies on the creation of new international reserves: 'Unless we make timely progress, international monetary difficulties will exercise a stubborn and increasingly frustrating drag on our policies for prosperity and progress at home and throughout the world.'

The richest country in the world had thus recognized that there were limits to its financial independence and that its existing power could only be maintained by co-operation with other states. But co-operation on what basis and using which instruments? An agreement on questions of world policy also seemed to be essential, since it was only too evident that the United States' desire to play a 'world role' had been a major factor in creating its financial dilemma and reviving the domestic controversy over who should control credit creation.

Europe's programme of action

The Europeans to whom the Americans turned, had been making their own recognition. The century and a half of revolution, reaction, violence, and wars, against an intellectual background of notions of conflict, whether ideological, social, or economic, have at least brought about a re-acceptance of action as a prime method of testing the validity of political and economic ideas. So where politicians and officials now concern themselves mainly with practical programmes, it is the intellectuals who have withdrawn into various forms of verbal solipsism. This is in contrast to Britain, where the public political debate is now dominated by the word fetichists—a complete reversal of the situation where the British once boasted of their capacity for compromise as against the inability of European politicians to co-operate in programmes of action.

In their day the British had justification enough as they saw Continental liberalism and social democracy stumble and eventually succumb to the belief that intellectual categories were more important than action, and activists, such as Lenin, moved in to secure power. In Italy, Mussolini chose action—any action—while Croce represented the futile end of the nineteenth-century notion of emancipation— freedom of inner expression, aesthetic freedom, and retreat into a Neapolitan palazzo to await an American landing. The French reaction to a century and a half of bourgeois love of martyrology, ceremonies of commemoration, and facile attitudinizing, for which the working classes paid dearly, was cynicism, collapse, and defeat in 1940. In Germany the field was left open to those able to exploit the types of affective communication to which growing self-consciousness, combined with a sense of individual insecurity, had made German society doubly susceptible.

So from the hangover of ideology only action remains. Even Marxism's twilight existence rests on a claim to have replaced random factors by objective programmes of action. The excitement over what once seemed an instrument of objective analysis has lasted so long that it has created that Marxist style of dramatic emphasis so useful to both shop-floor agitator and minor don seeking to impress his undergraduates. But at least the Marxist residue is a recognition that by nature men are more activist than 'image' and that economic power is a factor which must be utilized.

And it is as a programme of action, one for setting-up institutions to control the growth and direction of economic power, that EEC in the face of diversions and setbacks has begun the delimitation of national financial sovereignty and the definition of the conditions for inter-dependence. In the calculating and rational character of its attempt to create a new framework of European institutions, it is as unique in history as the establishment of the Greek *polis*. Even where older intuitive and emotional problems are involved, such as the future status and role of Europe's peasant communities with their tribal, instinctive, and traditional past, EEC reconciliations and proposed solutions require a rational balancing of factors. The Treaty of Rome is not based on the evocation of past traditions, as with most European treaties and conventions, nor on some essentially romantic appeal such as the United States Constitution, but sets out definable goals to be attained by the creation of rationally conceived institutions presiding over specified fields of practical activity.

This is fundamentally different in essence and terms from the British 'genius for compromise' which was in great part an instinctive unwillingness to face up to wider issues. In its latter-day version the spirit of compromise becomes something of a menace: it can be a shabby thing, preventing the wider recognition of rational thinking.

World issues are raised

The world has reached a stage where compromise can hardly be stretched further in contemporary sophisticated financial terms. Even one of the first areas of European settlement, Latin America, struggles with currency problems which appear to grow ever more hopeless, rejects any suggestion of solutions imposed from outside while proudly announcing plans for new Continental monetary units with romantic names like *andino* or *latino*. Prosperous countries such as Canada accept *de facto* that without the support of the Federal Reserve and of the International Monetary Fund they are unlikely to maintain their own reserves for more than a few weeks. This was disturbingly demonstrated in May 1962, when only rapidly organized international credits of some $1,000 millions enabled Canada to overcome a reserve crisis. For the sake of good-neighbourliness, the United States tolerates a leakage of dollars through Canadian institutions, and foreign interests extend their control of Canadian industry. But crisis can still recur while Canada persists in maintaining a banking system which restricts healthy credit competition but gives a licence for financial banditry.

New definition is also required between the money markets of the Western world and the capital position in Japan, where the trade surplus since 1963, sufficient to cover the short fall on invisibles, is nevertheless accompanied by a deficit on capital account. The funds have come not from an open market nor from savings but from the Bank of Japan whose gold and foreign exchange reserves of $2,000 millions in 1965 depended on Japanese exemption from United States lending restrictions and on Japanese access to a European capital market whose appetite for Japanese bonds must remain an uncertain factor.

Smaller countries, such as Austria, also find that a parochial policy of accumulating reserves begins to create its own problems and have to permit a loosening of restrictions on the movement of funds. Spain, motivated by autarchic self-centredness and reacting against political ostracism, is trying simultaneously to encourage an inflow of foreign funds and maintain national control over their use by creating a new system of industrial credit banks.

Even countries capable of maintaining modest positions of financial independence demand to play their part in shaping a wider order. As the world's leading supplier of gold, South Africa views the problem of liquidity in terms of the quality rather than the quantity of reserves, with the co-ordinated revaluation of the world's currencies on a gold basis as the most satisfactory solution. But the tenacity and ingenuity of its European inhabitants have also built up an industrial economy whose needs require a voice in the international control of credit arrangements. Australia at times sounds resentful at its exclusion from the Group of Ten and more select monetary councils. Its case for inclusion is strong, since at the time of the 1964 and 1965 sterling crises, Australian holdings of £660,000,000 were equivalent to those of all EEC and EFTA countries combined. With export income growing by £30,000,000 a year over the past ten years and backed by an annual growth in real terms of 4%, Australia's fortunes have become steadily enmeshed in the complex of modern international finance; $1,500 millions of Australian stocks maturing in London and New York during 1967 cannot be overlooked by Britain and the United States in ordering their own money and capital markets.

Canada, Japan, Austria, Spain, and Australia (South Africa's gold gives her a special position) may singly be in no position to exert major financial pressure on the United States. But the functioning of an interlocking international monetary system requires their active co-operation, and this by itself imposes limits on the freedom of financial action of stronger powers. The total United Kingdom private overseas investment of £11,500 millions becomes a hostage to fortune rather than a lever of power, and even more does this apply to the corresponding United States investment of $70,000 millions, of which $21,600 millions are in Canada, $17,000 millions in Europe, and $12,400 millions in Latin America. The predicaments of the United States Government balancing the pros and cons of a continuing deficit policy, encouragement or restraint of overseas investment, domestic credit expansion or restriction, can in theory be set aside by a policy of selective direct controls over its banks, money market, and the investment programmes of individual industries. But this would raise the same sort of questions over Presidential power which caused a virtual deadlock between Executive and Congress in Kennedy's last months. And the introduction of a full-blown policy of this nature would create the very crisis of international confidence, where a new gold-rush would begin.

So by 1966 the leading industrial countries of the world were all trying in one form or another to cope with anti-inflationary policies and higher interest rates without inflicting damage on each other's economies, yet also planning ahead for increased productivity. Governments which had happily allowed their expenditure to rise in easier times were all being pressed to cut back. The surpluses of grain and storable commodities and metals were disappearing at the same moment as the credits for financing the movement of higher priced goods were being tightened. In the past such an accumulation of warning signs would have meant—as in 1931—a *sauve qui peut*, when the weakest went to the wall, and unexpected political movements and dramatic shifts in power were the sequel to monetary crises, default, and unemployment. It is a measure of the advance of the Western world that the theme of co-ordination of financial policies sounded by M. Robert Marjolin of the EEC Commission in January 1966 when he made the 'Annual State of the Community' Report to the European Parliament, was echoed at international conferences throughout the year.

But who would be the co-ordinators? The governments of smaller European countries reacted sharply when the finance ministers of France, Germany, the United Kingdom, and the United States met at Chequers a year later to exchange ideas and call for lower interest rates. For the issues extended beyond the discretionary powers of civil servants and the skills of central bank officials. They extend to the direction of investment programmes, control of capital markets, interest rates, and even fiscal policies. The form of bluff played between central banks and commercial currency operators by buying an ailing currency and passing it back to its own central bank becomes not only increasingly expensive but also embarrassing to a nation counting its reserves at a time of credit restriction. The key currency concept has reached the end of its validity if the reserve currencies nominally supporting it have in turn to be supported by 'swap' credits denoted in other currencies.

Since Britain's main preoccupation was to repay its debts and credits by 1970, there was little its government could do beyond offering helpful amendments to the proposals of others. For the United States the issues involved questions of Presidential power and aims. The creation and control of new international credit machinery raised distracting questions for those attempting to realize the new conception of the EEC, whose joint gross national product of $271,000 millions was the nearest potential challenger in terms of total productivity to the United States. One conclusion could safely be drawn: no answer would be found within the national framework alone.

6. Search for wider solutions

Aftermath of war

As in so many fields of human activity, the main stimulus to central banking co-operation and to the search for wider monetary solutions came from war and its aftermath. Up to 1914 it was a question of acquiescence by central banks in each other's national policies rather than of joint action. If one bank needed to attract gold from abroad, this had in the short term to come from the reserves of the others, so that when one raised the discount rate, the others accepted this with an appearance of good grace. The flow of new gold through the London bullion market and the fact that the United Kingdom was a creditor and not a debtor on short-term account enabled foreign bank governors to feel sufficiently relaxed about withdrawals.

World War I left a rudely disturbed financial heritage. Britain had lost $4,000 millions' worth of foreign assets, most of them in American railroad stocks. France had sold $700,000,000 worth of securities and saw another $4,000 millions in Central and Eastern Europe reduced to worthless paper, while through sale or confiscation Germany had lost virtually all its foreign investments. The United States stepped forward as the world's creditor. Needless to say, gold had disappeared from internal circulation.

To meet the credit needs of a world without reserves, the major powers met in 1922 in Genoa and came to what now seems the only obvious answer (although it did not appear so at the time), that national paper money obligations should by mutual agreement be used as reserves. In so far as foreign banks had been accustomed to holding sterling in the nineteenth century, this did not seem so revolutionary. But there was now a difference: sterling had previously been held to facilitate commercial transactions and not for reserve purposes. Since only the United Kingdom and the United States possessed the banking facilities to enable a volume of foreign-owned short-term paper to be traded and London and New York provided an active market for every sort of currency, the pound and the dollar emerged from Genoa as the two 'key' currencies. The condition which both countries accepted as feasible was that their currencies should not depreciate in terms of each other or of gold. The simplest practical method by which the implied gold guarantee of key currency liabilities of sterling could be upheld seemed to be for Britain to return to the gold standard at the pre-1914 rate of exchange.

The officials and bankers of Genoa can be criticized for having underestimated the difficulties of the system, in particular that sterling and dollars would only be available if the United Kingdom and the United States were running balance of payment deficits. The world's annual output of gold could be fairly accurately forecast but the swinging trade position of two major manufacturing countries was obviously a less dependable factor for determining the operations of the gold exchange standard, as it became known.

Bank for international settlements

Still! It was the first conscious co-operative step forward by the world's leading states to create an international monetary order in some degree under conscious control and not left to unseen though presumably beneficial self-regulating economic laws. The immediate problem was price inflation in post-Versailles Britain, so deflation was to be the keynote until British domestic price levels could match those of the United States.

In 1928 France returned to the gold standard. From the repatriation of some of her former overseas assets and from a favourable balance of payments, she created a sizeable surplus which she proceeded to convert into gold. Paris enjoyed a moment of seeming financial power which diverted capital from London, and did not hesitate to use it to embarrass Britain if it followed European policies displeasing to France: conversion of French sterling holdings into gold was the favourite pinprick of M. Poincaré. Meanwhile the New York stock-exchange boom took in funds looking for good returns. London was caught between these two poles of attraction. International capital movements —it was only too apparent—no longer equalized interest rates: in fact they aggravated differences. By 1929 American capital outflow had virtually ceased. Since borrowing could no longer finance the imports of debtor countries and ever-new trade barriers rose against their exports, depression was the sequel. And once capital was withdrawn, confidence in exchange rates—the important element in the key currency system—was lost; funds did not flow to countries with large short-term obligations whatever rates they offered. Bank standstill followed in Germany and Austria in 1931, £200,000,000 worth of foreign-owned funds were withdrawn from London, and in September of the same year with only £130,000,000 worth of gold left in the central reserves, the Bank of England suspended convertibility of sterling into gold.

Adversity produced new measures of co-operation. The breakdown of the gold exchange standard had in practice created three *de facto* spheres—'the world of the dollar, the world of gold, and the world of sterling'.[1] This was largely the currency era in which we lived up to 1961, for the patterns of trade, diplomacy, and defence tended to harden along the limits of the spheres of British, Western European, and North American political influence. A sharpening of the delimitation was brought about by the 'management' of the sterling area, the deficit spending, and statutory price increases of the Roosevelt era, and the forms of autarchy and bilateral trade by which the Continent strove on one hand to revive commerce and on the other to husband its gold. By 1936 the situation had eased sufficiently for the United Kingdom, the United States, and France to enter into a formal agreement to cease competitive devaluation; by this time the price of gold had increased all round by 60%. But by then, too, political rumblings and threats had begun to overshadow economic and financial considerations: those who had transferable funds sent them for safe-keeping to the United States, whose share of the world stock of gold rose from 38% in 1929 to 71% at the outbreak of war. In retrospect this was not all loss. The massive resultant gold cover for the dollar enabled the United States to shoulder its reconstruction responsibility in the war-ravaged Europe of 1945.

The needs of the age had, however, brought about another co-operative forward move, the creation in 1930 of the Bank for International Settlements. A series of futile 'World Economic Conferences' had been held from 1927 onwards in an attempt to formulate a new framework within which trade, borrowing, lending, and debt settlement could be organized. The assemblies only demonstrated the complete inability of the world's politicians and statesmen to find a common language of analysis and description, much less agree on a common course of action. But from one of the conference proposals, that to establish an international central bank, came at least the BIS.

[1] *International Liquidity*, Ian Shannon (F. W. Cheshire, Melbourne 1965), p. 29.

This was finally set up after The Hague conference on German reparations in 1930. Its immediate tasks were to collect the annual German reparation payments fixed under the Young Plan, distribute them among the creditor countries, and service the Dawes and Young loans to Germany. The wording of its charter went much further: 'to promote the co-operation of central banks and to provide additional facilities for international financial operations: and to act as trustee or agent in regard to international financial settlements entrusted to it under agreements with the parties concerned.' Although its main shareholders were central banks, it was to function as a true bank, drawing resources from its own operations and not from contributions. Its balance sheet is still drawn up in units of account with a gold value equal to the Swiss franc of 1930.

Bretton Woods and the IMF

The lessons of Genoa had been learned. The Allies were still fighting their way out of the Normandy bridgeheads when on 22 July 1944 the representatives of forty-four governments drawn from all continents, neutrals as well as belligerents, signed at Bretton Woods, New Hampshire, the 'Final Act' of their deliberations and resolved to set up an International Monetary Fund and an International Bank for Reconstruction and Development (the 'World Bank'). Outwardly this seemed a revolutionary decision. In practice it was a compromise, a toned-down version of plans put forward by Keynes for a world central bank and new international currency, *bancor*, to replace the allegedly discredited gold standard.

Not all international financial personalities took kindly to the omniscient Keynes. The Americans, who were going to have to bear the brunt of financing any such scheme, did not particularly see why their stock of gold should be downgraded in utility nor what was wrong with the dollar as a denomination. Since Britain in turn desperately needed a post-war reconstruction credit (eventually fixed at $3,750 millions under an Anglo-American financial agreement), she had little option but to fall in with the Americans. It may have been less than Keynes hoped for, but it was probably as advanced a scheme as the world's officials and bankers could have administered.

So the International Monetary Fund was set up to implement the intention of signatory states to consult on monetary changes, outlaw practices harmful to world prosperity, and assist each other on short-term exchange difficulties. To assist post-war reconstruction and 'for economic progress everywhere', the International Bank for Reconstruction and Development (the World Bank) was to provide a portion of capital for 'international investment'. A balanced growth of international trade, high levels of employment and real income, the development of productive resources of all IMF members, removal of obstacles to trade, orderly marketing of staple commodities at fair prices, and the harmonization of national policies to these ends to 'aid political stability and foster peace'.

After such preliminary fanfares, the detailed arrangements have a pedestrian touch about them. They look very like—and indeed are— the old skills of money-changing, keeping a tally, and judging a customer's credit-worthiness. The Agreement laid down a system of fixed exchange parities for all its members in terms of gold as a common denominator, or of the United States dollar of the weight or fineness in effect on 1 July 1944. These parities were to be maintained by each member buying or selling gold or convertible currencies other than its own within a margin of 1% for all spot rates and for all other transactions within a margin which the Fund would regard as 'reasonable'. Each member received the right (limited by a quota equal to its subscription to the Fund) to buy foreign currency from the IMF against its own currency in case of balance of payments deficits.

Preserving a healthy balance between the lip-service due to equality and the realities of power, each member was given 250 votes plus one additional vote for every $100,000 of the quota of its subscription, but if a decision was required on whether it was abusing the Fund's facilities, it was liable to lose one vote for every $400,000 worth of its currency that the Fund was obliged to buy, or gain one for every $400,000 acquired through undertaking obligations to buy the currencies of other countries in difficulty. The spirit of the Bretton Woods concept was that of mutual obligation among societies with common assumptions. They undertook not to impose restrictions on current transactions, not to make exchange contracts contrary to those in harmony with the Agreement, not to use the Fund's resources for capital transfers outside the normal course of trade and banking, and to furnish full information on their holdings of gold and foreign exchange, their production of gold, details of exports and imports, international investments, and all clearing arrangements.

Such conditions were hardly likely to appeal to the secretive Stalin, and one of the first withdrawals from the Fund was that of the Soviet

Union, to be followed by its satellites. There may have been mental reservations among other signatories. But with the United States, the United Kingdom, China (still under Chiang Kai-shek), France, India (still under British rule), Canada, and the Netherlands contributing the main quotas, the assumptions of Ethiopia, Haiti, Liberia, Egypt, and others could be tactfully overlooked, while the Fund was specifically charged not to object to currency rate changes merely because of the social and political policies of its members.

The tasks and responsibilities of the Board of Governors and of the twelve executive directors were wide enough. All the powers of the Fund were vested in the Board, whose members and alternates chosen by each and every member, serve five years. The Directors who are responsible for the conduct of operations, must include five from the members with the largest quotas.[1] The Board can revise quotas, approve uniform changes in the par value of members' currencies, determine the arrangements for co-operating with other international bodies, declare when a currency has become scarce, authorize temporary suspension of its free exchange, and issue reports on members abusing the Fund.

The operations based on the quota system are in themselves simple and straightforward. The subscription to the Fund of each member is equal to its quota. This is reviewed at five-year intervals, requires a four-fifths majority of total voting power for any change which in turn must have the consent of the member involved. The subscription is paid partly in gold, either 25% or, in the case of founding members, 10% of their official holding of gold or United States dollars, whichever was smaller, and the balance in national currency. The Fund can at its discretion accept securities or other obligations in temporary substitution for currencies which it may not require for its current operations.

With the $7,720 millions of gold made available by 30 June 1947 the IMF started operations with the immediate aim of assisting its members to cope with swings in their balances of payments. A formal limitation was laid down that such transactions should not cause the Fund's holdings of any currency to increase over twelve months by

[1] The IMF now has twenty Executive Directors, of whom five are still appointed by the countries with the largest quotas (USA, UK, Germany, France, and India). The remaining fifteen are elected by all the other members of the Fund who combine in any way they see fit for the purpose of electing directors every two years. Voting for Executive Directors proceeds on the basis that every Director must have at least a prescribed minimum of votes and he cannot have more than a prescribed maximum. This minimum-maximum is changed every two years, depending on the number of members in the Fund and the size of their Fund quotas. At the end of 1966 the geographical breakdown of the fifteen elected Directors was Europe 4, Africa 4, Latin America 3, Asia 2, Canada 1, Australia 1.

more than 25% of a member's quota nor under any circumstances to exceed 200% of its quota. The excess of any quota may be sold for gold by the Fund or repurchased in gold by the member. Annual increases or decreases in a member's monetary reserves are taken into account in determining the extent to which a member may have to repurchase its currency: and if from transactions with third countries it has unduly increased its holdings of their currencies or gold, it must use these to repurchase its own currency from the Fund. A nice sensible arrangement for preventing the accumulation of unwanted currencies in other people's reserves, and for foreseeing situations where members' reserves drop below their quotas and where the Fund's own holdings are alarmingly below or above the quotas, 75% of the non-gold element being the danger signal!

Waivers in exceptional conditions, the additional payment of currency to allow for reductions of par values, and repayments for increases were all allowed for by the officials and bankers who drew up the scheme. Mysteriously enough, they recommended liquidation of the Bank for International Settlements at the earliest possible moment. The sentence of death was lifted quickly enough once the latter's President, M. Maurice Frère, had demonstrated in Washington that the Swiss management in Basle had scrupulously recorded all wartime transactions and that without an experienced banking agent to handle gold and currency dealing, the IMF and its associated creations would remain still-born concepts.

Even allowing for the heartwarming phrases in the Bretton Woods preamble about 'political stability' and 'economic progress', the IMF began as a strictly neutral mechanism conceived as the next logical step in functional monetary co-operation. The sister creation of Bretton Woods, the World Bank, with its initial capital of $10,000 millions subscribed by IMF members emerges with an utterly different ethos. Its purposes betray its Rooseveltian and New Deal origins. For not only was it to assist in the restoration of economies destroyed or disrupted by war but also in 'the development of productive facilities and resources in less-developed countries'. To this end it could guarantee or assist private investment, use its own funds to promote the long-range balanced growth of international trade, raise standards of living, improve conditions of labour, and ensure that in its loan policy 'the more useful and urgent projects, large and small alike, will be dealt with first'. Before even national governments had demonstrated that they had mastered the art of ordering their economic affairs, here was the confident proclamation of a world economic doctrine, the first formal embodiment of the notion of 'underdevelopment' which was going to acquire such obsessional overtones during the next two decades.

Marshall Aid and the European idea

However, there were more pressing problems in the years immediately following Bretton Woods. European reconstruction required a far greater capital expenditure than anyone had anticipated. Severe winters and poor harvests in 1946 and 1947, the shattered state of Western European industry, and the isolation of Eastern Europe posed questions which the IMF had never been designed to answer. The British reconstruction credit disappeared in a matter of weeks with nothing to show and Britain had to reimpose import controls and currency restrictions. With 85% of the world's gold in the hands of the United States, Canada, and Switzerland, only massive transfers of capital could enable Europe to begin a long-term re-equipment programme. Marshall Aid and related military assistance programmes were the American solution, pumping $43,000 millions into Europe, so that by 1950 the proportion of United States' gold reserves to the world's total had dropped 64%, by 1960 to 44%. As a means of spreading the world's capital resources, the Marshall Plan achieved a resounding success.

It also started off a process which had not been foreseen—the beginning of another international monetary grouping which, moving from one *ad hoc* role to another through a whole series of labels, has emerged as a major challenge to the IMF itself. The Organization for European Economic Co-operation set up in 1948 by the eighteen countries participating in the Marshall Plan, to allocate the generous American aid, depended on each member submitting fullest information on its national resources, finances, and economic policies. The recovery programme involved the liberalization of intra-European trade, so that Europe could make the best use of its own productive capacity: the first step in this process had to be the removal of discriminatory exchange restrictions and the provision of a multilateral payments system. For it was still a Europe of barter and black market where the smuggler on Alpine paths exchanging lighter flints against nylon stockings was matched by governments trading timber or metal scrap against wool or coal at arbitrary scarcity rates.

Thus were born the European Payments Agreements of 1948 and

1949, and a European Payments Union was established in 1950. The reprieved Bank for International Settlements was called upon to provide the clearing machinery for the system and the EPU proved to be a successful replacement for the $10,000 millions of gold and currency reserves lost by Europe since the outbreak of war. The Union operated as an overdraft system under which OEEC members gave agreed overdraft facilities in their own currencies and received corresponding drawing rights. The outcome was by 1959 a doubling of the volume of trade between OEEC countries. By 1958 most of the members had already agreed in principle to restore external currency convertibility, a clear demonstration that it is the movement of goods which ultimately determines financial strength or equilibrium and that there is no separate mechanistic monetary world with its esoteric laws and mysteries. The EPU was superseded in December 1958 by a new European Monetary Agreement which took account of the change in the economic scene.

OECD expands

In the meantime OEEC members had recognized the virtues of common endeavour in economic and financial affairs *vis-à-vis* the non-European world. Ernest Bevin's simple faith that working groups grappling with practical problems were preferable to the grand economic conferences called in the twenties and thirties by Ramsay Macdonald seemed justified. In September 1961 OEEC became OECD (Organization for Economic Co-operation and Development) with the United States and Canada, associate members of the old body, becoming full members. Japan, ever anxious to be seen in the company of 'advanced nations', acquired full membership while Finland and Yugoslavia were granted a special status entitling them to participate in certain OECD fields. Some links with Eastern Europe were being restored.

If Bevin had been alive he would have approved the new statement of OECD aims. These were first, to promote the highest *sustainable* economic growth and a rising standard of living in its *member* countries; second, to contribute to *sound* economic expansion of both member and non-member nations which are in process of development; and third, to further the expansion of world trade on a multilateral, non-discriminatory basis in accordance with international obligations. There was a certain caution and recognition of limits in this statement as against IMF and World Bank preambles with their easy promises to all mankind.

For one of the principal instruments for OECD co-operative endeavour has been its Economic Policy Committee. In this forum the policies of individual governments are submitted to a thorough critique by the others under the lead of a member specially selected as devil's advocate. Composed of ministry of finance officials and governors of central banks the Committee meets several times a year to discuss the international repercussions of national economic policy measures. To provide it with a basis of discussion, the Committee set up three specialized Working Groups, one on general economic policies, the second on balance of payments problems, and the third on price levels and stability in member countries.

It was Working Group Number Two to which the Vienna IMF Conference of September 1961 referred the problem of supplying backing for sterling. Since it consists of senior officials from the finance ministries and central banks of Canada, France, Germany, Italy, the Netherlands, Sweden, Switzerland, the United Kingdom, the United States, and after 1964 Japan, it became known as the Group of Ten. Its discussions, held every six or eight weeks, are devoted to analyses of balance of payments situations of members and what national or international measures should be taken to deal with them. The terms of reference extend to the determinants of international capital movements and the state of national capital markets.

Significantly enough, the consensus of European opinion in Working Group Number Three has been at variance with the view of British Treasury officials as to whether internal demand in Britain was too high. The Working Group majority remained consistently sceptical over the likely outcome of deflationary measures of successive British governments, considered that the scope of British incomes policy was exaggerated and that supporting British statistics should be regarded as highly suspect. The same disturbing discrepancy between OECD's view of the British and the British Government's view of itself was still evident at the end of 1966, when at a Ministerial meeting Callaghan anticipated some British growth in 1967 while OECD itself published a zero forecast. The dialogue and informed controversy on which British electorate and legislature should have been allowed to pass judgement has been transferred to international committees meeting behind closed doors.

Meanwhile the Bank for International Settlements developed a new role as executant for all financial operations of the OECD European Monetary Agreement. It provides to OECD its intelligence and analyses of international gold, foreign exchange, and capital markets, watching in particular trends of central reserves in relation to balances of payments. BIS officials, the senior ones still pre-war appointees, are neutral functionaries *par excellence* even in personality and mentality, apart from the odd licensed flamboyant. Since the BIS includes, in addition to its permanent staff of over 100, a number of seconded officials from national central banks, it has acquired the standing and *de facto* executive power which accrue to a competent professional secretariat. The accumulation of knowledge and experience is an influential guiding factor in the discussions of the Bank's board, representing the Governors of the eight European members, Belgium, France, Germany, Italy, the United Kingdom, the Netherlands, Sweden, and Switzerland at their regular meeting in Basle on the second Monday of each month.

Not that the BIS's own operations are themselves unimportant: it can accept deposits of gold and currencies from central banks, international organizations, and public institutions. Although the Soviet Government is not a member, it employs the Bank as a buying and selling agent for gold. The advances which the Bank can make, notably in dollars, to reputable commercial banks throughout the world are at any one time an important factor in the supply–demand relationship in international money markets. BIS assets which were the equivalent of £25,000,000 at the end of World War II have now grown to almost £1,000 millions, of which 43% is in gold.

When the Group of Ten agreed in 1962 to make available an extra $6,000 millions to the IMF, the so-called General Agreement to Borrow (GAB), the BIS was again nominated as the handling mechanism for the four-year arrangement. Its annual reports now include comments on the financial policies of its members, that of June 1966 asserting flatly that the United Kingdom's credit squeeze had been largely blunted by the monetary means used to finance increased public spending.

The Bankers' Club

It is a measure of how far Europe has come since pre-war days that the monthly meetings of the 'Basle Club' are treated as routine and, as often as not, fail to be reported in the world's Press. The 'Club' meetings are attended by representatives of the Federal Reserve Bank of New York in its capacity as American correspondent, while the Governors of the Bank of Canada and Bank of Japan have a standing invitation to attend should they be in Europe. Since the Governor of the Netherlands Bank, Dr Marius Holtrop, was current Chairman and President of BIS at the time of the sterling crisis of 1964, the threads of world monetary affairs could be picked up and speedily manipulated.

The mutual professional respect and confidence, and even the personal friendship which have developed between central bankers, are possibly the most important single factor making for co-operation at the present stage of the evolution of a consciously controlled international monetary order. During the sterling crises of autumn 1964 and summer 1965, there was an understandable over-dramatization of the day-to-day events, the transatlantic flights of British Cabinet Ministers and civil servants, the long-distance telephone calls and White House colloquies. But the outcome was never in doubt, and the machinery of consultation and co-operation functioned as it normally does. For routine loans and swaps of nine figures are nothing unusual between central banks and Basle.

The bankers have, of course, to pay the price of being as fallible as the rest of the human race. Once the immediate technical problems of parity alignment arising from the 1949 devaluation of the pound and other currencies had been cleared out of the way and IMF at least began to function, some of the common assumptions of European and American financial experts seemed to rest on a sound basis. Perhaps some of the elements of the 1949 devaluation were not fully understood, particularly by Her Majesty's Treasury. Whereas the devaluations of the thirties had been in terms of gold with the various currencies finishing up with approximately the same parities, 1949 represented a realignment of soft currencies against hard ones. There was no general writing up of reserves in gold terms throughout the world, although the devaluation gave a powerful stimulus to South African and Australian gold production. But in dollar terms world reserves dropped by 24%.

Key currencies and great swaps

The long-term consequences of this for the 'key' currency concept were not generally foreseen and were masked by the outflow of United States capital, well over double the inter-war years, while world trade in manufactures increased by two-thirds. For countries with a diminished gold element in their reserves, dollars were an attractive substitute and, if not immediately required for investment or trade, had the added advantage of bearing interest if lent to someone else. As far as sterling was concerned, if there were difficulties from balance of payments deficits the IMF stepped in with short-term operations.

In practice, from the inception of the Fund up to mid-1963 some 34% of the gross drawings of $7,000 millions by its members covered transactions with the United Kingdom. Sterling was thus ceasing to be a reserve currency and its appearance of still enjoying a world status came from its role as a unit of account in transactions handled through Britain's global commodity, banking, and insurance services. The use of sterling in such trade-invoicing naturally involves extensive covering of forward positions, and thus the risk of pressure on the exchanges, but for a time, as post-war shortages were overcome, the terms of trade moved strongly in favour of Europe. Sterling seemed at first to have a comfortable path towards convertibility. But since Britain was only a middleman, there was no significant increase in its reserves, and the British devaluation had therefore had a different character from that of France in 1958. The British trade surplus in 1959, the year when 'we never had it so good', was $449,000,000, but repayments on previous borrowings were $782,000,000. Britain was dependent not on its own power but on the restraint of others.

The dollar seemed to have entered on a more secure heritage as a key currency. The outward evidence of this was the Euro-dollar market based on the need of both central banks and private interests to hold a large proportion of reserves in United States banks to obtain credit facilities as well as to earn interest. By the end of 1964 these totalled $7,624 millions in demand deposits, $4,700 millions in time deposits, and $7,000 millions in easily realizable United States Government securities. The best estimate of dollar loans between Western European and Canadian banks and institutions and important private interests was by 1964 some $5,000 millions. In the decade and a half since the world had started its monetary salvage operations after wartime disruption, national money markets had once more linked up and a broad international market had emerged. The paramount role of the dollar is illustrated by the comparatively modest total of $2,000 millions equivalent of other currencies acceptable in this type of business, the so-called Euro-currencies.

Who were the owners of these media of international money business and did ownership represent power? Of the New York holdings, some $4,000 millions were held by non-American commercial banks and corporations and the remainder by governments. Of the Canadian contribution to the international Euro-dollar market, some $1,000 millions were probably owned by United States residents, and even in the European segment of foreign currency deposit markets, the American commercial banking and corporation share amounted at the end of 1964 to $700,000,000. The total short-term commitment of American interests, banking and private, in Europe, Canada, Japan, and Latin America approximated to $3,300 millions.

Of the other non-European contributors to this international pool of the world's mobile wealth, the short-term liabilities of Swiss banks, estimated at the end of 1963 as about $2,600 millions, remain the largest, representing the savings of wealthy families in various parts of the world, residents of countries where the currency is ever prone to devaluation or even cancellation, or the liquid reserves of large international enterprises. Oil royalties of Middle Eastern states and rulers bring an annual $2,000 millions replenishment to the pool, but an increasing proportion of this is dispersed in development plans, commercial transactions, and investment. At the end of 1964 British banks—including foreign banks based in London—appeared as holding some $4,000 millions of foreign currencies, but here again London acted mainly as a middleman.

There is little room for any sinister financier to operate the strings of the world's wealth. Ownership is no longer power except within a limited framework of enterprise and mainly a legal formula for the protection of management. Governments, central banks, or commercial banking systems dominate the whole international financial complex. With what end in view? Governments and their monetary agencies are concerned with liquidity and safety and providing their nationals with facilities for the financing of trade and investment. For them the interest return is secondary, and if there is an element of risk, the interest rate differentials will be ignored. But commercial banks must make a profit and international corporations and private interests must have a return—if they can find a way of avoiding risks. So where forward rates can be devised, the turn-round of covered arbitrage funds has increased.

Not all currencies command the same prestige however well their national economies may be run. The reason is 'technical'. No bank of standing allows its foreign exchange dealers complete freedom to exploit currency or interest rate disparities. But in dealing with normal requests for various currencies they may have to carry through two or three successive swaps and thus create in their books at minimum cost in the appropriate denomination the funds requested. This skill in arbitrage is only possible with currencies in major demand, either because they are continuously needed for trade financing or belong to countries where there are wide and active money and investment markets. However excellent the standing and backing of the Belgian franc, the Austrian schilling, or the Kuwaiti dinar, the demand for them is too thin or uneven for any monetary authority, bank, or private financier to be certain that trading in them over a period will offer a satisfactory yield.

So dollar, sterling, Swiss franc, deutschmark, and, to a lesser extent, the Dutch guilder remain the preferred units of account in international transactions. What is being exercised by commercial banks and private financial interests is a skill, not a power—that remains with the national authorities. Even central bank measures have been directed, not to establish an ascendancy for their own currency or for the issued securities of their governments, but to create equilibrium in rates and prevent undesirable inflows of currency.

The skills have brought great benefits. Liquid balances amounting to several billion dollars which might otherwise have been placed in short-dated government securities have been made available to commercial banks, which in turn have been able to use them to finance world trade on behalf of their clients. The speedy absorption of unemployed funds and the levelling of interest rates has in effect made large-scale currency speculation impossible. Whatever currency the borrower may in fact require, he begins by acquiring low cost currencies from the lending bank, which then sells them on his behalf, and purchases the desired medium with the proceeds and arranges for the appropriate forward repurchase.

In accepting this role for its currency, the United States has also shouldered burdens. Domestic interest rates, the Federal Reserve open market operations in government securities, the capacity of its gold and foreign exchange reserves to meet the sum total of its short-term obligations—all these involve an American responsibility towards the foreign governments who maintain a sizeable portion of their reserves in New York. The supply and demand for United States Treasury bills in New York is a matter for daily scrutiny by the commercial banks of Europe, Australia, South Africa, and other countries with highly developed money markets. The forward rates for the dollar affect the cost of financing trade. The ebb and flow of foreign deposits in the United States is linked with the liquidity of banks, corporations, and insurance companies registered in London, Amsterdam, and Frankfurt. President Johnson's Great Society cannot evolve in isolation.

So the Federal Reserve Bank of New York had by August 1965

already made swap commitments of $2,800 millions with eleven central banks and the Bank for International Settlements, to be able to acquire at call currencies to sell spot or forward to control the dollar rate. For in the previous month, the United States had made its first 'non-technical' drawing in five European currencies from IMF.[1] The United States Treasury had to explain that the drawing—the equivalent of $300,000,000 in French and Belgian francs, Dutch guilders, Swedish kroner, and Italian lira—was required because as a result of the American balance of payments deficit, foreign official holdings of dollars temporarily absorbed under the swap arrangements, had to be reduced still further by purchasing them with the relevant currencies. Although this drawing was made within the gold *tranche* and therefore had to be accepted by the Fund as 'automatic', this was a decisive step. It meant that the United States no longer wished to repay its swap from its own reserves and that in technical terms the dollar had reached its limit as a reserve currency.

This action also underlined—as had become apparent for other reasons—that sterling, too, had formally lost this status. For the biggest swap agreement made by the United States was with the Bank of England—some $750,000,000 by March 1965 representing the extent to which the United States was underwriting Britain's currency by holding it out of the international money markets. Compared to the United States, Britain's problems perhaps seem modest. The total of overseas short-term sterling holdings in the London money market at the end of 1964 were £3,107 millions, of which the chief items were £839,000,000 of Treasury bills held by central monetary institutions of the overseas sterling area, £862,000,000 bank deposits from the overseas sterling area, and for non-sterling countries £301,000,000 in Treasury bills and £791,000,000 in bank deposits. Non-official foreign investments in British Treasury bills amounted to no more than £56,000,000 testifying to the virtual eclipse of the role they had once played as the most important medium for short-term interest arbitrage between the financial centres of the world.

By the third quarter of 1965 the value of sterling held by overseas countries and institutions other than the IMF had fallen to £2,268 millions, reflecting not only a loss of confidence in the pound but also a payments deterioration in the overseas sterling area. The extent of the

---

[1] A purely technical drawing arises if the Fund is holding its limit in a currency (in this case United States dollars) and members who have to repay it for any reason cannot therefore do so in dollars. Another member can accommodate them by purchasing currencies from the Fund with its own up to the gold *tranche* of its quota.

'real' fall, probably some £1,100 millions, was masked by the sterling held by the United States under swap agreements, while an apparent rise of £42,000,000 in Western European holdings was accounted almost completely by £41,000,000 deposited by the Bundesbank in July under military support cost arrangements between Britain and Germany. The 'sterling area' was in practice being supported by the United States and Germany.

The process of shift and change will continue for Britain. In the autumn of 1965 New Zealand, the most loyal member of the overseas sterling area, announced its intention of drawing on the IMF to meet its short-term balance of payments problems rather than liquefy its London reserve portfolio of government bonds and bills. At the same time Britain was having to liquefy its own much-prized dollar securities portfolio as preparation for repaying the IMF. During 1965 a growing trade deficit averaging about £300,000,000 a quarter threatened further demands on the London reserves. Not all apprehensions proved to be justified, but if Britain trembles for its currency stability whenever a member of the sterling area has to consider making a claim on its own reserves, another chapter has come to an end.

Rightly it is pointed out that in spite of the 1965 drop the total of sterling balances since World War II has remained relatively stable. But even when the balances increase, as happened in 1964 and then in 1966, this is sensed less as a blessing than as a latent threat in case they are called at moments most embarrassing to Britain. The uncomfortable realization of what could happen with only a slight drop in wool prices qualifies even the gratitude the British should feel at Australia's contribution of £500,000,000 to sterling area reserves. An upsurge in exports of sterling area countries creates anxiety lest their next import figures will show an even greater rise, while United Kingdom exports to the less provident members require ever lengthier deferred payment terms, up to twenty-five years for India and Pakistan. A country with weak reserves must eventually call a halt to this. The June 1966 credit lines agreed with the Group of Ten and to be administered by the BIS to ease pressures and exchange losses arising from overseas sterling area conversions and settlements could offer a step-by-step method for a take-over of the sterling area under some other international support system: the mystery is that the recognition of the chapter's end was postponed for so long.

Yet against half a century of wars, revolutions, collapse of empires, reconstruction, global shifts in trade and investment, transfers of funds on a scale unthinkable three decades ago, the human achievement is considerable. With only the traditional skills of banking and exchange,

122

the international financial mechanism has been adapted to new dimensions of state control operated on a world scale. The human shortcomings can be forgiven, and indeed make the achievement since Genoa 1922 seem even greater.

7. Debate on the future

Liquidity or reserves

A situation where international funds and the central banks are accumulating currencies which no one wants can hardly be said to be one lacking in either liquidity or reserves. It is a question of acceptability. The continued creation of claims which cannot be met—the fundamental reason for the decline of confidence in sterling as a reserve currency—is not a creation of reserves.

If the working definitions of the Bretton Woods Agreement had been re-examined there might have been less confusion in that part of the debate which was carried on in public. 'Payments for current transactions means payments which are not for the purpose of transferring capital.' Under this concept the IMF included foreign trade, normal short-term banking business, interest on loans and investments, amortization and depreciation payments. Monetary reserves, according to Bretton Woods, are the net central holdings of treasuries, central banks, stabilization funds, and fiscal agencies in gold, convertible currencies, or such other currencies or securities as the Fund may specify.

Many of the schemes put forward for monetary reform are as workable in theory as the existing practices which, taken out of their historical context and discussed in terms of classroom logic, would be dismissed as impossible to operate. But a skill still has to be operated within a setting of common assumptions. Every scheme so far produced has presented some form of challenge to the social and political assumptions of those who would have to operate it.

The simplest method of increasing 'liquidity'—raising the dollar price of gold from \$35 a fine ounce—is ruled out because of the immediate short-term benefits to the chief challengers of the myths of 1776. The quickest method of easing the 'reserve' situation is to increase the number of 'key' currencies. For if it is impossible for all countries to have a balance of payments surplus, it is equally impossible for them all to be in deficit. So if a number of leading financial powers were to agree to accept each other's currencies without limit in settlement for their net credits, the probability is that over the years the swing between surpluses and deficits in their payments will prove supportable and permit further major economies in the use of the world's gold stock for final settlements.

But this latter solution would require all participants to permit funds to move freely between national money markets, abandon high interest rates, and allow reputable borrowers and lenders of all nationalities to use without let or hindrance the international market thus created. Since this would mean the end of Napoleonic centralism in France, loosen the tight grip of German commercial banks over industrial financing, give the Italian fiscal authorities sleepless nights, and jeopardize the Netherlands Bank's iron paternalistic hold over the country's banking system, a formal expansion of the key currency concept has so far proved unacceptable in both IMF and OECD contexts.

The currency-reformers

On one side, therefore, the debate has extended to include the proponents of a new supranational system and, on the other, those who prefer a gradual improvement of existing international machinery but introducing an obligation on each participating member to follow domestic economic policies which would enable the improvements to be really effective.

The former include Mr Edward M. Bernstein, one-time Assistant Secretary at the United States Treasury and IMF official, now an independent financial consultant. His plan for a new international currency takes the form of a reserve unit made up from fixed proportions of eleven important national currencies on a basis of fixed exchange rates between them. Professor Robert Triffin, economist and banker, who, like most Yale professors, can claim to have been at one time or another a 'Washington adviser', proposes bringing the gold exchange standard to an end by the compulsory handing-over of existing official dollar and sterling balances to the IMF in exchange for an equivalent value of Fund deposits.

British proposals for monetary reform have been somewhat along the Triffin lines. One put forward by a London banker, the Hon. Maxwell Stamp, proposes the creation of additional reserve assets in the form of IMF certificates, but would link these with the provision of development finance, either as an investment of currencies drawn from members' quotas or borrowed in the form of securities and notes issued by the World Bank. In the autumn of 1962, the so-called Maudling Plan put forward by the British Government at Tokio was based on a Mutual Currency Account. Prompted by the textbook British Foreign Office view that it is always tactically desirable to table some sort of document and elaborated by Bank of England officials, it aimed at attracting the widest support by being modest in its scope. In 1965 France advocated through her Finance Minister, M. Valéry Giscard d'Estaing, a modification of the Bernstein Plan, where the emphasis was on the control of the additional reserve unit by a small group of countries acting in unanimity.

Rueff and the Rhine-maidens

While mankind was not to be crucified on a cross of bullion, the counter-argument also came up from the depths, like the Rhine-maidens' chant in Wagner's *Ring*, that gold was guiltless and only the evil doings of men had tarnished it. M. Jacques Rueff, chief proponent of a return to gold, does not, however, preach the reconstitution of a gold standard which never was, but aims at a system where currency balances could and should be held for trading purposes and international settlements should be made solely in gold. This would be achieved by all countries refraining from accumulating further currency balances and agreeing to a simultaneous doubling of the price of gold in dollar terms. The United States would pay off its dollar deficits but leave its gold reserves unchanged in monetary terms, while the United Kingdom would redeem its sterling balances with the help of a twenty-year loan raised by the other countries, and met from the increased value of the world's currencies as a result of the gold price increase. The latter in turn would call forth an increased supply from mines and hoards and so meet new liquidity demands.

Rueff has come under severe attack, chiefly because his plan perpetuates contingental relations arising from the historical accident of the 1934 gold–dollar ratio. This would be consolidated by doubling the gold price, and those who happen to have gold now would receive an undeserved bonus, while South African gold supplies are too haphazard an element. To which one can readily reply that history *is* largely made up of 'accidents' and cannot be reversed, that the present is always the point of departure for the future, and there has been nothing haphazard about South African mining and selling policy. On the contrary, this last has been eminently predictable.

The commercial bankers who gather at every IMF conference to lobby ideas as well as tout for custom, pressed the point of view of those who cope with daily supply and demand. Their argument is a cogent one summarized by Dr Samuel Schweizer of the Swiss Bank Corportion of Zurich (who can probably lay good claim to the title of Arch-Gnome) that mutual credit arrangements are not technically an addition to overall liquidity because the credit position of one country compensates the deficit position of another. The gold monetary element thus remains central to a real increase of liquidity. If the main currencies continue to lose their purchasing power, a tension arises between the cost of gold and the prices of raw materials; this will sooner or later cause dislocations and eventually adjustments. A sharp inflation in the United States would precipitate this. President Johnson may have claimed: 'The dollar will always remain as good as gold' to which the Arch-Gnome retorts: 'Is gold condemned to be for ever as bad as the dollar?'[1]

But the pattern of serious debate gradually emerged less as a question of dialectic than of motive. The original dichotomy between those who had to take action and those who had assumed the role of urging others to act began to disappear. The latter were predominantly professors, writers, directors of institutes, and professional conference-haunters. The former were the officials and central bankers who had to operate existing instruments. Within the official ambit the dialogue turned increasingly round the participants' view of the world and how power should be exercised. Although the language of discussion—at times rather desperately—was still about 'liquidity', 'reserves', 'growth', 'balance of payments', and 'clearing arrangements', the issue was one of control, not a confrontation of theories.

This did not immediately bring clarity to the debate. When President Kennedy, welcoming the 1963 IMF Conference, laid stress on the measures being taken to reduce the American deficit, those who had been denouncing the United States for spreading inflation began to cry havoc at the prospect of the shortage of liquidity which could follow. When the Group of Ten set up a committee 'to undertake a thorough examination of the outlook for the functioning of the international monetary system and of its probable needs for liquidity', those who had been advocating just such a step protested that the whole

[1] *European Review*, Winter 1965–6 (The Birlet Press, 1966).

question had been overtaken by 'aid for the underdeveloped'. But two firm attitudes emerged and which demanded practical counter-arguments and not opposing theories. Since the Ten conducted 80% of net international payments and possess 86% of all reserves, the representatives of their central banks maintained that it must always fall to them to put up any new reserves to provide for any plan. Also, the United States claimed that in a world of sovereign states it must in the last analysis decide itself on what basis it would reduce its deficit. After 1963 the plans of the professors tended to be lost sight of.

Group of Ten gets to work

By June 1964 the Group of Ten had produced the assumptions which should govern any new system. First, there should be firm rules for the rectification of balance of payments problems; second, there should be multilateral supervision of swaps and accumulations of key currencies; third, there should be upper and lower limits to dollar deficits; and last, that in special cases loans in softer currencies could be allowed. The cause of inflation, it was emphasized, was a country's internal policy and not the consequence of the gold exchange standard. Funding of debts for key currencies, a general rise in the price of gold, and completely flexible exchange rates were ruled out as possible courses. In August 1964 the Ministers and Governors of the central banks of the Ten approved a proposal of their deputies to set up 'A Study Group on the Creation of Reserve Assets' under Signor Rinaldo Ossola, head of international studies at the Banca d'Italia. The three international organizations, Bank for International Settlements, IMF, and OECD, were invited to participate.

Mr Robert Roosa, former Deputy-Secretary of the U.S. Treasury, produced a more complicated Bernstein plan, by which the composite reserve units would be created in proportion to the extent national currencies were already in use as reserve currencies. Long-term loans, denoted in gold or dollars, would be granted to countries such as the United Kingdom, which had outgrown their present reserves, and be used as collateral for shorter-term credits between the lending countries, thus becoming a sort of 'secondary reserve asset'.

The 'Roosa Plan', apart from its obvious aim of making it easier for the United States to cope with its dollar deficit, struck the chord on which the Americans would continue to hammer in subsequent discussion. This was the insistence that it be set up in an IMF framework. Although the recommendations for the issue of 'Roosa units' would be made by representatives of the main contributors to the Fund (in practice, the Group of Ten), all IMF Governors would have to give their approval. While IMF voting still remained weighted in favour of the original chief Bretton Woods subscribers, its discussions, in company with other world bodies set up after the end of the war, were changing character, as it was joined by the new states of Asia and Africa. The IMF had never resisted any use by the latter of drawing rights: in addition it had sent expert missions to new states which found themselves in currency difficulties and had properly enough laid down conditions under which they would be permitted to make additional drawings.

But advocates of 'world solutions' were now objecting to the IMF telling Asian and African countries what economic policies to follow. This might be 'resented', they maintained. On one side the IMF was being called upon to play the role of a supranational central bank; on the other, the Fund was not to lay down the type of conditions which any banker is entitled to make to his clients. And this was not merely a question of the disparity of national monetary and fiscal policies. Drawing on any country's currency by others automatically increases its own IMF drawing rights: unless the increased liquidity is matched within some acceptable time scale by increases in productivity, the outcome would be world inflation. Since there would be little hope of most countries being able to restore their gold *tranche* at the same time, the Fund would end its existence with a mass of useless paper.

Not that the Fund had been denied fresh resources. From its establishment through to June 1963, the gross drawings of member countries had been $7,000 millions. All quotas had been increased by one half in September 1959. The aim of the $6,000 millions General Agreement to Borrow Fund set up under Group of Ten control had been to increase IMF borrowing possibilities. In September 1964 the IMF asked for a general increase of 25% in quotas to increase its resources to a total of $21,000 millions. Some countries even requested higher quotas, notably West Germany, Japan, and South Africa, as a recognition of the change in their relative economic importance in the world. By spring 1966 the required two-thirds majority approval for the quota increases had been received.

The first IMF Managing Director, Mr Per Jacobsson of Norway, who previously had held the same position in the Bank for International Settlements, had kept firmly to the Fund's stated objective of maintaining stable exchanges. His successor in September 1963, M. Pierre-Paul Schweitzer, at the time of his appointment a

Deputy-Governor of the Banque de France, seemed to be cast in the same orthodox mould. But by the beginning of 1965 he too had taken up the theme of the needs of developing countries, although the role of reserves in a country's 'development' is to maintain continuity and not themselves be used for the development. In fact during the period 1948–62, including the Korean war boom, the level of imports of the majority of IMF members had been determined by export earnings plus capital inflow, and not by short-term borrowing facilities. During this period of expanding world trade, most countries had felt themselves short of reserves.

Nevertheless by June 1965 M. Schweitzer was advocating that IMF should purchase obligations of the World Bank, which would then invest the proceeds in member countries, while he declared that 'the richer nations of the world should not appear to be clubbing together to create reserves—out of nothing as it were—for themselves alone'.[1] Stating his belief that it should be left to the Fund to create reserves, he did not go into details, adding: 'As a matter of fact these details are not in themselves very important from a broad point of point.' Since the reserves created by the 'richer' countries have enabled world volume of trade to increase twice as fast as world output, M. Schweitzer's remarks were disturbingly irrelevant for one holding such an appointment.

While the Ossola Group pursued its labours during 1965, the actions and pronouncements of governments left a surface impression of incoherence and contradiction on monetary matters. The French called repeatedly for gold as a basis of settlement. Rejecting the notion of a gold standard, Dr Carli stressed that a credit component had become a permanent element of external liquidity in the international monetary system, but he prudently put two-thirds of the Banca d'Italia's reserves into gold. United Kingdom politicians and economists repeated *ad nauseam* why a balance of payments deficit must lead to inflation, while on the other hand the Banca d'Italia's economic advisers expounded most lucidly how an external surplus creates inflation by pushing up internal demand. The Americans stood by the dollar as being better than gold, but President Johnson had to introduce legislation to abolish the 25% gold backing for the Federal Reserve System, so releasing $5,000 millions' worth of gold for dollar support operations. The Group of Ten agreed to continue until 1970 the General Agreement to Borrow, although at the same time all of them were carrying out measures to reduce domestic liquidity, a policy bound to affect the international availability of credit.

[1] Address to Institut d'Études Bancaires, 2 February 1965.

130

The Ossola Report

When the Ossola Report appeared in August 1965 there was an unjustified sigh of disappointment that it made no firm recommendations for monetary reform but merely listed the pros and cons of all proposals studied. What his study group achieved—and it was a major feat—was to set out a common language of assumptions on which the argument could be based at the policy-making level.

Leaving aside methods of financing external balance of payments deficits, the Ossola Group had devoted its main attention to ways by which central governments and their financial authorities could among themselves create new reserve assets for distribution 'across the board'. Its broad definition of a state's reserves was: 'All those liquid assets held by its monetary authorities which can be used, directly or through assured convertibility into other assert, to support its rate of exchange when its external payments are in deficit.' Attempts to measure by any quantitative formula the adequacy of world reserves were dismissed in the Ossola Report, which pointed out that there are other sources of liquidity which can be used in furthering economic objectives. 'The assessment of a country's reserve needs will therefore depend greatly on the degree of independence which it wishes to preserve in pursuit of its policies,' says the Report.

In the discussion of the various proposals, Triffin, Bernstein, etc., for collective reserve units, the question was raised again and again, not only in the Ossola Group but at every official and unofficial conclave: Who will decide on the issue and distribution of the new units? Will it be a small group of industrial countries who are the creators of the world's real resources? Will it be the Group of Ten or some larger grouping? If the Fund is to be associated with the scheme selected, will it be as a simple bookkeeper, as administrator of the transfers, or as the decision-maker?

It was hard to see how delegates of 103 disparate societies could collectively voice opinions on matters where even relatively homogeneous and like-minded groups of experts can barely agree on definitions. Still, Signor Ossola and his colleagues had to take evidence from clamant spokesmen in favour of all IMF members operating by simple majority vote in the creation and distribution of money. It is, of course, tempting to take an optimistic view of the power of objective rules of international bodies where the daily, if self-conscious, effort of maintaining goodwill and producing paper reconciliations creates its own special euphoria. Some of the operations do appear to pursue their own 'objective' path.

For example, in the calculations of the reserve assets of a central bank, other than gold itself, a 'gross principle' is generally observed, i.e. the dollar holdings of the bank are not deducted as a liability from the gold reserves of the United States. The IMF variants of this gross principle are in some cases so complex that they appear to be operating as part of a self-regulating mechanism. If an IMF member makes a first drawing, the member whose currency it draws gains a 'super gold *tranche*' equivalent to the gold *tranche* of the drawing member. If the latter makes a second drawing in its first credit *tranche*, not only do its reserves not decrease but the super-*tranche* of the second member is held to have increased, although the amount of gold remains the same. If callable gold certificates were substituted—as suggested in one of the many 'world solutions'—the same would apply. Similarly under another proposal—that of special currency operations by which the Fund would invest some of its currency holdings in World Bank or national schemes—this would be regarded as a doubling of reserve positions on both sides.

It is true that while the European Payments Union was in operation, as Signor Ossola noted, creditor countries did not worry about accumulated credits, although the process did not differ in essentials from the spending of reserves. This was, however, a convention among like-minded groups whose production was increasing and trade expanding. The acceptability of reserve currencies is based not only on their theoretical convertibility into gold at a fixed price but also on the circumstances that the issuing countries are major commodity, credit, and capital markets—a condition which only a minority of IMF members can meet. Any process of reserve creation implies the reciprocal granting of automatic drawing rights on real resources and even Signor Ossola, normally the personification of impartiality, had to describe as 'absurd' any suggestion that countries which could not offer this guarantee should participate. 'Reciprocal rights' also implies reciprocal surrender of rights on real resources, a process of restraint which makes the problems of industrial countries a completely different order from those facing primary producers.

Ultimately then, some form of gold value guarantee was held to be necessary, and in recognizing the indispensability of gold, the Ossola Group noted that in the last analysis any monetary innovation would consist in making a more economical use of it.

After the publication of the Ossola Report and prior to the 1965 IMF Conference, Mr Henry Fowler started a tour of Europe to canvass support for a world monetary conference. He received a cool reception. The debate had gone back into the inner councils of the Group of Ten and was increasingly dominated by the personality of Dr Otmar Emminger of the German Bundesbank, Chairman of the Deputies of the Group of Ten. With a cool, even severe manner combined with courtesy—essential when dealing with English romantic economists— he seemed to embody the views of his chief, Dr Blessing, that self-discipline would solve 99% of most human problems. When at the 1965 IMF Conference the Ossola Report had to be taken from the technical to the political plane, it was to Emminger that the matter was now turned over.

Outwardly the decision was an instruction to the Deputies of the Group of Ten to resume the discussions with active IMD, OECD, and BIS participation to find a basis of agreement on monetary reform and on the future creation of reserve assets. It seemed an anodyne outcome to what had been expected to be a controversial session. Indeed it was rumoured that the French Minister of Finance, M. Giscard d'Estaing, had arrived at the conference with two speeches, one accepting the need for a new system and the other rejecting the idea, delivery to be determined by last-minute telegraphic instructions from President de Gaulle. In the event, when M. Giscard d'Estaing did speak it was a vague dissertation on a doctrine of 'parallelism' between the creation of reserve units and the stabilization of commodity prices, obviously reflecting concern with French farm prices, rather than with aid for the underdeveloped. In public the Italians paid tribute to the dollar as a reserve currency but in private advocated a harmonization of the gold elements of the reserves of major states, not unexpectedly at the 50% level of their own.

The British had little to say. In public Callaghan could only maintain his well-known smile, although the problem of the long-term consolidation of sterling balances was the spectre at the feast. Candidates for an enlarged Group of Ten, such as Australia, Spain, and Mexico, received a brush-off, and the Ten agreed on no more than that there should be a 'forum for appropriate discussions' once their Deputies had reported in spring 1966. British and American officials assured Asians and Africans that this meant the IMF, an assurance they should never have given, since it proved impossible in practice and started an even more arid controversy in the summer of the following year. While the United States Congress produced its own plan for turning IMF into a world Federal Reserve System, President Johnson solemnly promised that the long period of United States deficits had come to an end. M. Pierre-Paul Schweitzer seemed rather impassive as the delegates dispersed.

But Dr Emminger went back to Europe in no doubt that the reserve currency system had reached its limits, some ten to twelve years previously in the case of Britain and in the case of the dollar at the end of 1964, when the United States introduced restrictive measures coming very close to foreign exchange control. The question of whether liquidity was short or in surplus had been shelved by the formula of 'contingency planning', which all participants understood as preparing some form of prophylaxis against the English sickness: the British themselves were told firmly that there would be no further support for the pound in a balance of payments context but only to counter purely speculative actions against the sterling rate.

The 1966 free-for-all

The discussions during the first half of 1966 were characterized by French skirmishing tactics and a dogged American insistence that IMF should play the central role. Provided United States' deficits remained within existing limits, the French indicated that they would not object to the dollar continuing as a modified key currency. Dropping their demand that any new reserve unit should be linked to gold, the French then proposed that it should be distributed in proportion to the percentage of national income devoted to development aid—by its own method of calculating this, France claimed the largest proportion at 1·6%. With their proposal that the IMF should have improved drawing rights only and that 25% of any reserve unit created by a restricted group such as the Ten should be administered by the Fund, the Americans seemed to be under the same conviction that they could 'handle' the IMF as they had once imagined over the United Nations. Since in practice such 'handling' has come to mean that the American-Afro-Asian-Latin American majority is increasingly invoked against European interests, there was reluctance to stomach the idea of giving a world organization a claim on a country's real resources and so reduce its range of economic policy choices. Dr Emminger seemed to go far enough, too far in the view of some of his European colleagues, in conceding that some proportion of any new reserve unit could be set aside for the underdeveloped world.

However, once the Americans had suggested that a gold link was not necessary for settlements in any new reserve unit, the Banque de France published in March its reserve figures showing that the gold element had increased to 86%, from $3,755 millions in 1964 to $4,730 millions in 1965, of which $884,200,000 seemed to have come from the United States' gold stock. Thereafter France simply dissented on the whole question of the necessity for new reserves and stood by the principle of reserve units to be based on gold and created by unanimity. The Italians continued to talk in wide formulae on the need for harmonization of reserve composition, although this would involve harmonizing national financial policies. As Belgians and Dutch looked at their domestic credit policies and considered how far they would have to help to foot the world's bill, they found the French standpoint decidedly more sympathetic. Outside the discussion, the Chairman of the Administrative Board of the Swiss National Bank told his shareholders' annual meeting in March: 'Instead of being happy that there is finally some prospect of dampening inflation, one is today calling for additional monetary reserves—artificially created with paper and ink and without real collateral—to increase the credit potential of international economies.'

Hopes of a solution in 1966 disappeared when M. Pierre-Paul Schweitzer and his officials under Afro-Asian pressure made a bid to establish the IMF as the controlling agency for reserve creation using their own Fund units. As the IMF officials' own plan was gradually dragged into the light of day, it proved to be the sort of carpentry expected to satisfy all 103 members at once while too complex for the majority of them to grasp. New 'unconditional reserves' would be distributed in the form of automatic drawing rights allowing for indirect transferability between countries either by purchase of currencies from the Fund or by the creation of reserve units, which could be transferred directly between countries under Fund guidance. To this was added a rider that IMF members already in debt by more than their 'unconditional' gold *tranche* would not have access to the new facility unless their 'conditional' borrowings were less than the amount of reserve creation decided on. The new reserves would be created by a straight IMF voting majority but only made effective for individual members under a two-thirds voting support from the largest subscribers or those whose currencies had been in most frequent use. The resources to meet normal Fund drawings and those on the new facility would be pooled and the Executive Directors would make decisions as to transfers. The 'conditional' and 'unconditional' proportions would be reviewed at the five-year re-assessment of Fund quotas.

The chances of a sympathetic reception by the Group of Ten for these proposals had been dispelled by Schweitzer's rejection of any suggestion that some IMF members were more (or less) equal than others. No doubt it is one of the disadvantages of world organizations that M. Schweitzer, or anyone else in a similar position, cannot bluntly tell one of his Executive Directors that the group of countries which elected him will never qualify under the minimum conditions permitting them to produce acceptable convertible reserves. Since the use of Fund resources by the United Kingdom in 1965 (amounting to $1,390 millions) substantially exceeded the British balance of payments deficit and enabled it to reconstitute reserves of $689,000,000, M. Schweitzer had a talking point when he proclaimed in April 1966: 'I can see no possible basis for dividing the member countries of the Fund into the reliable few and the less responsible many.' In May he launched a fresh attack: 'I consider that international liquidity is not the business of a limited group of countries but of the whole free world.' Dr Emminger retorted: 'I cannot see what difference it makes whether we conclude our preparatory work a few months earlier or later'.

And so, a small drafting sub-committee of British, Dutch, French, and German officials, whose names were unknown to their parliaments or the electorates whose fates were involved, produced in early July a basis for the appearance of Ministerial agreement, the French always excepted. Every conceivable phrase mentioned in past discussion was introduced, carefully offset by another about 'misuse' or 'safeguard'. Inspired Washington rumours of a new and aggressive United States monetary policy died out as the Ministers of Finance of the Ten gathered at The Hague on 25 and 26 July. The problem of sterling had been clearly differentiated from that of monetary reform and the agreed formula was that a series of meetings should be held with the twenty IMF Directors.

The general tenor of the document was that at that moment of 1966, there was no general shortage of reserves, but, as part of a contingency plan, existing types might have to be supplemented by a deliberately created new asset. Although this would have to be done on the basis of 'a collective judgement of the reserve needs of the world as a whole', the 'particular responsibility' of major key nations for the financial backing of reserve assets was recognized as against the 'legitimate interest' of all countries as to their adequacy; when needed they should be distributed to IMF members proportionately.

Nevertheless there was evidence of progress at the annual IMF Conference in September. The Group of Ten had given formal instructions to its Deputies to take part in meetings with IMF Executive Directors and consider questions affecting the world economy. If they had not accepted American and British suggestions to include in the instructions any reference to 'world liquidity', statistics were on their side. Over the past year 'world liquidity' as determined in terms of official gold holdings and readily transferable assets in central banks and IMF, had increased by $1,330 millions to a record total of $70,230 millions. In his address at the conference, M. Schweitzer himself had become more temperate. His own polemics had merely been exploited by Afro-Asian and Latin American delegates, who regarded 'liquidity' as a means of getting hold of more foreign exchange. Dr Carli too had been making converts for his doctrine of harmonization of reserves and there was general acceptance, and even a certain French acquiescence, in his view that the dollar portion of existing reserves should be maintained at approximately existing levels.

This had been demonstrated in a practical fashion just prior to the IMF conference by the great 'swap' agreement of August between the Federal Reserve, ten European central banks, Japan, and the BIS. Far from being a hasty improvization or stop-gap, this established a new point of departure for a joint financial policy by the participants. It could serve as the basis for determining future proportions of national currencies to be used in a *de facto* key role, or, taken further, the proportions of any new international composite reserve unit for which each country would be responsible. It also provided a ratio which could be used to determine the size of gold transfers to accompany future reserve unit transactions or settlements. In all but name this was an acceptance by the leading countries of the Western world that their currencies were all playing a reserve role and that they had undertaken a new obligation to control their domestic liquidities in the general interest.

The central issue or substance was now prevention of abuse of the system by deficit countries whether their troubles had resulted from maladministration, as in the British case, or because they were backward or savage communities—euphemistically described as 'poor', 'developing' or even 'modernizing' (to use the phrase of Mr Robert McNamara), but in effect incapable of sustaining a Western-style credit structure. If the United States stress was still on universality, Dr Blessing preferred to use the ambiguous phrase of 'the *global* needs of the *Western* world'.

Apart from a remarkable intervention by M. Debré in praise of gold, annual conference statements were muted. The Group of Ten–IMF discussions were authorized to continue for one year, with a clear distinction being drawn between the drafting of a plan and the definition of the circumstances of its activation. If the French objected that the existence of a plan would merely lead to the demand for its implementation, they were not without some experience of the devious ways of Anglo-Saxon diplomacy, and making the point that a new world monetary asset depended on the credibility of a world-wide authority, M. Debré asked: 'But who can imagine or believe in an authority sufficiently respected to create or manage monetary liquidity through daily uncontested decisions?' No one answered him.

Formally France was asking that IMF observe its own rule on which up to the beginning of the sixties the United States had also insisted, that each member acquiring other countries' currencies was entitled to ask the countries concerned to convert them into gold. No IMF member had been more ruthless than the United States in refusing to accept balance of payments difficulties as an excuse for departing from this convertibility principle. But statesmanship consists in recognizing new factors brought about by change, and an accumulated United States' deficit since 1960 of $21,000 millions reflected in central bank holdings of $13,000 millions and private holdings of $8,000 millions represented a new factor not to be wished away by formal logic applied to a past situation.

Towards compromise

The first joint meeting of IMF Directors and Group of Ten Deputies had been fixed for 28 November under the chairmanship of the IMF Managing Director. By mid-October the Group of Ten had made it clear that neither was M. Schweitzer to be permanent chairman nor Washington the permanent venue. The Fund quickly enough conceded that meetings should also take place in Europe under Dr Emminger. This procedural point crystallized the basic divergence of Europe's interest from those claiming to speak for the 'world'. But theoretically there seemed room for compromise within the broad concept of a gold transfer system, by which new reserve units could be used in settlement of inter-governmental obligations. Whether the Fund used its existing machinery or set up a new separate 'fund' to handle questions of additional drawing rights was a secondary consideration, and since the IMF itself had resulted from a compromise, any new general step forward would also involve one.

Nor was there any fundamental divergence of views between European banking experts and the Federal Reserve officials. Dr Emminger personally had come to favour an extension of the General Agreement to Borrow system, by which a proposal to open credits on behalf of any country is made on the initiative of the IMF Managing Director, the decision to open the credits is taken by those providing them, and IMF honour is satisfied by being able to give a confirming vote. The GAB and swaps provide an interim system which can in course of time be codified and the next step towards this could be, in Emminger's view, to put their use under formal multilateral surveillance. So far such schemes have not been attacked as discriminatory and represent a true creation of liquidity, even if among a relatively limited group of countries.

If the first stage of the Group of Ten–IMF talks seemed to get off to a friendly start this was not therefore so surprising. What was more worrying was M. Schweitzer's assurance that general agreement had been reached on the observance of principles of 'global needs', 'general trends', 'universal distribution', 'existing quotas'.[1] This seemed to point to the sort of compromise where the eventual documents and conventions would proclaim one end and aim and various signatories would console themselves with the thought that it would be different in practice. A similar situation was indicated by M. Schweitzer's categorical denial that the price of gold was to be discussed and the French Government's insistence that it had been and would be. The risks of formal concessions to 'universality', while trying to maintain a backstairs ascendancy, have been sufficiently illustrated by the relationship between Security Council and General Assembly at the United Nations. M. Debré's warning against the loss of power and control by one side before the other could meet the requirement of a credible and effective authority had considerable relevance.

He had also some foundation for his statement in July 1966 that minority was not exile, even if France's own voting strength in IMF was well short of the 20% needed to block changes in quotas. But the Group of Ten as a whole still had this power in the IMF Board, and so long as the United Kingdom and the United States had failed to put their balances of payments in order, it was the EEC countries who possessed it within the Group of Ten.

So the 1967 compromise plan of 'Special Drawing Rights' for increasing international liquidity, drawn up by representatives of the Group of Ten jointly with IMF Executive Directors, and submitted to the IMF Annual Conference in Rio de Janeiro in September, proved to be Dr Emminger's notion of an extension of the General Agreement to Borrow to meet balance of payment deficits. Embodying the Italian 'harmonization' suggestion, credit lines would be allotted in convertible usable currencies with the condition that countries would first utilize

[1] Washington statement, 30 November 1966.

their existing gold and foreign currency reserves in reasonable proportions. The circumstances for activating the plan were those insisted
upon by France, i.e. decisions as to dates and maximum value would
require 80% of IMF votes instead of the usual 85%, thus giving the
EEC countries with their 16·7% of voting strength, the possibility of
a joint veto.

Under the Rio proposals the first annual total of credit lines would
be between $1,000–2,000 millions and would be increased in the light
of experience. 'Reconstitution', that is, repayment in the currencies in
which the credit line was opened, would be for basic periods, initially
five years. The argument as to whether these should be 'rights', 'credits',
'automatic', 'transferable', or only 'repayable' was resolved by the
realistic admission during earlier 1967 discussions in Munich and
London that credits can always be renewed and in practice are
transferable between central banks so that it would be possible to
represent SDR's as first-line reserves. Recommendations for such
rights, which would have a fixed gold parity (that of the present United
States dollar) and the type of currencies to be used, would be made by
the IMF Managing Director and authorized by the Group of Ten. As
Emminger told a journalist in Rio: 'What was needed was a zebra, an
animal which could with equal truth be described as a white animal with
black stripes and as a black animal with white stripes!'

Prospects for the plan were clouded by the disingenuous claim of
the United States Secretary of the Treasury, Mr Henry Fowler, and
of the IMF Managing Director, that the scheme was not conditional
on a reform of existing IMF rules. Since it had been agreed in the
Munich and London talks that the two issues of SDR's and IMF
reform were interdependent, the French and German delegates at Rio
reacted strongly against Fowler's statement.

However, the IMF Executive Directors were instructed by the Rio
Conference to submit to the Fund's Governors not later than 31 March
1968 the necessary amendments to the Articles to establish SDR's and
any necessary amendments to IMF rules and practices. A process of
ratification by national governments will thereafter be necessary, with
the understanding that the United States and the United Kingdom
remedy their balance of payments deficits by traditional economic,
monetary, and budgetary means.

Still pursuing his Rhine-maidens, M. Rueff in *Le Monde* of 18
September 1967 had denounced SDR's as only an extension of existing
central bank swap arrangements, which is, of course, precisely their
virtue. And given the growth rate of international reserves in latter
years, $1,000 millions per annum represents a useful additional working

margin while the building-up of the SDR system would permit a gradual opting-out of sterling by countries no longer wishing to hold it in their reserves. In the long-term, the European Economic Community would be under a continuing powerful compulsion to maintain a single monetary policy *vis-à-vis* the rest of the world. For in the meantime another programme of action was cutting across the various world notions, that of the integration process of the Treaty of Rome. Stumbling at times, coming up against the same French obstructionism whether motivated by bargaining or merely to maintain the widest preserve of French sovereignty, the process was now extending into the field of finance.

EEC looks ahead

Early EEC preoccupations with internal trade barriers, agricultural prices, and external tariffs have obscured the significance of the financial developments, particularly as under the Treaty of Rome purely advisory status was accorded to the Monetary Committee set up in 1960. But regular meetings began between Ministers of Finance and Governors of central banks. Paralleling the progress made between 1962 and 1966 to change the concept of EEC from a customs union to an economic federation, discussions in 1962 had resulted in a formal announcement that full monetary union was the objective, that the Governors of the banks would by 1970 form the central organ of a banking system, and in the same year capital movements within the Community would be completely freed.

Even during the difficult years this programme was not halted, and 1964 saw four important decisions of the EEC Council of Ministers, the first being to set up a Medium Term Economic Policy Committee to reconcile economic policies and aims. To further this, the second decision was the creation of a Budgetary Policy Committee to do the same for national budgets. The remaining two decisions were the formalization of the Committee of Central Bank Governors as a consultative body on credit, money, and foreign exchange market problems and an agreement that no major decision or attitude should be adopted in the field on international monetary relations without prior consultation, particularly on currency parities. So far these agreements have been kept.

October 1964 also saw the formation of a panel of experts under

Dr Claudio Segré to study the integration of European capital markets. The separate national traditions of banking and finance had revealed their deficiencies during the Italian economic difficulties of 1963 and 1964, and only the reversion to various forms of concealed exchange control had prevented critical pressures on the lira. The alternative was a Europe-wide money market where surplus funds could move easily and re-establish equilibrium in short- and long-term rates. The potential of the existing embryonic unofficial international European market was such that in 1965, when European national bond markets were looking bleak, a series of non-European borrowers were able to raise $1,000 millions. It had been an impressive demonstration, but rising interest rates in European capital markets during 1966 illustrated that the inadequacy was not in the short-term credit supply for trade but in the longer-term investment requirements of the Western world.

These requirements will grow more pressing as European companies expand and as the European Investment Bank, set up under the Treaty of Rome, increases its issuing activity and seeks a market to support its paper. The balance of payments surpluses arising from Europe's steady expansion will create the same investment potential as the City of London possessed during the nineteenth century, and can engender a new outward thrust of the same order. The encouragement of this potential becomes as important as the development of weapons and the marshalling of armies. For here are involved the means by which the sinews of industrial power are strengthened while, as with the English sickness, underinvestment reveals itself in weakened postures in international trade and finance.

The sagging of the French franc rate in the autumn of 1966, reflecting the need to acquire some more easily transferable unit of account by those who had gained francs from trading and investment, was another reminder that by itself an immobilizable hoard of gold at best supplies a defensive weapon against economic dictation by others. But funds are put to work and new productive capacity is created through the attraction of a profitable and freely accessible capital market. The analogy of eighteenth-century Spain with its monopoly of Peruvian silver is still valid. After a year of international obstructionism, M. Debré held the spotlight at the December 1966 meeting of the Council of Ministers with a call to eliminate tax discrepancies in the Community which could impede the functioning of European capital markets once the movement of funds was freed.

This represented less conversion than his foreknowledge of Dr Segré's report, published a month later, which laid stress on the need for EEC countries to overhaul taxation and public finance and borrowing before they could evolve an integrated capital market attractive to the investor and accessible to public and private borrowers.[1] In 1966 there had been a clear misdirection of purpose in European capital control measures. The 'excess' domestic liquidity over which European central banks were trying to maintain control resulted in great part from a new growth of savings which could find no corresponding outlet in investment. The skilful procedures only concealed a sterility of thought when foreign currencies piling up in European central banks had to be made available to commercial banks and private enterprise to lend abroad on short term. The resultant appearance of foreign exchange earnings was being maintained at the price of internal official interventions in the relations between investor and capitalist, manufacturer and trader, producer and consumer. As far as Europe itself was concerned, the distribution of a relatively small quantity of a new official reserve unit would not meet its high and growing requirement for private investment. IMF solutions which would add to the inflation of economies outside Europe without increasing investment capacity could provide no answer to a situation where there was no shortage of official domestic liquidity: it could even aggravate it. Europe had reached a point where for its own further advance a new framework was essential for its whole money and capital system.

And M. Debré, dropping his shadow-boxing over the price of gold, flung down a further challenge at the January meeting of EEC Finance Ministers—one directed both at his Ministerial colleagues and at those who supported the 'world view' on monetary reform. Let the EEC Monetary Committee now prepare proposals for revising Bretton Woods, amending the functions and methods of IMF, and giving recognition to the increased importance since 1945 of Europe's 'hard currency' countries in matters of quotas and drawing rights. The issue had been gingerly raised before and dropped usually because of American or British disapproval. But the large-scale drawings of European currencies by deficit countries such as the United Kingdom and the United States had increased the effective European quotas without adding to their voting strength—still 16·48% as against the American 22·29%. The prospect of an EEC veto power in IMF might be the answer to the long debate. It could be something more—the reassertion by Europe of a controlling voice in a world body instead of the passive acceptance of the rule of numbers. Professor Zijlstra did not appear displeased as he announced the EEC Finance Ministers' decision. But he clearly disapproved of Callaghan's attempt to set up another rival grouping of Euro-American finance ministers.

[1] 'The Development of a European Capital Market' (January 1966).

Unanswered questions

There still remained the long-term question of sterling. The total of
$1,050 millions reconstituted in August 1966 by the Bank of England as
'reserves' from all the swaps, central bank loans, and Basle credits
could not meet all the theoretical demands, including the sterling-area
balances of $3,000 millions. To this, devaluation offers no answer since
its case rests on there being spare or rapidly mobilizable manufacturing
capacity which can, without delay, be diverted to exports. And with
higher interest rates the cost of servicing the balances also rises. The
suggestion—first voiced in 1945—that the balances should be funded
or repaid by a large low-interest or even interest-free loan from other
industrialized countries arranged directly or through the BIS was put
forward in 1965 as a definite proposal by the Italian Finance Minister,
Signor Emilio Colombo. In September 1966 M. Debré aired the idea
again.

For if Britain is serious in its desire to join EEC, something along the
lines of the Colombo–Debré proposals must follow. Europe could
hardly take over the sterling-area concept while to wind it up would
require a long-term substitute for the Basle credits. Once separated in
monetary terms from Britain, the economically stronger members of
the overseas sterling area, such as Australia, South Africa, Kuwait, and
even Zambia with its copper resources, could bring a powerful
strengthening to the Basle settlement machinery by making it their
main agent for international clearances and gold transactions. It is
unrealistic to assume that once the British balance of payments has
been brought into equilibrium, whether in 1968 or later, increases in
sterling balances can ever again become an acceptable source of
international liquidity. The continuing trend of a balance of payments
over the years rather than each annual quantitative situation forms the
basis for confidence and anxiety, and by 1966 there was little international confidence in British ability to formulate long-term national
aims and policies.

The Labour Government had removed the linchpin of the sterling
area by suspending the free outflow of capital from London to its
overseas components. Leaving the White House in August 1966, Mr
Harold Wilson still tried to bluff unbelieving reporters and cameramen
with talk of a 'world role' for Britain, but his Chancellor's action had
been the renunciation of any such posture. The Australian Federal
Treasurer, Mr McMahon, home after the 1966 IMF Conference, told
the House of Representatives in Canberra on 12 October, that in

international monetary matters he unhesitatingly supported the French rather than the British view in the interests of 'world liquidity and world sanity'.

And if the American deficit is not effectively reduced, the United States' gold holding will, in a two-year time scale, theoretically drop to the minimum domestic note-cover requirement.[1] Not only would the President then have to ask Congress for legislation to suspend convertibility but the United States' drawing rights of \$4,000 millions on IMF would be exhausted. In 1966 only \$230,000,000 of its gold *tranche* limits remained. Britain's proposal to repay its \$1,000 millions IMF drawing from the sale of American securities had already presented the United States Treasury with the embarrassing possibility that under its charter the Fund could refuse to hold any more dollars: a fresh appeal to Europeans to provide the currency might have to be made. With the prospect of little gold going into official reserves, something would have to give—the price of gold, perhaps—unless a contingency plan were ready to operate.

Yet the obstacles overcome by the Western world along the path from Genoa are also arguments against those who prophesy doom if their favourite monetary theories are not immediately adopted. European nations which have come through the wars and revolutions of the past half-century will not so easily collapse. The machinery of monetary and credit collaboration is now functioning strongly with an increasing power of control in joint Continental European hands.

So one comes back to the questions raised by Valéry Giscard d'Estaing in August 1966: 'Basically when an international monetary conference is held at present the United States think of the dollar, the British of the pound, and Europeans of gold. Why do they think of gold? Because there is no currency corresponding to the renaissance of their economies.' As with the internal United States' debate on the merits of 'disinflation' by fiscal as against monetary means, this involves a restatement of political aims. For even in the financial field, the EEC programme of action can scarcely advance further without such clarification. Will this be found in some wider confrontation such as the 'global needs' which now provide the recurrent theme in the whole monetary debate?

---

[1] Of the \$13,109 millions in the United States gold reserves in January 1967, only \$3,000 millions can be considered 'free'.

8. World fallacies

Europe becomes universal

The globe certainly has its needs. But are these identical with the European's self-projection of himself as 'Universal Man'? Are we really concerned with world needs or only looking for a principle of action by which we can resolve our inner contradictions? The world has been a veritable oyster-bed for Europeans trying to revalidate all the consequences of the past in the emotional unity of their present. The current Western liberal-humanitarian preoccupation with world needs and with 'objective standards' for assessing them, is no different. Dr Blessing spoke truer than he knew in letting slip his reference to the global needs of the *Western* world.

During its formative centuries no region could have seemed less likely to produce world notions or concepts of a Universal Man. Europe's own chances of survival at times appeared pretty slim. Yet in less than three hundred years, the peoples had sorted themselves into remarkably similar political units, had driven out or contained the Arabs, were busy exchanging wordy missives in the same written language, passing much the same sort of laws, erecting the same style of great stone cathedrals to the same god, and bringing up their young with the same curriculum. The Germanic and Illyrian slaves having outnumbered their Magyar masters, had changed the latter's culture, economy, and religion. In the process *solidus* dissolved into ducat, crown, and thaler.

And from the process too came the unique European endeavour to establish and confirm individual identity in terms of objective creations, or at least what we assume to be such. The classical inheritance cannot provide the explanation since it was freely available—and in a slightly more intact state—to other peoples in Asia and North Africa, and the late Roman Empire in the West had lacked speculative ideas. Nor can Christianity, since that too had spread East and South without similar results, while all the human qualities, courage, skill, loyalty, affection, cruelty, and greed continue to be found in all races. The combination of historical and human factors which has created the European passion for objectivity has not been repeated elsewhere. But our sense of permanence rests on the authority of objective creations and to release hold on them would throw us back into insecurity.

'The more injustice abounded, the more urgent it seemed to keep formally to the proper courses of law,' says Professor Heer.[1] The wretched peasants fought for the 'good old law', although it may have oppressed them in its day. If pikes and billbows had to do the actual work when ineffective law-givers were overthrown, the actions had always to be justified afterwards by a restatement of authority and reason with preambles invoking divinity and sovereignty. The growing body of bills of exchange and credit contracts, whether between private individuals, rulers, or the banks and *monti* of the Italian cities, carry the same invocations, pious or reasonable, as the diplomatic.

Those who, by temperament, preferred action to speculation found abundant opportunities for the release of physical energy and had no need for objective explanations for action. There were plenty of outlets, such as the German penetration and settlement of Eastern Europe, the Baltic coast, and the Danube basin, which the British regard as slightly indecent and the cause of so many of our troubles, in contrast to the corresponding Westward expansion of the European seaboard peoples, which every schoolboy knows to have been a civilizing mission.

There seemed no valid grounds for questioning the political abstractions of the Anglo-Saxon world, of France, and of the Netherlands. The victories were proof of their validity, and if the Confederated States also tried to justify their system in the name of the same ideas, the surrender at Appomattox demonstrated that theirs had been a misinterpretation. Against that the North could prove its concern with 'human values' as the poor and hungry of Europe flung themselves into an open land where physical effort brought quick reward and there were first-class organizers of 'values' in the shape of Andrew Carnegie, Grover Cleveland, and Boss Platt. There was something in it. The myths of 1776 provided the best incantations in circumstances which guaranteed the quickest results over the biggest area by the greatest number of people and justified both strike-breaking and trust-busting.

And the compassion awakened by our self-projection on to others hastened the softening of *moeurs* which the external restriction of arbitrariness had begun. The easement of life through material improvements and invention encouraged a sense of free interplay within the individual consciousness and facilitated further comfortable self-projection. Turgot's concept of the historical individuality of every

---

[1] *Das Mittelalter* (Kindlerverlag, Vienna), p. 26.

man as the substance from which the whole of humanity was built was something which a rational bourgeois could by 1750 afford to entertain. Our self-conscious concern for our own standing could now be proudly restated as the principle of respect for human dignity. It could, of course, lead to that form of transferred masochism which is sadism. But at least slavery became distasteful and so did torture and public execution—in quiet times.

But as we could not overnight call a halt to our physical conquests, so we went on seeking new hope of dominion and certainty by universalizing our aims and trying to impose them on others as values. The transmutation of Christian ideals into politico-social Utopias had already created the notion of civilization as secularized salvation. And as we nourished our hopes of being universally loved or respected, our personal need for human relationships hardened into hard and fast rules of morality. Discreet sensible arrangements of the Concert of Europe and of chancelleries were apt to go agley in this cockpit of conflicting universal certainties, particularly as the process spread among peoples of great emotional intensity such as Germans and Slavs.

A sentimental projection of ourselves on to distant or harmless objects was easy—free the slaves, convert the heathen, more pamphlets by Miss Hannah More on the shepherds of Salisbury Plain. But if the objects stood for another idea which threatened the peaceful security of our own identity then it was another story. 'Oh, that our skins were black!' cried the Irish leader, Daniel O'Connell, and later in the century *Punch*'s stock Sinn Feiner was a brutal gorilla armed with a shillelagh. Human beings identified with opposing ideas were quite definitely objects to be obliterated, and today's 'gallant little Ruritania' protected by a big-bosomed Britannia was tomorrow liable to be the 'Evil that is Ruritania', with only sturdy little John Bull to stand up to it. Victory only clinched the moral issue.

UNO seeks to rule

The coincidence of Allied triumph in 1945 and the establishment of world institutions such as the United Nations and its agencies, the International Monetary Fund, and the World Bank gave the latter a fine send-off of moral authority. Since the first United Nations resolutions, over Palestine and the Dutch East Indies, were directed against European states such as the United Kingdom and the Netherlands, who were in no position to stand up to American economic and financial pressure, the illusion of authority was reinforced—at least in Afro-Asian eyes. If at no time had United Nations' authority been enforcible over non-European states, the Western liberal conscience worn externally like Afro-Asian shirt-tails, found ready excuses, and it suited United States' power policy not to have confrontations with Asians. So long as Americans, and on occasion the Russians too, could ensure majority support in the United Nations General Assembly for their own policies, power and majority resolution were combined under a façade of authority.

But when the Americans lost this advantage (and it was one of the cardinal errors of John Foster Dulles and Henry Cabot Lodge to imagine that in wooing Assembly approval over Suez they were consolidating it) they were themselves at the whim of a majority which by then had sensed that the United Nations could be a valuable instrument for its own designs. If occasionally defeated or exhausted parties accepted a United Nations local 'presence', as did Nasser after Suez and Makarios in 1964, it was with the blatant intention of reforming and re-equipping under its protection.

The growth of United Nations' bureaucracy is often mentioned as the 'objective factor' which will develop into an authority not to be ignored by individual members. In theory functional bodies such as the Postal Union, Telecommunications Organization, World Health Office, IMF, World Bank, and commodity agencies could develop a regulatory and even a legislative role in which the handicaps of low calibre and biased officials could be overcome. But the trappings of sovereignty do not legitimize sovereignty itself: the prince hired the *stato* and not the other way round. And the façade of functional impartiality collapses as at the International Labour Organization when a screaming mass of Africans break up some specialist discussion, or in the Food and Agricultural Organization, when statistics fail to conform to accurate observation, or in peace-keeping observations when 'impartial' observer teams take sides as in the Lebanese civil war or the Egyptian invasion of the Yemen. On the same day in October 1966 that the World Bank opened its office for implementing the Convention for Settlement of Investment Disputes, the African and Asian countries which had signed it and were clamouring for aid-donations, demanded that the Bank break off its own engagements with South Africa and Portugal.

The Suez crisis, where both sides chose to observe face-saving formula as a means of withdrawal, misled Hammarskjoeld into thinking that untruth could be justified as an instrument. Nasser and Ben-Gurion blandly accepted his verbal assurances about the nature of the United Nations' occupation of Sinai without worrying overmuch about their degree of veracity. One needed the protection of the United Nations Emergency Force and the other had the satisfaction of knowing that for the next decade Egyptian plans for invasion had been disrupted by the Israeli spoiling attack. But the Congo was a different tale. No verbal conventions could conceal the intrigues and the gun-running of Indians and Egyptians. Hammarskjoeld's attempts to buy them off with increasingly anti-Belgian moves became more obvious. When he could no longer deny knowledge of what his subordinates were up to, he pleaded: 'My office depends on their support.' Under Afro-Asian pressure to act against Katanga, he produced one set of instructions for Western consumption, issued a second to one group of subordinates, and gave a third set of verbal orders to another, an unwise arrangement in an age of wireless communication and inter-ception.

The United Nations and similar agencies, although admirable intellectual formulations of the liberal-humanist concept of Universal Man, describe the end of the process of emancipation but not the beginnings of authority. To most of the United Nations members the notion of impartiality which underlies European jurisprudence and the older Islamic notions of law is lacking and always will be, for all are committed to their interests. Non-alignment or neutrality may have some meaning in keeping out of Russo-American or Russo-Chinese disputes but there will be no hesitation about harrying those who are seen as vulnerable. Here none are neutral. Where there are no other common assumptions there is rapid regression to the pattern of behaviour of the animal on which mankind modelled itself during its first and longest span as a separate biological species—that of the jackal.

The reversal of the Western attitude to the fate of its legal concepts has thus disturbing implications. When the first tentative steps were taken to extend the jurisdiction of international law to the acts of sovereign governments, great care was taken to ensure that the International Court of Justice should function under an optional clause by which countries are entitled to make reservations before accepting its jurisdiction. But now in an era when the concepts of international law have been cut off from the European tradition in which they originated, they have lost their attribute of 'law' and acquired its opposite of 'arbitrariness'. The concept of a legal personality extended to international organizations such as the United Nations, so that they could be endowed with rights *vis-à-vis* national governments and thus theoretically be bound by the same obligations, is now converted into a United Nations 'law of nations', which was twisted to condemn Britain and France while Nehru and Nasser were absolved. While the European process of privilege was a continual re-assertion of legality whenever it had been sensed as breached, Western 'progressive jurists' now hail breaches of agreement by the United Nations and its newer members as 'dynamic concepts of law'.

The extension of the powers of any world organization under these conditions leads into a dark maze where the objectifying has to stop. The Anglo-American assumption that the 'others' can be humoured by lip-service to misleading and untrue notions, that control can still be maintained by voting arrangements or by behind-the-scenes persuasion, has proved to be a slippery slope where Britain and the United States are finally robbed of freedom of policy choices. Not only may 'legality' no longer be affirmed but even general political or philanthropic propositions may not be challenged. Nothing illustrates this better than the postulate of 'world hunger', which has now been accepted without dispute in the framing of policy, and, breeding its own spawn of institutions, has achieved a special momentum of its own.

That there is local distress and famine is evident enough. The cause of malnutrition is generally adherence to religious traditions or a preference for easily produced non-nutritive foodstuffs, while local calamity is more usually the consequence of bad administration than of natural catastrophe. But that one half of the total population of the world is suffering from hunger and malnutrition is such a blatant untruth that the question is how it has ever been able to gain circulation.

It persists after factual and statistical refutation, as demonstrated by the controversy which flared up in January 1963 when Dr (now Sir) Norman Wright, Deputy-Director-General of the United Nations Food and Agricultural Organization, took issue with Professor Colin Clark, who had remarked at Loughborough that the figure had been arrived at as a result of miscalculations by Lord Boyd Orr and perpetuated by FAO officials who had a vested interest in doing so. Dr Wright did not attempt a direct rebuttal of Professor Clark's lecture but merely repeated the assertion about the 'half'.

The Bible of the United Nations 'Development Decade'[1] rests on a false premise, namely that there is a group of 'low income countries' which suffer from malnutrition as a result of an insufficient intake of animal protein. How one can ever establish what is the normal requirement of average consumption of animal protein in any African or Asian district must puzzle any European who has ever administered one. The

---

[1] *Agricultural Commodities—Projections for 1970.* Special Supplement to FAO Commodity Review, 1962.

low-income countries include West Africa, where the majority of inhabitants enjoy a more varied and nutritious diet than Soviet Central Asia, ranked as a high income country. Diet is as diverse as the human race, and there can be no universal ideal intake based on some corn-fed, hickory-smoked, riboflavin-flavoured American model scale. The intakes regarded by world organizations as 'adequate' would cause constipation or breed parasites in most of the human race or create unnecessary fluid in the bodies of nomads. In the same fashion, 'economically non-viable' areas of the world have been discovered: the Horn of Africa is a favourite one. Since these harbour healthy human populations and an intact ecology, the phrase would appear to mean nothing more than that men can live without benefit of economic theory.

The FAO assumptions for future *per capita* consumption of food are based on 'income growth' which is a meaningless concept over most of Africa and Asia. There is even a contradiction in the FAO survey itself which does allow that in 1970 *per capita* calories intake may approach normal requirements all over the world if production targets are reached, and that hunger will be the result of 'inequalities of income distribution'. In other words human affairs look like taking the same course that they have always done and 'world hunger' and 'world food supply', in the terms in which FAO postulates them, offer no fresh challenge at all. However, four years later the FAO produced 'The State of Food and Agriculture, 1966' and an 'Indicative World Plan for Agricultural Development' which, still based on the notion of 'income per head', proposed that overall help by United Nations agencies should be increased to $1,500 millions per year against the needs of some expected more 1,600 'mouths' by 1985.[1]

UNCTAD lays down the law . . .

Similarly the notion of 'development', first formally enshrined in the World Bank's charter at Bretton Woods and since then justified by a series of logically contradictory arguments based on philanthropy, morality, self-interest, expediency, and plain threats, emerged finally

---

[1] The plans cannot, of course, give any accurate estimates of the relative virtues of and needs for cash crops, food crops, industry, fertilizers, trade, or 'aid'. An 'optimistic' estimate was set beside a 'pessimistic' one and the only firm view was that the FAO should have more money.

as a straight priority claim, the premises for which were no longer to be submitted to challenge or scrutiny, on the resources of the West. This was the United Nations Conference on Trade and Development (UNCTAD) held at Geneva from March to June 1964. Promoted by a United Nations official, Dr Raul Prebisch, one of the many Latin Americans who find world planning more attractive than ordering the affairs of South America, it was regarded by the United States and United Kingdom as requiring the usual general expressions of goodwill appropriate to such occasions. Faced by a series of resolutions by seventy-five Latin American, Asian, and African countries setting claim to European and North American resources, the American and British delegates, the latter led by Mr Edward Heath, lost their nerve, and falling in with the mood of the conference, accepted forms of words which at their face value signified a new departure in international relations.

For the official outcome was a United Nations Trade and Development Board, a Committee on Commodities to work out how to replace international agreements for stabilizing commodity prices by a new principle of linking the export earnings of developing countries from commodities to their rates of economic growth, a further Committee to study how industrialized countries should give preference to the manufactures and semi-manufactures of developing countries, and a new notion—'the principle of industrial transformation', i.e. the transfer of export industry from developed countries to developing ones. The proposition, in fact, was that Latin Americans, Asians, and Africans, unable to organize their trade and development, would now lay down rules to European authorities still struggling to find an accurate language of description and analysis for their own national planning. Undeterred by the global prospect of the blind leading the blind, Dr Prebisch in an address in 1966 to the Fourth Session of the Board of UNCTAD was calling for a world economic development policy with plans to be assessed by an impartial group of international experts.

Fortunately perhaps, global reality continues to move in a completely different direction. Once Dr Prebisch had set up his headquarters and summoned his committees, other needs intruded. Even on cocoa, which has centralized producer-selling agencies and a dominating group of manufacturing purchasers holding their own stocks and in a position to make reasonable forward requirements, there was no agreement. Hoping to clock up a quick success, Dr Prebisch organized a United Nations cocoa conference in New York in May 1966 to set up a system of 'floor' and 'ceiling' levels with a buffer stock to absorb surpluses and financed by export levies. African and Latin American political jealousies, suspicions that no safeguards could prevent cocoa being sold at a premium through parties outside the rules, and consumer fears of production increases to profit from 'floor' prices wrecked any hope of establishing regulated relationships between sales quotas and reserves stocks. No firm statistical bases existed for any long-term buffer-stock financing agreement and no one was willing to put up the $80,000,000 suggested by UNCTAD officials.

And so with other commodities! When coffee prices rose in 1966 producers began to chafe at the quotas allotted them by the International Coffee Council, balked at contributing to a $100,000,000 diversification fund, and refused to hold back plans for increased production. In June 1966 smaller cotton producers at the International Cotton Advisory Committee in Lima firmly turned down proposals for limiting production proposed by the giant cultivators—the United States, the Soviet Union, and Egypt. With sugar there is no neat division between 'poor' producers and 'rich' consumers, since growers range from European beet-farmers to South American cane-growers, and at the same time all are consumers. The 1965 International Sugar Conference in Geneva failed to reach agreement, and in June 1966 Brazil suddenly unloaded 600,000 tons on world markets. That was the challenge of Latin American reality to another Prebisch dream.

Nothing abashed, he pressed on with a permanent twenty-eight-country Sub-Committee on Commodities which at its first session announced an expensive programme for a series of studies on international commodity markets although Mincing Lane can provide these at any time to any legitimate caller. UNCTAD also forwarded a report to the Group of Ten demanding that new reserves be created for use by developing countries, while the World Bank prepared for it a $400,000,000 a year scheme to be administered by an international agency, for lending to developing countries whose export earnings fell short of 'reasonable expectations' or for taking their surpluses on deposit.

The pretences of UNCTAD and other bodies can perhaps be tolerantly regarded as the beginnings of the process which from Genoa in 1922 led through many setbacks to reasonably well-functioning international monetary and credit arrangements. If the motives of some of the participants are not quite identical with their public professions of faith, can this not be treated as a contemporary illustration of progress as a dichotomy of rational documentation and contrasting reality?

But here the underlying motivation clashes with reality. For it is not in the 'underdeveloped' tropical and semi-tropical areas of the world that the bulk of commodities now originates, but in 'rich' developed temperate countries.[1] Since 1945 the soya bean has become the biggest source of edible oil. The conditions of production are determining factors: the political upsets which may occur in the three years it takes for a palm tree to give a full commercial yield can have disruptive consequences for large-scale manufacture over a greater period of years. If, thanks to science, yields have been increased, they vary—and with them the costs of production—between different regions of the world. The growing demand for animal feeding stuffs favours soya oil since four-fifths of every bean becomes soya meal and less than one-fifth becomes oil. Specification favours the large-scale temperate producer of commodities so that the United States provides over one-third of all other countries' imports of oils and fats as against 2% before World War II. Over the past ten years while world exports of oil and fats have increased by over 44%, those of African origin have barely risen by 20%.

Those who so confidently embark on 'world commodity planning' need only pause and reflect on the cereal surpluses of the thirties, with the New Deal paying farmers to plough back their crops and with Latin America as the world's leading grain exporter followed by North America, the Soviet Union, and Australia in that order. Under the much-maligned colonial regimes Asia and Africa then made a bigger contribution to world food grain trade than Australia. By 1966 only North America and Australia were significant exporters, while the Soviet Union, China, and Asia were dependent on them for vital supplies. And North America still retains vast resources of uncultivated land. Against all this background of world change, grain has been one of the few world commodities whose price has fallen over the past few years. Without world planning mankind has received its daily bread and eats it cheaper.

If prices fixed under any commodity agreement were to exceed long-term market price forecasts, there would soon enough be a large surplus of production in the developed countries, above all in the United States, and also in the Soviet Union and China. An excessive price would mean a subsidy from the European consumer to the American producer, and it would be the United States which would have to play the key role in the creation of buffer stocks. In practice the

---

[1] Statistics and main facts in this paragraph are condensed from 'Raw Materials and Pricing', an address given in London by Lord Cole of Unilever Ltd and in Rotterdam by F. J. Tempel of Unilever NV at the annual general meetings of the two companies on 27 April 1966.

producers of the world's main commodities have been well served by their consumers, for the latter discount so far ahead the possibility of something happening that the reaction is comparatively small and short-lived. Where the situation is beyond their capacity to rectify, the threat of substitutes looms up, as with copper in 1966, in spite of the existence of large quantities in the United States' $8,000 millions emergency stock-pile of some seventy-six raw materials.

End-usage must therefore determine the operations of any system for ironing out fluctuations in commodity prices. Whatever resolutions may be passed at conferences, no calculus exists by which social needs of producers can be linked to the Western concept of finance as a means of settlement ultimately determined by consumable resources. UNCTAD's demand that industrialized countries set aside funds to be drawn on by developing countries when their imports decline requires some sort of coefficient, in the sense of a quantity placed before and multiplying another quantity, known or unknown. But where Nkrumah squandered his cocoa income on prestige extravaganzas and Nasser spends his cotton on Russian weapons, no objective determination is possible.

This did not prevent UNCTAD officials from producing the figure of $20,000 millions, alleged to be the difference between development requirements and probable income by 1970, maintaining ingenuously that accuracy was less important than the general idea! This statistical parthenogenesis unfortunately crops up too often in world bodies, as, for example, in the 1966 Annual Report of IMF Executive Directors, which blandly states:

> 'It is generally agreed that the growth of world reserves should reflect an international judgement as to the needs of the world economy, rather than emerge as a by-product of certain other facts such as the need for balance of payments assistance on the part of particular countries . . ., the actual balance of payments deficits of reserve centre countries, or the decisions of particular countries with respect to the composition of their reserves.'[1]

A similar paracletic descent now surrounds the figure of 1% of net gross income which industrialized countries are expected to allocate to aid, not counting repayments on previous loans. Formally incorporated in an UNCTAD resolution at the March 1964 conference, this 1% has ceased to be queried. It happened to be an approximation, based on a somewhat insecure statistical foundation, of what was believed to be the normal overseas investment rate of some Western countries. It bears no relation to need or adequacy: some countries include arms

---

[1] Chapter 2, p. 10.

deliveries in the figures. Although the United Kingdom has not been able to calculate accurately to within 5% what is its own gross net income, Sir Roy Harrod has even turned the 1% into a moral obligation, an interesting quantification of morality as taught at Oxford. Professor P. M. S. Blackett, who as President of the British Association in 1957 had already threatened us with 'moral doom' if we did not aid the underdeveloped, upped the target to 2% in an address to the American Association for the Advancement of Science in December 1966.

. . . And the World Bank has enough

The burden of trying to validate the invalidable has fallen mainly on the World Bank and its two associated bodies, the International Development Association, with an $1,000 millions endowment, and the International Finance Corporation set up with an initial capital of $100,000,000. On 30 June 1966 the subscribed capital of the Bank itself totalled $22,426 millions with reserves of $953 millions and a net paper income of $143,000,000. In the twenty years since the Bank was founded, the three agencies had made $11,122 millions available for reconstruction and development with new commitments running at over $1,000 millions a year. The post-war reconstruction tasks of the Bank have long been replaced by its role as a channel for aid, and in the process it has steadily lost its character as a bank and become a sub-scription fund. Although its charter requires that its role be marginal, the Bank and its associates now handle one-tenth of the flow of finance from industrialized countries to those classified as underdeveloped by international agencies. Asia and the Middle East take 40% of the finance, the more backward European countries 25%, and the remainder is shared more or less equally between Latin America and Africa.

The first two Presidents of the World Bank, Mr Eugene Black and Mr George D. Woods—both Americans—have directed its operations with skill and conscientiousness. If their appeals for development aid have at times been couched in the fashionable jargon of philanthropic melodrama, they were doing no more than following the line of their own governments. The IFC officials undertake seriously not only the corporation's own charter of making equity investment in approved private sector projects, but also the wider role of scrutinizing all industrial projects to be financed by the World Bank group. Dams, power stations, communications, and factories across the globe bear testimony to the soundness of their judgement and their critical control.

But the pressure by the Afro-Asian-Latin American world to extend IMF drawing rights is now matched by a similar demand to inflate the lending capacities of the World Bank. This comes at a time when IDA uncommitted funds had at the end of 1966 been reduced to $115,000,000, IFC had to be supplied with a $400,000,000 credit to carry on operations, and the Bank itself, when floating bond issues, was having to pay the highest rates ever and charge correspondingly higher rates to borrowers. The amount of money available from the profit-making loans of the Bank's first years to countries such as South Africa, Japan, and Yugoslavia and available for free loans to other agencies, is dropping as the credits are repaid: during the year 1965–6 total principal repayments dropped from $1,732 millions to $328,000,000. By January 1967 the Bank had approximately $1,000 millions in liquid funds and commitments of $2,500 millions.

Although multilateral financial aid was still the proclaimed doctrine, the balance of payments difficulties of its chief proponents, Britain and the United States, prevented its extension. Mr George Woods encountered stubborn resistance to a straight increase of IDA's capital to $1,000 millions. Since the World Bank estimated already in 1965 that $3,500 millions, representing 40% of the grants and loans extended by itself, other international agencies, and as direct 'aid' by industrialized countries has now to be returned annually to service existing debts, the end of a chapter of world-lending is in sight. Such repayments absorb 15% of the developing countries' export earnings and half-way through the 'Development Decade', nowhere were the proclaimed 5% growth targets being met. The Bretton Woods concept could no longer be validly applied.

A statistical 'gap' can theoretically be statistically filled. The gross national product of the industrialized countries is probably rising by $2,500 billions a year, and in 1966 may have totalled $50,000 billions. If at the same time external finance for the developing countries has reached some $9,500 millions a year, including that from the Sino-Soviet countries, according to World Bank estimates, then in book-keeping terms another $3,500 millions can be provided by cancelling previous interest payment undertakings and making new loans interest-free. But not all industrialized countries are necessarily in a position to take their share of this on the top of their balances of payments, while such a sum implies a diversion of capital resources on a scale which would affect the national products from which the aid itself must

158

eventually be provided. The effect would also be felt on the World Bank's own capital-raising activity, and at that point it would probably have to abandon its status as a bank. Its regional imitations, the Inter-American Development Bank established in 1960, the African Development Bank in 1963, and the Asian Development Bank expected to go into operation with $1,000 millions capital in 1967, would rightly claim the privilege of interest-free loans from the West. The pattern of World credit would break loose from that of world trade and any attempt by the IMF to establish a tenuous hold over new reserve creation and liquidity would end in confusion.

For in the end one comes against the hard reality that after $60,000 millions categorized as aid since 1948, the number of countries regarded by the World Bank as unsafe for further borrowing is rising. The Bank's economic adviser, Mr Irving S. Friedman, has had to admit that approximately one-third of the $9,500 millions a year flowing to such countries had been lost without a trace.[1] Meanwhile the annual purchases of gold for Asian hoards at least equals the amount of new commitments made for Asia by the World Bank. Our notion of the world's need is evidently not how the world conceives it.

Quantitative fallacy

But the Western view of the world has committed us to the illusion that mankind can be treated quantitatively, that if certain 'objective' factors can be brought into play, whether calories, rates of investment or growth, all men can be developed into a version of our Universal Man. The liberal-humanitarian view of the world reveals itself as a perversion of power, as a desire to possess all men by remaking them in its own image. If there has been some growth of criticism over the detail of aid and whether it is of the 'right' kind, few voices dare raise themselves to query the validity of the concept itself. For it has now been surrounded by self-flattering or guilt-creating words such as 'richer and poorer nations', 'young peoples of the world', 'human misery', 'duty', 'commitment', and so forth, analogous to Blackett's moral doom. If both plans and aid are based on illusions, theirs and ours, the outcome will be confusion, and a deeper sense of distress from hopes cut back. In the process, too, rural masses move from what was at least a subsistence level to urban conurbations, where the cost

[1] Address of 22 July 1965 in Washington.

of existence is higher and the sum total of misery is increased. The countryside, losing its most enterprising elements, becomes a slum. The outside experts call for plans to be reversed and for development to begin with agricultural improvement and fertilizer factories. If religious and social customs stand in the way of this, then they must be swept away so that our Universal Man can emerge from his chrysalis. Education is put forward as the means of his emergence, although unemployed and unemployable diploma holders and graduates are becoming one of the sad features of life among backward peoples. Outmoded privileges and institutions are therefore to blame and must be got rid of. To develop a society it must be destroyed!

Although Europe's own industrialization followed domestic agricultural improvement and the development of great new food overseas supplies, this became possible through investment, i.e. postponed expenditure and withheld consumption. Even private capital investment in backward countries, although it brings welfare to the inhabitants and gives the entrepreneur a profitable return, can only stimulate local development if at the same time it helps to create a local capital market. The expenditure from aid will not encourage this unless the atmosphere is conducive to saving: otherwise receipt of aid only leads to either indulgence or hoarding. And since the political process in most aid-receiving countries is one of centralizing power through personal authority and expropriation of private interest, there is no broadening base for the free saving and free choice which are the prerequisites for capital creation.

India's plans that never were

If there could ever have been a 'World Truth Year' it should have been 1966. It was the year when India's planning finally collapsed, when the critical food situation which had been threatening since 1964 seemed to have come to a head, although the Indian Government itself was still unable to say whether there was true famine or mismanagement of supplies, and when central administration showed signs of disintegration. Even without the war against Pakistan and the suspension of American non-project aid, the reserves had fallen to the minimum required for rupee-backing, so that repayments of $125,000,000 to the IMF in 1966 would have finally emptied them. In spite of $1,000 millions in annual aid, the share of imports paid for by exports had fallen to little more than half—a $1,200 millions trade gap

—and a British industrial mission found industry working at 60 to 70% of capacity because of the lack of foreign exchange. The virtual monsoon failure of 1965 was not a fundamental cause (1964–5 had been a record year for harvests and imports of grain, enough combined to meet the needs of population-increase), but only an additional critical factor. Thirteen years after launching the first of its five-year plans supported by a continuous flow of $12,000 millions of Western aid, India had in Western terms reached financial and economic collapse.

There was no acceptance of the obvious—that in an Indian context development and planning were meaningless notions. Some $280,000,000 credits and loans were produced or promised by Britain, Swiss banks, and the IMF. Mrs Ghandi came back from Washington with a $300,000,000 educational project to be financed from rupees set aside from previous aid shipments, although it was estimated that by 1966 some 50,000 Indian graduates and 700,000 matriculates were unemployed. When the World Bank convened its Aid India Consortium in April 1966 the only item on the agenda was to consider either a moratorium or a rephasing of Indian debts amounting to $1,500 millions over the next five-year planning period.

To no avail! In June 1966 India devalued the rupee by 36·5% at the wrong time, in the wrong fashion, and unaccompanied by the simultaneous fiscal and monetary measures necessary to prevent inflation resuming at an even faster rate. The devaluation had been recommended by the World Bank ever since 1963, and for many years the rupee enjoyed only half the official rate in free markets and gold was sold at twice the United States' fixing price. But the elaborate system of import licences, tariffs, export subsidies by which the pretence of the official rate was maintained, was too tied to the filigree of giving and taking favours by politicians and officials and described as Socialist planning. The decision was postponed as the reserves drained away and dhows from Dubai brought in ever more gold ingots for private hoards. When devaluation was finally carried through, the various concurrent measures proposed by the World Bank—such as two-tier rates, price adjustments, import liberalization, special tax scales—failed to materialize: they were probably beyond the capacity of the Indian administration, and by July the gap between free and official rupee rates was still about 40%.

Not that over the years the Indian economy had been completely stagnant, even though by Western calculations at its 1966 growth rate it would require 137 years to reach the Japanese rate of income. India possessed the greatest private hoard of gold in the world, and by the standard of the Reserve Bank of India's statistics its national income had been rising from £6,000 millions in 1948 to £10,500 millions in 1964, new industries had been set up, and both exports and output had risen. This growth more or less matched population-increase, confirming what any observer can see for himself, that Indians work sufficiently hard to keep alive and not much more. But no possible valid relationship can be established between these phenomena and the investment programme of the Plans, in theory rising from £2,500 millions of the First to £7,700 millions of the Third, nor to the quantities of foreign aid. Even the 1966 halt in the increase of industrial production and fall in official tax receipts may only have reflected concealment of goods prior to devaluation and tax evasion. Whether the Fourth Plan involving an investment of £16,125 millions would be launched or not seemed as irrelevant as to whether or not it would ever be completed. In fact when the Aid India Consortium was debating whether to meet India's new request or accept postponement of payments for its £1,000 millions debts, Indian leaders were debating whether they should dissolve their Planning Commission. It was not unlike the indignant denial of the Minister for Food and Agriculture, Mr C. Subramaniam, that anyone had died of starvation, although he admitted that they might have died of under-eating. India follows its own way in the manner put by President Radhnakrishnan to President Kennedy: 'We cannot control events but we can control our attitude towards events.'

India may be the most dramatic instance of where the case for massive aid falls down. But over the same period three of Asia's most prosperous countries, Burma, Ceylon, and Indonesia, were reduced to beggary as a result of internal struggles for power, the last left with $2,200 millions of debts to the outside world. African upsets left hardly any basis for a rudimentary framework of current commercial credit transactions, much less for the forward planning of investment. By 1966 the Africans even began to discover that the resolutions they had passed at UNCTAD for wider preferences and non-discrimination for their products in the Western world were clashing with their need for assured markets with the erstwhile metropolitan powers. More of Dr Raul Prebisch's 'world ideas' evaporated in Geneva committee-room arguments between African delegates and Latin Americans who had always disliked the African trading privileges in Europe, although signally failing to implement their own resolutions to set up common markets on their own continent. Against all this, Japan and the Chinese cities of Hong Kong and Singapore, without natural resources but endowed with great human ingenuity, reached new levels of prosperity. There was cause enough to query liberal-humanitarian quantitative egalitarianism.

Falsehood digs in

But 1966 brought no fundamental reappraisal, although if a total of aid as great as the central reserves which enable Europe to sustain and expand its credit basis has been spent without a fruitful return, there was reason for one. If the financial load was no longer acceptable, the United States Government sidestepped the issue by shifting the onus of examination and recommendation on to World Bank officials and sought refuge behind 'multilateralism'. Forced by the most severe balance of payments crisis in its history to hold its aid programmes round the £200,000,000 a year level, the British Government's attitude towards aid still remained: 'We give aid because in the widest sense we believe it to be our interest to do so as a member of the world community. . . . The basis of the aid programme is a moral one.'[1] In other words, the practical outcome was less important than British feelings of self-righteousness.

It is not only the national forum of public discussion which is monopolized by those with a vested interest in development institutes, aid schemes, overseas service, and world charitable appeals. Sceptical voices at international conferences are soon silenced. While the American Secretary of Agriculture, Mr Orville Freeman, pointed out that in practice developing countries were increasing their agriculture at rates higher than the United States, Professor Gunnar Myrdal, a leading 'world figure', angrily denounced the inadequacy of the 'rich' countries' efforts.[2] One FAO official accused the Western world of allowing its demand for agricultural produce to fall, thus depriving developing countries of foreign exchange. Another called for a new $5,000 millions agricultural programme to increase the domestic consumption of the developing countries. The 'rich' are therefore required to be both greedy and charitable at the same time. 'Tied aid', i.e. that it should be spent on the purposes for which it is intended, arouses the particular wrath of both United Nations' officials and liberal advocates, but 'tied trade' in the form of special preferences in industrialized markets for particular lines of developing countries' exports, is now official UNCTAD doctrine: in the latter case the absence of competitive biding is a virtue, in the former it is a vice.

When all the rhetorical points are exhausted, the final flesh-creeping warning to the West is that world population will increase from 3,000 millions to 4,000 millions in 1980, and 6,000 millions by A.D. 2000. Either the West will be overwhelmed or mankind will perish from

[1] Ministry of Overseas Development White Paper (Cmnd 2734, August 1965).
[2] Speeches at 13th FAO Conference in Rome, November 1965.

universal hunger. However, given the decided preference of the 'developing' countries for organizing conspiracy and war against each other, such an increase is unlikely, to say the least of it. The strain of numbers is likely to be felt first through social tensions, inability of government to maintain confidence and order, and internecine strife: it will emerge as a problem for the policeman, not for the dietician.

In the face of such inconsequentiality, such a vested interest in falsehood, such well-entrenched international racketeering the temptation is strong to lapse into a weary cynicism and put up with the double-dealing of the United Nations and its agencies. But it must be resisted. For the Western world is faced here with the global infection of some germ akin to that which brought about the English sickness—an obsessive determination to maintain a universal illusion about ourselves whatever the cost.

Nor has power disappeared elsewhere in the world. In spite of Russian miscalculations and setbacks, there is a growing Soviet ascendancy in regions and matters where a decade or so ago the name of Russia was hardly known. Whatever the nominal terms of the eventual military and political settlement in South-East Asia, it will be China and not the United States which at the end will remain physically present. It will be Japan's skill which will dominate the operations of the Asian Development Bank and in 1966 it launched its own plan for economic development in South-East Asia, and as its first major international initiative since the war dispatched a succession of Ministerial envoys to the Philippines, Malaysia, Singapore, Thailand, Laos, and South Vietnam to work out the conditions for extending them state credits. Where Indian parliamentarianism failed, military dictatorship in Pakistan apparently succeeds. There are thus other impulses, by no means liberal in origin, which are impingeing effectively on the consciousness of the peoples of the globe.

But the Western liberal still dare not let go his obsession with the world. The concept of a continuing emancipation of 'Man' has landed him in an intellectual trap: *men* simply do not conform to his image, so he is driven into an intolerance of himself and becomes the man, in Robert Frost's phrase, 'who cannot take his own side in a quarrel'. In the end he abandons intellectual effort to the notion of 'inevitable pressures' such as conquest, independence, hunger, and cataclysm, although these are merely the creations of his own neurosis and there is nothing inevitable about any of them. Accepting the inevitable has its reverse form, the doctrine of fallibility, which leads to making allowances for everything and even justifies relapse into indulgence as the only gesture of freedom which he feels he can make as an individual.

164

A new morality is thus made out of the inevitability of human appetites. So the liberal insight has run to an end. Relief can only be had from its oppressive image if it is projected on to some object remote in time and place, such as the Bushman and Balinese. The liberal himself even relapses into animism by finding 'evil' in those who point out the smudges of reality on his idealized bushman.

Can trade be aid?

But in practical terms the path of reality and action is not difficult to observe. It has never been hidden. Since nine-tenths of trade and investment between industrialized and primitive societies are conducted to the profit of both by the private sector, it is under trade, not aid, that a solution will be found. Yet the crude slogan needs qualification. For no one can just 'trade', least of all with countries unlikely to pay for the goods. In the international context of the second half of our century the permitted risks and profits of trade come up against the limits of public credit policy, and trade cannot be considered in isolation from domestic investment, now everywhere submitted to some form of public control or priorities. Even the successful return on existing overseas investments may be singled out for special penalty, as under the British Labour government's corporation tax.

As the world groups itself into new trading areas, such as Common Market, EFTA, and French-African associated territories, and as special trade incentives, credit arrangements, and quotas are introduced by one state after another, the General Agreement on Tariffs and Trade in operation since 1948 (GATT) and by which the Signatories agreed on equal treatment in tariffs and their abolition, reveals its lack of substance. The circumstances under which the great 'Kennedy Round' launched in Geneva with many tributes to the late President, and aiming at a 50% cut in industrial tariffs and freeing of trade in agricultural produce, had disappeared before its discussions had made any advance. When Kennedy obtained Congressional authority under the Trade Expansion Act of 1962 to propose tariff-reductions, the European market seemed vital to American farmers, the American economy was relatively slack. Now the situation is reversed. The GATT discussions became another round of tariff-haggling and the carefully drafted and edited 'concessions' add up to the same outcome which normal talks between governments would have reached.

But even the 'Kennedy Round' in its original concept would have no more brought paradise on earth than its failure would have meant catastrophe. Although some fifty countries are members of GATT, IMF calculations showed that of the overall increase in world imports in 1965, almost half ($3,000 millions out of $7,000 millions) went to West Germany, while $2,000 millions were taken by the United States, South Africa, and Australia. The remaining $2,000 millions of the increase were accounted for by the rest of the world, most of them by the European industrialized countries and Japan. Even with the backward countries, import programmes are increasingly determined by the credit terms granted them by exporters not by annual fluctuations in their export commodity prices. Longer-term financial and credit policy is becoming the major determinant of patterns of world commerce, not the 'terms' of 'trade', i.e. the price ratio of manufactured exports to commodity imports. Traditionally this was the result of London's setting world commodity prices so that incomes and prices abroad moved with changes in British prices and costs.

Although the 'terms of trade' is still officially regarded as a decisive factor in estimating prospects for a country's balance of payments, it is rapidly declining in importance. Raw material costs are becoming marginal and in some cases minimal in determining export prices. The ownership of transport and shipping, as the Japanese were among the first to establish, can be more important for a country's earning capacity than that of mines and plantations. Since 1950 industrial countries have been expanding *their* exports of primary products, largely as a result of deliberate policies of agricultural support, twice as fast as traditional producers. Virtually every nation has, or is trying to have, some local industry, so that exports of machinery and transport equipment are the biggest single item in world trade. Straight manufacturing conversions of primary products, such as cotton textiles, which represented 40% of world exports in 1900, are now only 10% of the total.

The sources of energy in industrialized countries and the basic supplies of their giant chemical and synthetic industries are met by massive movements of crude petroleum at stable prices. The decision to develop alternative sources of energy, such as nuclear power and natural gas, which will be available at economic rates by the end of the century in OECD countries, depends on political factors. By A.D. 2000 it will not be the possession of oil which will determine the economic advance of Middle Eastern countries, but the deliberate preferences of Europe.

The expansionary demand for foodstuffs and raw materials after the wartime and post-war years of shortage was largely responsible for reinforcing the belief, current at Bretton Woods, that the rough pre-war balance of trade between manufacturers and primary producers was basic to the pattern of restoration of world trade. The shortage has been overcome, and is unlikely to recur except after some future catastrophic destruction of resources. The IMF concept of credits up to five years to rectify balance of payments deficits, like the post-war British hopes of re-attaining full convertibility, therefore rests on an invalid basis, as would the related concept of flexible exchange rates. The UNCTAD demand for the preferential treatment of the manufactures of developing countries and for compensatory financing to maintain the purchasing power of their primary commodity exports would be more than 'two standards'. It would create two radically contrasting systems of world trade—one based on subsidy with continually inflating prices and the other theoretically based on competitive prices. A real 'trade gap' between industrialized and backward peoples would actually be created.

So trade is in as much need of re-examination as other 'world' concepts. Since it has no self-equilibrating basis, its continued expansion must be directed within some consciously conceived framework of financial policy determined by the industrialized creditor countries—in effect the Group of Ten. Because of the strains which can be put on the reserves by large outflows of capital, convertibility itself depends in the last analysis on capital movements. If this has hitherto been largely facilitated by the American deficit, we have seen that this has its limits and does not meet the periodic needs of creditor countries for higher reserve levels to support overseas private capital investment during periods of trade slackness. This is the real global financial need, and must ultimately be met in terms of the European capacity for capital creation and not of the pseudo-problems created by world bodies.

Is there a global need?

This is not to ignore the needs of other peoples. Since European consciousness requires a continuous dialogue, a recasting of ideas, and their practical application in new techniques, Europe's relationship with non-Europe can never be an inactive one. It must have a creative aspect to satisfy our restlessness and cure us of our own obsessions.

And the sheer size of EEC means that certain questions are being raised which sooner or later will have their global significance.

As the Six complete the programme of action which under the Treaty of Rome served them as a set of aims for the first decade of their Community, the need will arise for a reformulation of goals in a form which will satisfy the individual Belgian, Dutchman, Frenchman, German, and Italian as to the worthwhileness of his own part in the whole scheme and give him a more secure sense of identity than that of being the possessor of a Mercedes or a Fiat. Sooner or later certain choices will have to be made which will concern the quality of his society. In an age when techniques themselves can become instruments of power for controlling every physical and mental aspect of human organisms, no opportunity for political knowing dare be missed. Given the *rechtstaat* basis of European political life, the political debate and its outcome could prove as rich in constitutional precedent and practice as that in the United States a century and a half ago.

And what of the others? The orderly social, political, and economic evolution of Asia, Africa, and Latin America and the development of self-reliance by their peoples are also Europe's interest. If the assorted Catholic, Lutheran, Anglican, Wee Free, and Auld Kirk gods are now rocking unsteadily on their African pedestals, this is because the process the West regarded as universal turns out to have been unique. But 'mankind' is more than the vacuous phrase of Christmas messages of monarchs and popes. There are other 'unique' processes at work. The primitive animism of Japan would seem to be the most unlikely social context in which Western technology should flourish. Yet it does. With the imaginative Arabs bound by no rigid social structures, Western ideas and techniques are never sustained.

These instances should make us pause. Much of the apparent chaos of the world may only be our own chaotic minds grappling with fallacious ideas. Even Africans in their own societies can conduct their lives with competence and pride in contrast to the posturing and clowning United Nations delegates representing, in Professor H. A. Turner's phrase, 'broken backed states—foreign offices attached to domestic chaos'.[1] Their need to recover identity is as essential for their own survival as for our solvency.

[1] *Wages Trends, Wages Policies, and Collective Bargaining: Problems for Under-Developed Countries* (Cambridge University Press, London, 1965).

9. Return to diversity

Where rationality stops

The fallacy which has bedevilled Britain's ordering of her economic affairs, committed the United States to a tragic error in Asia, undermined the foundations of international law, delayed the improvement of the international credit system, and now even threatens the Western capacity for rational recognition, is the belief that in every non-European there is a European waiting to get out. The intellectual stratagems to which we are prepared to resort to persuade ourselves of this seem as limitless as the illusion itself.

On the assumption that Asia and Africa are in a pre-industrial stage analogous to eighteenth-century Britain, the doctrine of 'Intermediate Technology' has been enunciated and enterprises formed to supply obsolete or second-hand equipment suitable for village craftsmen. Seminars are held to study which Western administrative techniques or tax systems will be suitable for societies believed to have reached other stages in a historical process akin to that of Europe. If social, cultural, religious, or political differences stand in the way of application, new seminars are set up to study how they in turn can be removed. Education is the ultimate cry, although the industry and techniques of the Western world were developed by men with little formal schooling, some of them illiterate, but highly endowed with temperamental abilities such as love of risk-taking and power of command, which they translated intuitively into organizational skill. Mass primary education in Britain dates from 1872, long after it was the workshop of the world, and the best minds of the European educational system have devoted themselves to research and academic teaching, not to technology, administration, commerce, or finance.

The Western world seems to be in some danger of overlooking the distinction between a simple sequence in time and a chain of causal relationships. At times we appear to be trying to transmute *our* aims into the origins of the others, our excuses about ourselves into explanations for their *raison d'être*. When endeavours to 'modernize'

12

a backward society fail utterly, the excuse is offered that it is passing through the equivalent of *our* Dark Ages, *our* Middle Ages, or *our* Renaissance. All countries, we claim, have transitions of arbitrary rule, suppression of freedom and law, and financial corruption and chaos before reaching *our* state of 'maturity'. Only European history is valid for Universal Man, and we finish up apologizing for our past savagery to the savages of today.

The suggestion that they should be judged by other values than our contemporary ones is not unnaturally resented by the 'savages' themselves. And it has its subtle backwash on our own behaviour. As a West Indian puts it:

> The main effect of people persuading themselves that Africans are different from other people, is that they abandon normal standards of decent behaviour and end by thinking that anything is good enough for Africa even though they would not for one moment consider it for Europe and North America.[1]

The resentment is understandable, but Professor Lewis's argument does not dispose of the fallacy. For it is the attempt to prove that we are all the same which has led to the state of affairs which annoys both him and the Africans.

The belief is only tenable if we can establish that consciousness of self is being heightened in exactly the same way for all the peoples of the world, that objects enter their consciousness in the same patterns, and are retained in the same conscious setting of aims and notions. Whatever the stage of skills of different societies, some basis of common assumptions could then be accepted. This is particularly essential in the case of finance, since the media of exchange and credit have ceased to be pieces of gold to be counted or hoarded, or simple tallies to be totalled up: they have joined the body of abstract notions, generalizations, and calculations which require convincing demonstration through logical forms and the cause and effect relationships of rational language —in short, through words. As much as social and political assumptions, they require to be sustained by compatible argument as well by the practical test of market-place acceptability: like them, they are threatened with disintegration by fallacious argument. A loss of political confidence and a breakdown between credit and trade produce the same social phenomena.

Indeed the long interplay of language and memory culminating in the European framework of tense and the rational acceptance of time

---

[1] *Politics in West Africa*, Professor W. Arthur Lewis (Allen and Unwin, London, 1965), p. 35.

and causality embodied in our institutions and documents, are such essential elements of existence that we take them for granted like air and water, and forget their presence. But beyond the tenuous boundaries of European rationality, consciousness seems to be expressed—as language shows—not in clear-cut systems of tenses but as dominated by moods. The philologist notes the phenomenon without sensing its significance, while the philosopher is too concerned with ascribing *his* significance to words to note the nature of the phenomenon. The development of temporal rationality is not merely the result of European culture having become mainly a literate one, nor of the invention of print itself, although this has hastened the trend. Neither literacy nor the conscious ordering of syntax can redeem for the Arabs the defeat of time by mood.

Even our doubts are peculiar to our own culture. Perhaps the verbal fusions which link up aspects of experience, especially under a phonetic tradition of literacy, must for ever remain imperfect. Our philosophers in particular, concerned more with words than with experience, have never fused 'is' with 'ought', although this is no problem in human decision. The verb 'to be' and the personal pronouns associated with it emerged late in language, long after full consciousness of self existed: in some languages it does not exist. Our doubts, accentuated by separation of speech and visual code, do not exist for the Chinese, to whom such separation is alien. They have other causes for uncertainty.

And now a fresh self-consciousness, a revived desire for a recognizable identity, is emerging among all races and societies of mankind, creating new problems not only in their future relationships with the Western world but among themselves. Can we regard them as moving into our world of tense? Dare we yield to the temptation of projecting sentimental images of ourselves back in time, thinking thereby that we can join them in some common conscious process?

Africa restores cunning

It may be that other races can tell us something about ourselves before we entered a mental world of temporal rationality, and when skills and cunning seemed more important than conscious knowing. But this is no pointer to tomorrow. The sensing and sharing of moods may well be the compelling characteristic of negro communities, New World as well as African, but Europeans can only share those moods through denominators which were common to all races of mankind before they progressed to heightened forms of self-consciousness. The negroes of Africa—and for that matter all other races—are not in the childhood of mankind, waiting to take off. They are as old as the Europeans and have grown, 'matured', or deteriorated in their own social contexts. Much of African experience may still possess something of the directness and absoluteness we associate with the pleasures and pains of child life. But while romantics and neurotics may believe that Africans can bring back 'spontaneity' into our thinking, the essential character of our concept of time is its irreversibility, and our memories cannot now flood in on us in a manner which is both spontaneous and rational. We cannot so easily combine our perimeter of rationality with someone else's magic circle.

For in Africa there is little pure 'knowing' or 'understanding'. There is a predominance of 'knowing how to', i.e. cunning, and under the changing moods even that is in continual transmutation, especially where all words possess an evaluation quality and even particles and prepositions are so expressive of purpose that misjudgements over their use can lead to regrettable misunderstandings. The growing element of comparison in our thinking has hardly disengaged in the languages of negro African societies: for most of mankind the process is in practice one of juxtaposition, mental or physical. One learns to say in Bantu tongues 'This is good beside that' instead of 'This is better'. So two goods can exist simultaneously, like two wives, and if an African chooses one in preference to the other, we have to learn his reasons for ignoring our preference. It may be easier not to try comparison but insist on good and bad. The test of quality is not in time but whether a thing serves the immediacy of present purpose. As Professor Lewis suggests, solutions may require pluralism, not the imposition of a notion of a general good, a European concept which demands a totalitarianism equally foreign to African life.

Once in the realm of general notions, rational communication becomes well-nigh impossible, as with *uhuru*, that popular East African cry meaning literally 'not being a slave'. For self-conscious Africans it may express a genuine aspiration to be no longer regarded as the white man's inferior and for the unself-conscious holds the promise of plunder. But once *uhuru* is attained, it will carry no status of rational privilege and will be accompanied by no concept of rights. The 'rights' acquired by the Africans from European law will vanish along with the European masters, who in their time had really freed the peoples from Arab slavers. Whatever the African identity, it will not be asserted through some framework of rationality but be shaped by the moods of rulers whose struggle has been not for equality but for power and superiority over their fellows.

What sort of identity will this be? The heightening of African self-consciousness as a result of the impact of European rule and trade cannot be reversed. Once Africans have become conscious of their differences they pass, as all men do, a point of no return. Some things can no more be taken for granted by them than they can by us. At least 'Pan-Africanism', a nice invention of European intellectuals and taken up somewhat fearfully into the currency of state papers by both British Foreign Office and State Department, has in Africa itself only lasted as long as the mood of anti-colonialism, which even Lord Caradon is finding difficulty in presenting to London as a serious factor. The Europeanized African described in the opinionated writings of those who flocked out to new African colleges and universities fits the bill just as little as the African of Rider Haggard's romances. Naturally the Africans are as ready to conform to what they think is required of them by the professor from Nebraska as they once were for the district officer.

The prospect for the Africans' future is blurred by the Western determination to find excuses for their backwardness. First, they were isolated from the Mediterranean world: they were not, in fact. Or it is an outcome of slavery. But we have all been slaves through long centuries of our own history. If the negro has not been a slave, colonial paternalism is to blame. If under his own rulers he followed traditional ways, then reactionary feudalism is the cause. Or else it is maintained that he is not backward and at one time surpassed us in civilization. Since someone else is always responsible for his past, we are therefore to be held responsible for his future, although at the same time we are not to regard him as anything else but an equal, i.e. as responsible as ourselves.

But cannot the gradual replacement of African languages by those of Europe create a rational framework for African minds and thus endow them with a capacity for conceptualization? Europeans too have changed their languages, albeit generally with cognate ones, and the quality of our thinking has been thereby affected, creating a wider gulf between emotion and intellect. But will Africans be Cartesian if they are francophone, or Humeans if they are anglophone? Or, as has been the historical experience over the past two centuries, will the European languages be reduced to Creole forms? In African society within any foreseeable future, the experiences which will have to be conveyed in words will not be those of the winding stream of European linguistic heritage. The responses to experience and the sense of satisfaction to response will have little more than a common denominator of sense perceptions: supported by gesture and intuition, this suffices well enough for daily communication and the teaching of skills. But there will always be moments of incomprehension. For even in the case of simultaneous events where no question of rational causality arises, Europeans are continually rejecting or overlooking present elements in favour of past objective creations. Interconnecting them all in mood, the African thus often appears to be living so much more in the present.

Our languages can be adequate functional means of communication with non-European societies in matters where no general issues of human purpose intrude. The words can acquire a pidgin aspect by assuming an immediate relationship with non-European thought-structure, and over a sufficient period of time such a relationship may bring changes in both native language and mind. But this is not the transference as an autonomous object of the linguistic cultural heritage in which Europeans are both product and process. Here identity stops short. Not only does the concept of 'Man' of our political rationale provide no bridge but we shall be hard put to fathom against what reality the African is testing his own notions of 'humanity': at least he will not be using an abstraction but 'men' in the plural.

If instead of making excuses we accept the evidence of a half-million years of human evolution, it would appear that an African adjustment to a stable instinctual order was effected during the eons of pre-history. The acceptance of circumstances rather than the development of a need to change them has created the moods of indulgence and inertia of African society. 'Self' in the sense of secure identity, has been sought not through separation as an individual but by reinforcing the feeling of belonging to a group. 'Self-government' has never been part of the African consciousness because he has needed only government, which is what he will get once more. The fulfilment of family and personal obligation, even if we call it corruption, may prove more abiding in Africa than the letter of contracts and be for us a reminder that 'ought' derives not from 'being' but from possessing.

The predominance of instinct means that new experience arouses lively and unrestrained curiosity and a readiness to bring great mental concentration to bear on any new object. But it also gives Africans a flexibility which rationality lacks. We may at times be surprised at the decisions by which a trusted Minister is suddenly gaoled, a treacherous one reinstated, plots are discovered and then forgotten, and while the demands for European aid are without measure, European culture is denounced as destructive of Africa. These are the acts of intuition and

174

not the outcome of defective logic. But if *we* try to stretch our own logic to accommodate African argument we weaken our own rationality. And institutions built up on confidence in the observance of European-type rights, contracts, obligations, and restraints will not be maintained.

For in such a society personal ascendancy will be asserted, as it always has been, by cunning; with growing self-consciousness this will be intensified. European self-denial has always seemed to the African as slightly ridiculous. He saw only its outer aspect, which was something he could exploit to his own profit, while its element of inner control escaped him. His own instinct for human motivation will always encourage him to use mystery even after he has been taught our causal explanations. So while happily learning such techniques as may be within his capacity for skills, a fresh world of secrecy and myth will have to be created by the African. This may not be the European idea of the 'good', but we lost the power to convert Africans to this when we abandoned our rule.

Japan extends its skills

Cunning too may in great part account for Japan's capacity for developing skills to the limits of intuition and instinct without the necessity for continually re-assessing them in a conceptual framework akin to ours. There is no obsessional emotion engagement with objective creations since no process of objectivation has been involved. As the archaeological and anthropological records reveal the steady lengthening of human ancestry and how abiding are human characteristics, the secret of Japanese achievement begins to emerge as the long unbroken refinement of the adaptive instincts of the Sibero-Mongol peoples, with their highly evolved capacity for and delight in mimicry of the habits of their quarry. Such cunning combines high sensitivity to substances, forms, and actions without emotional involvement.

When Japan's rulers sensed that their power could be enhanced rather than undermined by acquiring Western skills and techniques, the achievement did not stop short at the adaptation of industrial and laboratory processes but has extended to the structures of management, procedures of book-keeping and accountancy, and Western routines of credit-giving and taking. It is a reminder to us how far our creations can be handled as non-conceptual skills.

But the Japanese direction of economic and financial affairs shows more than slavish adherence to procedure. In the post-war boom years, its industry, based on new and scarcely exploited Western electronic technology, soared ahead. From a careful study of the needs of Western industry, Japan established itself as the world's leading builder of giant tankers and bulk carriers, while its own heavy industry was reconstructed just in time to profit from a world shortage of steel and chemicals. Under government regulation and direction of the economy, by the restoration of the *zaibatsu*—the financial and commercial combines—and by national habits of hard work and saving, the skills have given Japan an annual growth rate rising as high as 15% while exports climb yearly by percentages of up to 32%. In the 'stagnant' year of 1965, industrial production was 174·8% against 100% in 1960, and the growth rate was still 4%. Japan's plans foresee annual growths of over 8%.

The essentially quantitative application of skills gains effectiveness from the animal-like solidarity of the Japanese people. Any Western participation or qualitative notion which might disrupt this is firmly excluded. When Japan conformed to the letter of OECD membership obligations, and in 1964 adopted in theory an open-door economy after thirty years behind protective barriers, its Ministry of Finance and the Bank of Japan brought down a tight, crude, quantitative monetary control. If consumption fell and inventories rose, so did exports (by 30% over the previous year, to a total of £3,047 millions equivalent), and imports rose by only 2·1%. By 1965 some £3,000 millions equivalent of modern industrial capacity was lying idle and of 500 leading Japanese companies, 110 paid no dividend and another 77 cut their payments to shareholders. Against normal bankruptcies of 1,000 a year, the totals for 1964 and 1965 were 4,000 and 6,000 respectively, involving debts of £500,000,000.

In a Western country there would have been panic or at least a widespread loss of confidence. But in Japan enterprise was allowed to form 'recession cartels', a Corporate Rehabilitation Law enabled the authorities to take over bankrupt industries which they considered could still serve the economy, while the collapse of the remainder was accepted. Industrialists patiently awaited the government's next moves, which were a controlled reduction in taxes, a quantitatively determined allocation of public funds for spending, and a major share-purchasing operation by the central authorities to support stock exchange levels and thus encourage new company financing. In spite of the bankruptcies, there was no rush to draw savings. The Japanese authorities followed what would now be regarded in Europe as an out-of-date economic textbook operation impossible of application in a modern industrial economy, and all conformed. Intuition and action produced a solution which European rationality would have disputed.

The methods by which Japan draws on the financial resources of the Western world ensure that the solidarity is not broken. The banks and large companies have acquired nearly $2,000 millions of short-term credits from abroad, and in the belief that the United States dare not permit Japanese default, foreign banks and lenders are ready to let them take the credits—at the highest rates. In Europe Japanese industry raises bond issue after bond issue. But no direct equity participation by foreign capital is permitted, no foreign interests— with one exception which slipped through many decades ago and is now carefully hedged in with effective restriction—may set up their own companies in Japan. When pressed to take the next step under OECD agreements permitting direct investment, the Japanese authorities talk in evasive terms of phased liberalization. If government does lift restriction and introduces some system of regulated participation by foreign capital, Japanese industry will probably be found to be uninterested or equally evasive.

In Western eyes there may seem to be strange unworkable anomalies in the Japanese economy. It is normal to find that 70% or more of industrial finance is in the form of bank loans with interest rates of 10% and above. Profits can drop and even disappear, although business sales go up by 10%. But the insulation from world forces remains effective. If interest rates are high and the invisible balance of payments on patents and licences from the West shows a large drain, Japanese industry still realizes average yield *increases* of 10% to 20% on the foreign techniques so acquired, and no new technical product is launched on world markets without a cost-absorbing home demand on which to fall back. Small wonder that Japanese industrialists hesitate to introduce foreign elements into management.

In theory a prolonged slump in world trade could expose the whole economy. As the Japanese appreciate the joys of high consumption, savings habits may fade, and as labour becomes scarcer, wages may break loose. The growing complexity of a modern technological society may require controls and direction based on qualitative ratios with which Japan's rulers could not cope. The intrusion of Western-type gadgets may eventually have emotional and social consequences which would disrupt Japan's combination of a language of concrete imagery, instinctive coherence, a high capacity for skills, and customary, indeed primitive, ways still based on the magic world.

But so far this has not happened. Japan conducts its financial co-operation with the outside world without shedding its identity, even re-affirming it. The programme of overseas aid and credit which had risen to $414,000,000 in 1965 aims at $1,000 millions in 1970. Conducted in the name of 'development' it will not take the form of private investment or deferred payment exports, but as government to government loans to strengthen the hands of Japanese officials in their dealings with South-East Asians. No secret is made of Japanese hopes to supersede Western nations as the leading power in the area. And while the latter have to dissipate resources by defence commitments in South-East Asia, Japan seeks its opportunity through peaceful methods.

The Chinese search for balance

If negro Africa and contemporary Japan, both illustrating different extremes of human consciousness determined by magic, intuition, and juxtaposition, indicate one form of limitation to the illusion that Universal Man can be created by means of rationally conceived Western institutions, there are even more significant lessons to be drawn from societies where consciousness has a defined and detached form and where there is a duality of human experience and of highly evolved systems of symbols. In such societies one would expect to find a form of conscious cunning comparable to that of the West and consciously expressed ordering notions of human purpose. But when we examine earth's oldest extant civilization, that of China, we find that once the basic animal needs which are the starting-point of human purpose have been satisfied, society rests not on an uncertain basis of restless conceptual change but on a conscious striving for balance.

The interaction of mind and language in the course of Chinese civilization has bequeathed a heritage of emphatic words playing a triple role as nouns, verbs, or adjectives and arranged so as to emphasize the practical and affective aspects of an emotional whole.[1] There are no concepts, abstractions, or generalizations, but evocations. Correct designation takes the place of logic but the words indicate neither

[1] 'Le chinois, il est vrai, possède une force admirable pour communiquer un choc sentimental, pour inviter à prendre parti. Langage rude et fin à la fois, tout concret et puissant d'action, on sent qu'il s'est formé dans les palabres où s'affrontaient des volontés rusées. Peu importait d'exprimer directement des idées. On désirait avant tout arriver (discrètement tout ensemble et imperativement) à faire entendre son vouloir.' *La Pensée Chinoise*, Marcel Granet (Editions Albin Michel, Paris, 1950).

178

time, number, nor gender. Since the employment of each word corresponds to the rules of a social order, the wrong use can bring fatal consequences: to ensure that the correct name is used, the qualities of the thing must be studied.

Chinese is thus a language in which to formulate pleasing paradoxes but not to analyse ideas or express causality, admirable for a traditional culture or a hierarchical society but impedes new derivatives. Our linguistic philosophers crying: 'What do I mean when I say . . .?' would in such a society be locked up as lunatics, for the truth is in the word and the word may not be questioned. The traditional Chinese equivalent of the Cambridge school would have been the commission assembled by the Emperor every nine years and made up of scribes and blind musicians to verify that there had been no departure from the orthodoxy of the designations by which the virtues of his reign were assured. Society rests on a feeling for the fitting.

The morphology of mind thus revealed was already shaped before the beginnings of written Chinese culture leaving no room for the development of the abstract metaphors and analogies from which the body of European intellectual discourse has evolved. The earliest literature of proverbs, anecdotes, and biographies derived from funeral eulogies served many diverse opinions: for they were used not to define ideas but to give prestige to a totality of conduct. All judgements are thus subjective. Time and space derive from the observation of the *times* and *places* in which certain acts will prove fitting or otherwise, and since they are grasped by intuition and not by abstraction, they could never stimulate the development of philosophies and sciences such as Europe has created from its consciousness of a separation between subject and object. Numbers originated as symbols for aspects of totality and were not measures of quantity but of value. High intuitive skills visible in the earliest relics of Chinese tool-making and a powerful capacity for pictorial memorizing serve well enough in the application of technology. How, then, in the face of the well-tried wisdom which is the way of life for a fifth of mankind, can we maintain that a rationality tenuously evolving in the framework of European syntax can have universal validity?

Attempts on the Western part to find concepts to which both European and Chinese ways can be subsumed collapse, as did the seventeenth-century Jesuit attempt to produce a grandiose synthesis combining Confucian ethics and Roman Catholicism. Innocent X was not mistaken in sensing their incompatibility. Similarly Chiang Kai-shek's 'New Life Movement', with its pathetic blend of Protestantism and Confucianism, proved stillborn. We cannot combine, we can at most destroy each other's systems, as happened to the Manchu Empire. Only hatred was born from this clash of incompatibles. The despair and primitive range of Chinese peasant risings linked up with the resentment of intellectuals over the plight of China. In this almost spontaneous situation of despair, Lenin's 'Theory of Imperialism' offered Mao Tse-tung and Chou-en-lai what the Chinese mind most needed at that moment, a complete explanation for the development of society and technology, a descriptive interplay of all the forces in society, and a reason for rejecting all the schools of Western thought which were associated with the humiliations imposed on the Chinese people. But neither need it astonish us that it took less than fifteen years from the triumph of Chinese Communism to the doctrinal break with Moscow.

For the Chinese nature of the movement required that there should be no 'revisionism', no tampering with names, however much the realities of power might demand tactical flexibility in personal conduct. The need to control mass movements may have committed Mao Tse-tung to a course which caricatures the tradition of restoring correct designations for the emperor and the dynasty. The extravagances of the 'Red Guards' are a measure of how far the emotional balance of China has been upset over the past century, and whoever may be Mao's successor, it will fall on him to find means of restoring this balance, assuaging the outrage to the Chinese sense of the fitting and reconciling party, administration, and communities. But we need not hope that this will take the form of some partial *rapprochement* to Western ideas, for Chinese thinking does not admit logical structures with subdivisions which can be considered separately from the whole. Even modernized 'High Chinese' language has to take into account this past of China, while the romanized script has still to cope with the emotional connotations of the juxtapositions of words. Language reform will not automatically provide the same abstractions and generalizations which have grown out of the European interplay of syntax and phonetic script. China is striving to restore her own mode of consciousness and return to a world where time and space are subordinated to the instinctual balancing of moods.

In a society where correctness is all, the promissory note and bill of exchange have flourished since the earliest records, justifying China's claim to be the first state to use something akin to a paper currency. But where personal obligation could be counted upon there was no need to erect vast structures for credit creation and discounting. The virtual exclusion of foreign banking and finance since the Communist advent to power has meant the return to a system almost traditional in its simplicity and uniformity, and where the domestic economy can be insulated by an invisible Great Wall. The Bank of China functions internally as a nation-wide savings bank for individuals and enterprises, and acts externally as the tally-keeper in foreign exchange for the export-import corporations through which trade is conducted, converting the occasional surpluses into gold for the central treasury. China's $1,300 millions of annual exports to the non-Communist world—a mere fraction compared to the great days of the China Trade —reflect the marginal external requirements for an economy where 70% of the population of over 700,000,000 is likely to remain engaged in food production for the rest of this century.

Mindful of the fate which overtook the finances of the Imperial government, China has preferred a modest pace of industrial development to opening a mass of long-term credits to facilitate import of Western equipment. The £63,000,000 total of loans virtually forced on Imperial China from 1874 to 1898 by European banks was secured against the customs and salt-tax revenues, the main assured sources of income for a government which published no budget. Customs bonds had to be deposited with British and German banks, and the loan of 1898 stipulated that no tariff changes could be made without their permission.[1] The Hongkong and Shanghai Banking Corporation and the Deutsch-Asiatische Bank even drew up a convention in 1899 to divide up China into 'zones of interest' for future loans: the German Government refused to ratify it because the German share was too modest. This remains the classic example in modern times of the financial domination of a weak state. So now China conducts the minimum outward financial effort necessary to keep a domestic balance while its leaders struggle with the proposition that economic problems, like social, political, and military ones, are ultimately solved by the inner cohesion of a properly indoctrinated human spirit. History has not proved them wrong.

Indian concern with self

If the Chinese thus reaffirm their sense of identity, what is the prospect for the Indians, who represent Asia's other well-defined form of consciousness? Instead of Chinese worldliness with its sense of the

[1] *Du Temps de l'Émission d'Emprunts Chinois en Europe*, Fritz Seidenzahl. *Études* (Deutsche Bank AG., Summer 1966).

close relationship between nature and society, there is here a tradition of minds identifying themselves within a subjective order. How much of this tradition has survived the period of European rule? Or has it gone the way of India's past empires and kingdoms? And in this latter case, what is taking its place—something with which we can share our conceptual order? The older India had no place for Western rationality. The Aryan invaders had not arrived at a clear divorce of mood and time in their utterances when they first conquered, and were then engulfed by, the myriad peoples of the subcontinent. In their languages animate forces had not begun to take the form of abstractions. Myths did not acquire a chronology but evolved into cosmological fantasy, where cycles take the place of time, and introspection absorbed them at an age when there was a total indifference towards history and the passage of time. Mind and speech are opposed and language has never been consciously conceived as a means of grasping reality.

This did not mean that Indians ceased to concern themselves with the affairs of this world. For direct perception and intuition can cope adequately enough with the contingencies of human existence and enabled a conquering race to create military kingdoms and develop the instinct for barter and trading. The superior military tradition, the flexible script, and a coherent religion gave the rulers an ascendancy of several hundred years over the tribal societies of South-East Asia, while the instinct for racial difference hardened into the social stratifications of caste. Under the conscious systematization of moral teaching the individual could ponder on personal qualities, and, turning away from the external world, remain innocent of the mental conflicts which arise from the conscious antagonisms between myth and reason, feeling and logic. As a closed system it offered solace from the miseries of human existence and a certain tolerance of diversity.

In European terms stagnation never seems far away. For Indian 'thought' consists in choosing a word or mental image, concentrating on it and creating the illusion that it is in some way changing the nature of the subject. The result may be described as profundity by its devotees. To Europeans concerned with logical connections and objective analysis, it appears a jumble of fantasies, even though some of the aphorisms may appeal to their sense of poetic imagery. But introversion results in a preoccupation with libido and breeds self-pity and hypocrisy. If one refuses to be conscious of time, unpleasant memories can be suppressed and the lessons of past experience ignored. The numerical riddles which were part of the cosmological fantasies gave the Indians symbols which we took over through the Arabs as descriptions for our mathematical concepts. But our algebra and our calculus are as far removed from Indian riddles as are the Upanishads from the Platonic dialogues.

Subsequent invaders were accepted as rulers and found willing tools but the system itself had hardened against them. The cruelties and human hardships of caste might mean that a more attractive religion such as Islam could make limited inroads but conversion by force was prevented by the very numbers and diversity. British rule, introducing a new official language and unifying creations such as law courts and railways, has added a new superstructure which for a time has helped to sustain the slender pretence of a parliamentary system. Modern commerce and manufacture offer high profits to the able merchant classes, and if Indian skills are not of the level of China and Japan, they are sufficient to operate Western-style equipment when avarice can stimulate interest for long enough.

But in a long enough time-scale administrative anarchy will follow the return to linguistic and educational chaos. Whatever the transitional political forms, the Congress Party continues to deteriorate into a collection of unprincipled self-seekers, hardly conscious of the discrepancy between their proclaimed social aims and their plans for personal gain. Why should they be conscious of them? The collapse of older social obligations under the impact of the West, has resulted in a corrupted version of the wisdom of the *Bhagavad Gita*: 'Give thought to nothing but the act, never to its fruits and let not thyself be seduced by inaction. For him who achieves inward detachment, neither good nor evil exists any longer here below.'

So Western aid disappears in India with hardly a trace, and in the villages the *panchayati raj* struggles along on the basis of local action. The Plans get bigger and bigger and so does the urban unemployment they are intended to solve. Yet economically and financially the system does possess its own inner coherence. Vast agricultural plans and food estimates are produced for India by the United Nations Food and Agricultural Organization, whose former Indian head, Dr Sen, had, like Dr Prebisch, a preference for planning for the world rather than operating in his own country. But the Indian system produces its own solutions, for the most efficient use of its land is in small-holdings of under five acres.[1] As many as seven times the number of man-days were put into holdings under two acres as into those over twenty-five, and output per acre was three times as great. Family labour obviously can be used more lavishly in small than in big farms, and while the marginal product of the labour may be small in cash terms, it is never zero or

[1] *Agricultural Production Functions, Costs and Returns in India*, C. H. Hanumatha Rao (Asia Publishing House, 1965).

negative. The relatively poor performance of large farms arises from the difficulty of supervising day-labour, so that the owners prefer to use less labour and accept lower returns. It is the small farmer who increases the land under sugar cane, cotton, or groundnuts, whereas the larger farmers are reluctant to use fertilizer intensively and increase cash crops. The Indian works for himself, not for a plan. With a vast gold hoard, a system of personal obligation rather than contract, and the spur of scarcity, the Indian capacity for self-preservation can cope with governmental chaos and state bankruptcy. Drought and famine may strike one year: and there will be appeals for help. But there will be good years. The West's hopes for India will never be realized, but neither will its worst fears be justified.

In the first clash between India and China, the two civilizations revealed the contrasts of their unchanging aspects. In their invasion the Chinese followed the rules of strategy laid down by Sun Tzu in *The Art of War* some 2,500 years before. 'Remember,' he wrote, 'military art is just a device to enable you to acquire an initial ascendancy. Once your position is strong, you will get what you want without having to fight for it.' Having shown the Indian Army its own limitations and humiliated Nehru in the eyes of the rest of Asia, Mao Tse-tung displayed his proper qualities as a Chinese classicist and superior person and offered a cease-fire with suitable protestations of peace. And Asia either applauded him or was discreetly silent.

It was not Krishna Menon's responsibility, since 'responsibility' is not an Indian concept. If Chief of Government and War Minister had been two other members of the upper caste, the Indian Army would still have had to pay the price of holiness, and the ordnance factories would still have been busily making civilian goods for profitable private trading. The collapse of 'Panch Shila' and of 'non-alignment', like the brutal actions in Hyderabad, Jumagadh, Goa, and Kashmir, the subversive plotting in Nepal and the Congo, the whining appeals for Western arms and aid coupled with bland lies about Russian aircraft—if need be, all these can be excluded from the mind as hindrances to spiritual realization. Our short name for it is 'humbug', and in calling it thus we may be wrong in Asian terms: but Nehru was wrong in ours. The two forms of consciousness—Indian and European—cannot interpenetrate in this sphere.

Can objectivity break down?

None of this is written in any patronizing spirit. The Chinese and Indian casts of mind have had the same span of human existence as the European in which to define themselves and have produced their own social systems to meet the emotional needs of the individual. In recognizing their delimitation, our own identity stands out by contrast. Indeed, in our desire to see Asian societies in terms of 'Right' and 'Left' and to convert, 'civilize', or 'develop', there lurks a form of possessiveness. Once the Asian has a European suit, or university degree, our scale of calories, or worships one of our universal gods, he will be ours. For European consciousness must assimilate objects: that is the logical consequence of objectivation. In our subconscious we may even resent Asian resistance and would prefer to break up their societies. There is something akin to the mentality of Nazis in those who preach 'Man' or demand 'Love' for all mankind.

The Chinese and Indian, and this may apply to other non-Europeans responding largely by instinct, sense the implicit threat to their identity, and while accepting some of our material gifts, maintain their inner reserve. United States officials are at times baffled when they discover that the Asian recipients of their aid imply that they are conferring merit on the donor by accepting it. So far from incurring an obligation themselves, they have relieved him of one. The Eastern reversal of 'it is better to give than to receive' has a certain touch of civility lacking in the cruder Western version. But it hardly justifies Mr George Woods calling for ever more World Bank resources, while it would seem to rule out the IMF Executive Directors' demand for 'objective standards' in the distribution of newly created reserve assets to all members. Reconciling in strict monetary terms the criteria of borrowers and lenders is difficult enough in a purely Western context.

Confronted by other highly developed forms of self-consciousness we can thus begin to recognize well-defined perimeters of human identity. What we are not, what the others are not—these are not contingent matters of yesterday. If the archaeological and anthropological record has been read aright, some of the differences are as old as disengaging human consciousness. If Chinese and Indian societies and the European world had all remained instinct-based we could find wider compromises, and in the spheres of function, technique, and natural needs where instinctive imitation and adaptation predominate, exchange continually occurs. But where the acquisitions of the past have become part of a self-conscious present, such an exchange and interpenetration cannot take place without endangering one or both of the societies.

The West is for ever recreating its picture of the past, and our conviction that it is possible to remain the same in the midst of change and that change constitutes the only means of maintaining one's identity is now deep-rooted in European thinking. This is the conscious endowment of tense. Evolution in itself may be an indifferent and neutral process, but in European consciousness it has become for men a form of self-presentation. Eastern moods ensure that achievement is treasured in states of consciousness. Tense requires that we construct it anew as an object.

Since human evolution has gone beyond the biological and become the evolution of consciousness, is it possible that the process could break down or get out of control, as have other essays of nature? Our narcissistic obsessions have already brought incoherence. Could the concept 'Man' so block the way to the creation of new objects, that rational identity would collapse, and we should be driven back into an uncontrollable emotional existence? It may be that this has already happened more than once in human history, particularly if one turns from further Asia to consider the Arabs.

The drama of Arab emotions

For here we are confronted by a state of consciousness which finds it difficult to sustain ordering notions of any kind. The Arab mental effort to grapple with external reality is ever and again swept away in an endless drama of the emotions, in an indulgence in mood where time and causality play only intermittent and spasmodic roles. There is a cry for identity in a 'unity' which is unrealizable. Arab preference for the dramatic rather than the real has both shaped and been fostered by the language, so that all utterances are liable to become emotional discharges. European governments and journalists find after each *coup* or 'revolution' that the proclamations and public utterances bear the same flourishes as those of the overturned regime and sometimes after a few weeks, the same men seem to be back in charge.

'Truth' for the Arabs is emotional intensity and *imma* (literally 'verily'), which launches their utterance, has little to do with verity. The proud declamation of the verb which normally begins an Arab sentence sets everything into a drama of movement: the alliterative force of the repetitions of prefixes, the clicks, expulsions, gutturals, and palatals heighten the emphasis. The countless permutations, alternatives, and varieties of plurals call up new associations for the speaker, the preference for genitives rather than adjectives permits a satisfying dallying over the quality rather than the thing itself. Impact is everything: meaning is subsidiary. What we translate from the Arabic as abstractions are not concepts: they are attributes.

Where indeed, as the Old Testament says, can wisdom be found? How can truth and reality be unravelled along the threads of thought in this arabesque? Here is no role for time, only an infinity of moods hinting at subtle relations between actions or suggestions for action. The causatives which make intransitive verbs into transitive and transitives into double-transitives do not convey causality in any sense which European languages can describe. This is a language for the drama of human intercourse.

So what we call Arab fecklessness is not the consequence of Mongol invasion, Crusader destructiveness, Turkish conquest, European ascendancy, or present poverty. It derives from a form of heightened self-consciousness apparent at the beginning of Arab recorded history. This may be the key to the inexplicable rise and fall of other Semitic peoples. Had they risen from the purely instinctive world to the fringe of time only to see their first attempted assertion of rational identity collapse in mood? The great military sallies, the wide-ranging trading ventures, the prophecies and fanaticisms, the gruesome slaughters, and the suspicions and intrigues which robbed daring generals and admirals of the fruits of victory—these have been the destiny of vanished Semitic societies as well as of living ones. Although ruling over a fertile land, the Amhara display the same characteristic, awaiting a revival which never comes while their society remains in a perpetual state of cruelty and treachery.

Western influence could disrupt Arab traditions without bringing rationality. Reformers such as Mohammed Abdu, Ahmed Lutfi el-Sayyid, and Saad Zaghlul tried conciliation in vain: not that Europeans showed much comprehension of their problem. Europeanized Lebanese and North Africans struggle to produce Western-style studies and solutions for Middle Eastern situations, explaining away the surface phenomena in terms of nationalism, socialism or the alleged moral defects of the West. But the Arab mood defies them. It has infected the non-Arab peoples on whom conquest imposed the language: some of them were of Semitic stock, others enjoyed even in Roman times a reputation for violent emotional traits to which the Arab tongue has given new intensified utterance. When the mood fits,

Arabs can produce empirical answers, while their daily needs are served by quick wits and nimble fingers. If evil consequences result from the accumulation of short-term self-seeking, religion encourages a mood of fatalistic acceptance.

Within Arab society all this makes sense. Even if suspicion and perfidy emerge from the inner labyrinth of thought to which the outward tortuous expression corresponds, emotional engagement never lasts for long. Political hates are satisfied by minor blood-letting, and there would never be any logical 'final solution'. Nor, on the other hand, was there any sustained follow-up to the most favourable Arab opportunity for building up a civilization to match Europe's in achievement—the period of post-conquest consolidation in North Africa and Spain. The architects of some half-dozen mosques and palaces (if they were Arabs at all) evidently lacked the capacity to evolve further styles. The handful of 'thinkers' from whose cribbed *olla prodrida* the learned doctors of Padua patiently extracted the original kernel of hellenistic scholasticism would have been forgotten had not the Averroeist label been a convenient smear to use against their opponents by those medieval McCarthyites, the Franciscans and Dominicans. Today the rulers of the oil-rich states send their youth abroad for education and draw up enlightened domestic and overseas investment programmes with expert European help. But among both leaders and young technocrats there broods a pessimism, an underlying refuelling of the emotions, which will bring about fresh combustion.

Is the Arab case also unique? If we are finally separated from an instinct-based way of life and our reasoning becomes introspection, may we not suffer the same fate and be for ever condemned to a life of emotional frustration and self-destructive savagery? Could this only have happened in some intermediate stage of self-consciousness in ages long ago?

Latin American divergencies

But it has happened to human communities in our own time, to the former subjects of Spain and Portugal in the New World. Since Canning called in this world to redress the balance of the Old we have seen only relapse and descent. A continent with a profusion of natural resources, intelligent leaders belonging to one of Europe's oldest and most stable intellectual traditions, a vigorous new nineteenth-century immigration, and as generous a European *per capita* investment as was received by North America—the era of Latin American independence began with all these. Yet revolutions destroy their creators, the armies which proclaim their intention to restore law and order breed further anarchy. A fierce self-conscious pride rejects partnership with outsiders and even the minimum obligations for orderly trade, and makes Latin Americans rush perversely to those they know in their hearts to be their enemies.

In Brazil the lack of any social homogeneity makes rational communication well-nigh impossible, so that knowledge is buried beneath rhetoric, and facile café-writing is dubbed 'philosophy'. The racial diversity so much praised by devotees of multi-racialism as a combination of sturdy European pioneer stock, negro vigour, and Indian exotic colour means that even a common mood cannot be sustained, much less a rational perspective of time. If in the relatively homogeneous Argentina, every man remains a Señor Yo, the situation seems even less curable in lands where Spanish and Indian descent are inextricably mixed and self-consciousness takes its savage form of *machismo*, the need for a male to prove himself by some bloody and pointless display of courage. Ego has degenerated into hopeless narcissism expressed in violence, and has nothing to do with poverty.

The Spanish colonies broke with their motherland because of the need to differ and diverge. Representative government fails because Latin Americans cannot accept that the image of another should represent them. The basis of political activity has been the quarrel, the struggle, the conspiracy, and the act of rejection is the symbol of manhood. Bolivar and Morazan can remain as historical symbols but contemporary successors are not wanted. The question is therefore not one of first solving social and economic problems so that political stability can be created: the problems themselves are the creations of diversity and instability. Unrest and distress create the appeal of a strong man but he can only rule by posing as a rebel. Peron and Castro are not malignant tumours impeding healthy growth: they are the process. Forecasts of the emergence of a new class, bourgeois, intellectual, or professional have so far been falsified.

So if hunger and desire stimulate a clamour for possession, expropriation only throws away accumulated reserves and halts development. Trade revives temporarily to be stifled by export taxes, restrictions on output, and discrimination against agriculture. 'Common Markets' are always pending, and the Organization of American States signs new protocols but the Alliance for Progress remains still-born since the illusion of 'Spanishness' maintains its air of reality by having an enemy, a role for which the United States is only too satisfactorily cast.

Hopes rise, however, in the case of Mexico. After half a century of civil war, arbitrariness, and carnage horrifying even in Latin American terms, the Partido Revolucionario Institucional had by the twenties imposed an iron authoritarian rule, displayed an unusual solidarity of leadership, suppressed clerical intrigue, and brought the soldiery to heel. The oilfields and mines expropriated under a Communist ideology provided the means for imports and development: population increase and peasant clamour for land were met by the distribution of state lands confiscated from pre-revolution estate owners. Mindful of past Mexican grievances, the United States Government gave benevolent behind-the-scenes assurances to New York investment houses underwriting Mexican loans, ample foreign exchange was available for debt-servicing, and tourists flooded in. The Mexican central state finance institution, set up in 1934 with a capital of $1,600,000 after the carnage had subsided, had by 1966 accumulated assets of $1,300 millions. A lively if superficial intellectual life began to burgeon.

Like Japan in Asia, is this the case which belies the generality or proves the rule? As a Mexican generation which recalls the horrors of revolution passes from the scene and the old guard of the PRI yields to new personalities within the ruling party, there is an anxious testing of the points of strain. Students and schoolboys begin to challenge authority, opposition groups emerge, state governors quarrel and intrigue against each other. Will the assured attractions of office and material advancement win the day over the needs of self-expression? For, once a sense of crisis develops in Latin American thinking, no leader dare halt to ask: Who am I? What does my identity require of me now? For *machismo* may echo back his words.

Must Europe throw over time?

Now Europe too, Britain in particular, is under pressure to throw over time and abandon itself to mood. 'The end of great empires is always sad,' said Sainte-Beuve. But the notion that 'Europe' or the 'West' has in some way come to an end or that we have reached some completely novel turning-point needs critical examination. We are always discovering that some development of our own time—or often one which occurred a little in advance of it—has been a decisive point in human history—the wheel, printing, gunpowder, the potato, the magnet, Bacon, the steam engine, or splitting the atom. But even when some contingency has acted as midwife each new development was implicit in what had gone before. The 'Dark Ages'—a fine piece of historians' egocentricity—were an active period of discovery and invention. Human consciousness knows neither breaks nor periods of darkness. Through turmoil and disruption its attributes become more strongly marked.

Nor need this surprise us if we accept that human consciousness is self-consciousness. Even 'historical parallels' may be nothing more than our self-images, with little bearing on the factors of consciousness operating in the age under study. The image of 'Asia Awakening' may exist only in the minds of Europeans who have adopted the comforting philosophy of *der gute schlaf*, the newly discovered 'technological unity of mankind' may reflect the Meccano minds of our scientists and sociologists, and 'intermediate technology' be the refuge of those whose mental development was halted while they still played with nursery toys.

The misnamed 'nationalisms' which served local power-seekers well enough to cause imperial embarrassment or withdrawal depended on a mood which the passage of time is changing. Soekarno, clowning in his Dutch uniform and waving his swagger-stick, is poised to vanish, leaving the prosperous domain created by Dutch rule with $3,000 millions of debts, and turning once more for IMF help. In a few years' time Britain will wonder why it expended men and money to protect Malays against Indonesians: even before *konfrontasi* had ended, the British had become the target of Malay ambitions and resentments. Burma's ejection from the sterling area in 1966 had already been delayed too long: the Burmese had always thought of access to reserves as a right, never as involving a corresponding obligation. As the mood subsides we shall find that nobody has either awakened or fallen asleep, but that life in the instinct-based farming and fishing communities of Southern Asia is continuing as before with a more strongly exclusive flavour about it.

This will be gain. For the European view of diversity and inconsistency as mere contingency, and of our unifying concepts as being the essence of the matter, has not been seen or sensed by others in the same light. Quarrelling missionaries who preached love, scrupulous administrators on friendly terms with unscrupulous traders, just judges, and high-handed soldiers—Europeans accepted all these in the days of physical empire as natural to the functions of the individuals. The colonial subjects sent to Europe to study, encountered philosophies which denied the religions, economists who sneered at both, businessmen who dismissed the economists, and scientists who worked for 'truth' but cared nothing for the social applications of their discoveries. Europeans can cope with this. But this variety which we flatter ourselves is Europe's greatest strength had a profoundly shattering emotional impact on peoples whose mental security depended on the orderly juxtaposition of things and events within natural instinctive societies. Confused by the contradictions, non-Europeans misread the internal emphasis and take over the notions without any sense of the context in which they acquired a meaning.

Even the 'pre-conditions' allegedly necessary for the 'take-off' of underdeveloped countries are part and parcel of the European process and not the base of our own 'take-off'. Law, order, a sound monetary system, impartial administration, social services, utilities, and transportation which form these pre-conditions are disappearing as part of the rejection of colonialism. There is, of course, a rational mean between the self-righteous acceptance of the Irish potato famine as a divine visitation on the inhabitants for their thriftlessness and popish superstition, and our present-day maudlin concern with the material welfare of non-European peoples. Our own society may need regular demonstrations of altruism to preserve it from callousness, and there can be no objection to individuals and groups enjoying the satisfaction of having enhanced their self-imagery by participating in the relief of distress.

But when suffering in the mass is encountered, the need is for good government and not for charitable acts; Narcissus with his fluttering wrists cannot help. Here European governments must decide their policies in terms of their own expediencies, political and economic, and in the long run the greatest material benefit to both West and East will come from the renewal of private risk-taking and investment. But the representation of Europe's tasks *vis-à-vis* the world at large as a 'moral responsibility' indicates that self-righteousness and not compassion is the impulse, and that all the potential ferocity of inversion is liable to be released against our own peoples.

The recognition of diversity does not mean a world of chaos. As Japan and China demonstrate, intuition and skill can create stable orders. Even less peaceful aims produce achievement: the prospect of a great military sally across the frontiers of a disintegrating India inspires Pakistan's military-bureaucratic rulers with the purpose and foresight in administration, investment, and diplomacy which their neighbour lacks. 'Man' as a creation of the European objectifying consciousness proves to be only one of several forms evolving through human diversity. At most, his devotees will be left with a sort of universal sub-man, formed from the black-brown proletariat spilling over from the disintegrating Commonwealth, bringing down already low urban standards, and threatening the recuperative powers of the British people. This problem requires another type of recognition, one which can only be brought about by Europe re-opening the dialogue of contrasts and challenging the debased rhetoric of emancipation and egalitarianism.

And the maintenance of the credit, swap, and reserve situations between governments and central banks as well as the creation of a new international capital investment mechanism depends for the next decades, and perhaps for all time, on the framework of Western concepts. No global basis of human confidence exists which would sustain a credit and monetary order under existing world bodies, disintegration and collapse would only follow as is happening with Western notions of law and truth. The effective instrument may prove to be a strengthened OECD, bringing in other countries in the European tradition. Japan's association may be a functional one, profiting from the money markets of others while pursuing its own aims through a new outward economic thrust. But provided we recognize Japan's intent and scrutinize its acts, this too can be accepted. For it will still be through the Western tradition that new power will be engendered.

10. Crossroads of power

America chooses action . . .

But the problem of identity also faces the two major contemporary powers—the United States and Soviet Russia. Both are emerging from an era of myths and groping uncertainly towards a new role without any clear conception of what this may be. American and Russian grasp of the techniques for acquiring knowledge and control of external physical reality—to the very rim of space—is excellent. But to what final aims of policy the techniques should be applied remains an open question for them both. But the answer concerns most of the peoples of the globe, since the confrontation between these two powers has been the ultimate reference in political, strategic, and economic assessments over two decades by every major, and most minor, governments.

But some things can be said with confidence. It has been first and foremost through action that Americans have learned to know. Although there have been American disciples and imitators of all European schools of thought, if there has been a clearly identifiable direction in the indigenous stream of thinking it has been the search for an objective philosophy of action. Academic world and the realm of public policy have both been characterized by this quest. If human factors can be objectified, error will be excluded and correct action should follow. It is the complete antithesis to the philosophy of traditional China. It has not even been easy to reconcile epistemologically with the basic myths of 1776 and with the appetites of the rational monster 'Man' who sprang fully formed from the heads of the Founding Fathers to give their posterity headaches for the rest of time.

Certain initial difficulties about the reality of 'men' were swept under the rug by making two and a half voteless negro slaves the constitutional equivalent of one white voter, while the Indians were excluded by 'treaties' which the Supreme Court reconciled as best it could with other legal fictions. So that 'Man' would prevail there was always the last resort of extermination. In the ontological underworld which was busy opening up the West, organizing immigrant workers and voters, buying up steel mills and railroads, breaking strikes, and laying the foundations of power, intuition and action were sufficient guidance. Applied reasoning in the form of 'know-how' was more important than general rationalization about human purpose: it was a happy amalgam of 'cunning' and 'knowing'.

So is anything wrong? Have we any right to cast doubt on the Americans' capacity for objectivity and on their identity as men of action? Allowance must always be made for human shortcomings and misjudgements of ignorance. As both Grant and Eisenhower found in turn, the army system of passing the buck is the negation of action, and a President delegates his functions at his peril. Chance factors of politics bring to the top men such as John Foster Dulles, who was dominated by all the suspicions and resentments of a stupid man, so that when things went wrong it was always somebody else's fault— Kruschchev's, Eden's, Nasser's, the Jews'. Yet Dulles' stewardship as Secretary of State reflected to an exaggerated degree the reverse side of the American tradition. Self-justification, hypocrisy, and plain lies towards the outside world were paralleled by cowardly abandonment of his State Department subordinates in the face of McCarthyism. When United States policy commits itself to the destruction of European achievement in the world, to the disruption of Buddhist societies in Asia, to the wilful opening of the Middle East to Russian penetration, to undermining tenuous notions of order in Africa, and to postures of opposition to Latin American despair, there is good reason for doubt.

Given a situation where the factors of action can be taken in isolation, the American capacity for quick and courageous assessment is evident. The two contemporary occasions which stand out are Truman's decision to intervene in Korea and Kennedy's challenge to Kruschchev over Cuba in autumn 1962. There were important qualitative differences, however. Truman knew little of the intentions and strengths of the Communist powers and whether or where they would stop if challenged. True, the United States had a monopoly of atomic weapons, and in the last analysis it might have had to use them rather than accept total defeat. But the President could only guess—nothing more— whether his intervention would have as sequel a world war in Europe as well as in Asia. Stalin's role remained a mystery. Truman had only instinct, came to his own decision, and showed the modesty and resolution which have traditionally been the hallmark of greatness.

Kennedy had first-class intelligence on Russian intentions and capabilities. If this time Russia also possessed atomic weapons, the United States Government could reckon with certainty that Kruschchev would not launch a world war over Cuba and in conventional terms could not impede a major American action in Cuban waters or territory. The risk was minimal, the ballyhoo unlimited. The practicalities of action, in accordance with the best American tradition, were excellently conducted. Where Truman's decision was intuitive, Kennedy could assess the factors objectively, but he and his entourage struck attitudes best described by the Yankee adjective of 'phoney'. The concomitant of the achievement of objectivity *in rebus* seems to be the falsification of the human factor.

. . . But cuts itself off from instinct

In becoming increasingly self-conscious, America has been cutting itself off steadily from the crude though sure instinctive capacity which was its strength in action, and the nature of American economic and social evolution furthers the illusion that human factors can be assessed and presented as objects. The new 'objective' strength is there, the consciousness of the destructive power of the weapons, first-class radio interception and electronic detection, the calculators and computers. In situations which can be isolated as 'models', courses of action can be clearly defined, and the intellectual *kriegspiel* of United States nuclear strategy does not merit the sneers of British staffs, who consider playing it off the cuff an adequate substitute for the accurate calculations necessary to follow the complicated stages of technical preparedness for defence. The recurrent 'Cold War' confrontations of post-war Europe, where the computer could conduct assessments of Russian strategic intentions within the framework of conventional general staff planning assumptions, meant that the terms of reference for a United States ground-force commander's room for local manoeuvre could be 'objectively' presented.

The security which past ascendancies, such as British sea power, could offer was also a physical one, but the ascendancy itself was based not on domination but on a balancing act in which Britain, France, Germany, and Russia participated in terms of their narrower self-interests. The balance may have been unstable—balances usually are —but there was an inherent factor of restraint born of the long tradition of power politics inherited from dynastic intrigue. Ultimately it was a policy played by instinct: it may not have been a perfect one, since it did not save the world from two major wars, but it did not rest on the assumption that world power meant complete domination. This traditional type of ascendancy was not surrendered to the United States when Europe lost its primacy in 1945. It ceased to be relevant for a decade afterwards, and during the United States nuclear weapon monopoly and economic predominance, world power meant literally 'power over the world'.

The concept of 'Cold War polarization' lost its meaning when the policy of 'negotiation from strength' began to be questioned, and 1953 was the last year when the objective power factors existed for such type of negotiation. In 1954 brinkmanship failed to work in South-East Asia, and Dulles' rankling over the failure—for which he naturally blamed Britain and France—was still, two years later at the time of Suez, stronger than his desire to profit by the unique opportunity of the Hungarian uprising to roll the Iron Curtain back to the Rumanian frontier. When Kruschchev told Kennedy at their first encounter in Vienna that the relation of forces had changed, and later commenced the Berlin Wall to prove his point, he was voicing something which the United States Administration had barely started to admit to itself. But the Eisenhower line on the all-out use of nuclear weapons could no longer be maintained, nor the simple confrontation of Man versus Anti-Man.

Power stalemate

Has this proved the classical power stalemate obliging the United States to re-examine its policy in the more conventional terms of historical balance, of the aims of other peoples and governments, in a word in human terms? Recalling only too well from their own days as great powers that the price of compromise is paid by allies whose value has diminished, the Western European states were quick to voice their doubts as to whether the United States could be counted on to risk its own destruction for their sake. In traditional diplomatic terms they need not have worried. For it was still through the will-o'-the-wisp of a global objectivity that White House and Pentagon sought to pursue a community of interest with the Kremlin. As the two top-leaguers, the President of the United States and the head of the Soviet power hierarchy could surely treat the question of all-out nuclear warfare rather like a matter of external reality, a technique which maintained a status quo for which neither side cared overmuch but were not prepared to change at the cost of complete destruction! Even where both sides had to maintain a tricky local geographical contiguity, as in

Germany, the risk of a Russo-American clash could theoretically be lessened by the fact that they could afford to be less ambiguous in their policies than smaller powers.

However, Russian and American power policies are less easy to synthesize than the flavours of a Thanksgiving Dinner. For ambiguity, and not objectivity, is the basis on which the Kremlin conducts its foreign policy. Russia's negotiating line for a non-proliferation treaty gave no indication that she saw it as a step towards some form of Russo-American world co-dominium. By supplying Hanoi with moderate quantities of weapons and equipment, the Russians were deliberately pursuing a policy designed to weaken United States power and discredit its world standing, and if there was a price for calling it off in the form of some Central European settlement, they gave no indication that it would be one which the United States would be prepared to pay. Russia could clearly follow its own power policy without risk and with considerable success.

The recognition that 'Man' was not to be found in Africa or Southern Asia should have proved easier. No great American illusions were involved and the American love-affair was of too short duration to build up the same type of myth which existed over China and Cuba. The American involvement was only in small part a miscalculation of Cold War risks: it resulted from a need to hit back at the European image. It was too hard to believe that Captain Kong-Le's *coup d'état* in Laos could be anti-American without being pro-Communist, or at least French-inspired: the disbelief led irrevocably to the involvement in Vietnam. Courage, loyalty, and generosity were thrown in too, as they will be wherever are Americans, but there was no open admission that what the United States had really been seeking in South-East Asia and Africa had never been positions of strength but only opportunities for taking out old resentments on Europe. The need is so great that the cost is ignored. If the follies of Adlai Stevenson brought about the bloodshed of the Congo, those of Arthur J. Goldberg could lead to massacres in Southern Africa.

Here is the underlying confrontation which seems most dangerous to the American sense of identity. For not only does Europe fail to fit into the American dream: Europeans have their transatlantic illusions as well. The United States is never neutral in European consciousness: it is either admired or hated, complimented or insulted, sheriff or outlaw. The discovery of America was preceded by myths about Atlantis; Columbus thought he had discovered something else, the aboriginal customs were first described in the century of Defoe and Rousseau, the white American was endowed in imagination with the virtues of the Noble Savage, and is hardly to be blamed for failing to live up to somebody else's idea of how a savage should behave. When Europeans finally witnessed a member of the United States Government, in the form of Mr Mennen Williams, actually dancing to African tom-toms, they found him neither noble nor virtuous.

There were too many subjective scores to be paid off. 'The outside pressure on free peoples' which the Truman Doctrine professed to counter turned out to be American as much as Communist, so that between June 1947 and April 1948—between Marshall's speech at Harvard and the passing of the Foreign Assistance Act—a scheme conceived in a spirit of genuine farsightedness was applied ruthlessly and treacherously to force the Dutch to evacuate the East Indies. As far as the concept of 'Man' was concerned, Soekarno fitted admirably, but not the stock which had settled the Hudson River valley. The British were given the illusion of a special relationship so long as they had a useful though minor technical contribution to make to defence and intelligence. But they had no right to feel disillusioned at Nassau: Palestine and Suez should have been sufficient warning. The American relationship with France and Germany, just because there are fewer elements of myth-making about it (in spite of Lafayette!), may prove a more solid base on which to redefine a Western alliance which has to depend for its existence on something more than the fear of Russian land armies.

The Western world badly needs such a definition. Under both Eisenhower and Kennedy administrations, American sympathy for the Treaty of Rome and the aims of EEC rested on the belief that here was a federal experiment on American lines and a beneficent economic grouping which would strengthen the West against Russia. Contemporary Europe does not fit into such designs, and in spite of the fumblings and mistakes, EEC attempts at creating a new unity within diversity aim at meeting twentieth-century realities and not the myths of 1776. Traditions of authority as well as liberty are involved in the reconciliation of national policies and institutions. Even if President de Gaulle's technicians are not very up to date in their plans for a *force de frappe* and his own economic notions somewhat crude, he has at least brought an end to some illusions on both shores of the Atlantic and introduced the element of rational limitation which has been lacking between the United States and Europe for two hundred years.

Letting 'Man' go

But to the communal disintegration and fragmentation and dehuman-ization of thought which are common to the whole Western world are added in the American case two formidable barriers to a restatement of general ideas. One is the coarsening of instinct and blunting of intuition which have gone further than in Western Europe, and the second is the lack of homogeneity in American society. The transition to new assumptions appears a risky and fearsome venture, so that even dehumanized lies about 'Man' are held on to as at least an anchor. For the grim truth will keep popping up like some unruly element in a Donald Duck film, that there are different sorts of men who are not fitting together very well and Utopia is no longer possible, even in Atlantis. This possibility was always present, but once self-consciousness passes a certain point it becomes inevitable.

When belief falters one of the oldest atavistic human urges asserts itself: 'Find a sacrifice. Don't just stand there. Crucify somebody.' Like the priests of Ancient Egypt speaking in hollow tones through the hole in the idol's niche, the manipulators are there too. 'If the rest of the world believes it, Utopia may still come true again.' So the South has to be shaken out of its backwater of prejudice, less from any genuine desire to better the negro's lot but so that the rest of the world in general, and Africa in particular, will not be able to point a finger of scorn and that the President will be able to demonstrate the purity of his intentions in the Congo and Rhodesia.

Meanwhile the descendants of the once voteless slaves are demanding at least two and a half identities. In a self-conscious world their demands are never likely to be satisfied. Once the outward legalistic forms of humiliation and discrimination have been removed, the negroes come up against the tougher and unspoken forms of white exclusivity and also against the limits of their present capacity. The causes of the latter are arguable—genetic, the complexes of two cen-turies of inferior status, rural slum existence, or the near-underworld urban milieu into which negroes have been confined. Two American generations have to face a hard reality that in any time-scale within which they can operate, negro integration will probably mean the disruption of already weakened assumptions on social conduct, wide-spread breakdowns in precariously maintained standards and even more violent forms of lawlessness, not necessarily of negro origin. The United States would be on the way to becoming the biggest ever banana republic.

The alternative may be difficult of achievement. At least pluralism is at the basis of American political organization. Men prefer order to arbitrariness, and the extension of federal powers necessary to bring about separation will in the last analysis prove no more formidable than those required to enforce desegregation. A lingering hang-dog cult of guilt has not been in the Americans' nature. They are not likely to accept James Baldwin's invitation to take the negro as their therapist 'in coming to terms with evil in themselves'. Slavery was only one aspect of the common brutality of past naïver ages, and the Americans fought a bloody war to remove it, while real progress in removing personal humiliations from the negro has come from quiet persuasiveness in both South and North. What the Americans have come up against is the clamant need of human diversity to be recognized and sterility of 'Man' as an identity tag.

The Russian renewal

The years of American adjustment to the evolution of Russian power pressures also offer opportunities which will not recur. While North America's identity was created by an expansion in space which permitted free rein to action and intuition and where ideas were never much more than a parsley surround, the Russian people have been following a slow progress in time. Human relationships have retained their strong intuitive nature, but the ordering and directing of Russian institutions has been by calculation from above. The framework of Marxist formulation may have supplied an instrument of authority for the ruling group but their people remain uncompromisingly Slav.

Now the framework of verbal concepts, largely the creation of men who acquired in exile a certain intellectual detachment and perpetuated as a tool for Stalin's conspiratorial mind, is under his successors being submitted afresh to the impress of the Slav mode of thought. Time, aspect, and mood with their threefold inflections of reasoning, action, and intuition pass in one process through the consciousness of Russia's rulers. They can cope with the apparent logical contradictions involved in the many facets of maintaining tension on the reins, now loosening centralized controls, sometimes strengthening the hand of Party appointees, at other times that of officialdom, continually probing between direction and autonomy for some mean of effective action, and always trying to sense popular emotional needs. The top rulers of

Russia must thus be men, and not assemblies. They will, of course, make errors, and these too can be threefold; errors of calculation, errors in action, and errors in responding to the moods of others. The lowest price a Russian ruler pays for error is eclipse.

So however much factual intelligence Western governments may acquire on Russian economic affairs, harvest returns, industrial bottle-necks, and weapons development, their interpretations of Russian statements and actions as well as of Russian reactions to their own moves remain uncertain propositions.

The answer to the riddle is to be found neither in Machiavelli nor in Marx, nor by intellectual projections of our analysis on to a Russian 'model', but in Russian consciousness itself, as it moves between deep introspection and hard objectivity. In Macmillan's last encounter with Kruschchev, the British Prime Minister's insensitivity to changes in the Soviet leader's moods resulted in what he doubtless thought was the impeccable logic of his arguments, reinforced with wit and skilful allusion, arousing only greater antipathy. To Kosygin, Wilson is an irrelevancy. At most, one can say that Russians always take themselves seriously and expect to be taken so by others.

The intense emotional life of the Russian, which his language nurtures into adulthood, enhances the pleasurable aspects of guilt, so that instead of outward revolt there is adjustment, agonizing enough in itself, between subjectivity and external reality and eventually masochistic acceptance. Insight, so far from inhibiting harsh treatment of others, can make the Russians readier to punish others in their own image. 'Bedniee Rossia' laments the idiot, as the pillaged cities flame on the horizon, and the flood of emotion brings its own consolation. That the Ashkenazi Jew has acquired from his sojourn in Russia an unrivalled capacity for revelling in misfortune need not surprise us. Because Russian identity in society is thus not dependent—as it has been in great part in Western Europe—on the maintenance of time-honoured incantations, emotional release and satisfaction are all the more essential for inner security.

The new self-conscious 'Soviet man' will not be so easy to describe in Western European liberal-humanitarian terms. He may be brash and aggressive in his confidence in achieving skills and over his material progress and possessions. Memories of his elders' behaviour under Stalin and his own naïve delight in novelty will inject a cynical element into Marxism without rejecting it entirely. Like the stewards in the pre-Revolution stories, the obsequious final sibilant will be mentally added or dropped, depending on what company is present: Gromyko's son will obey orders like his father. The steward who learns to be more ruthless towards his subordinates and more cunning than his equals will provide the succession.

But the men who direct Russian policy will bring the same cast of mind to their task. And a policy which has shown such consistency in broad aims and flexibility of tactics under the direction of men so different as Chicherin, Litvinov, Molotov, Kruschchev, and Brezhnev is unlikely to take new and unexpected turns tomorrow. Even the more representative nature of the Party and bureaucracy and the restoration of 'legality', which means the charter law acquired from the German settlements, are a promise of continuity, and not of departure from precedent. After almost half a century of Russian experience, Marxism seems perfectly reconcilable with the social transition from peasant farms to scientific agriculture, from rifle warfare to space exploration, from obscurantism to modern analytical techniques. The unending controversy with the peasants over the produce of their private plot is the continuation of the struggle they began as serfs over their *allod* at the end of the Dark Ages. The official has taken the place of steward as the enemy.

Yet Russian awareness still betrays itself by an aspect of uncertainty. The Marxist framework of ideas required the myth of a realizable world-wide revolution. There may also have been in the last century an apocalyptic strain in Russian thought, but it was balanced by a general pietism. Does the unrealizable myth still imply a potential risk of miscalculation in the strategy of power? Does Russian self-consciousness still need a final assertion in the face of what is non-Russian, or can it find satisfaction within some larger grouping of identities?

Within the Sino-Soviet bloc there has been no such accommodation. The patterns of nineteenth-century linguistic or ethnic self-consciousness in Eastern Europe are too set to fall into any Russian mould, except perhaps in the case of the peoples of Czechoslovakia, who console themselves with inner brooding as drab as their outward being and make no great difficulty about conforming. Where identity is sharply defined—as with Poles and Magyars—the passage of time only intensifies self-consciousness and can add to the force of explosion if emotion breaks loose, as happened when the Petöfi clubs of 1955–6 started their movement of protest. Whatever has taken the place of the romanticism imported a century ago by Rumanian gentry and bourgeoisie to give an air of nationalism to their sectional interests, it is certainly not Marxism.

The eroded revolution

And the relative insulation of Russian domestic economic and financial developments is being pierced at a number of points. This parallels the introduction of profit-linked management into Russian industry. The quiet tone in which the speeches were given at the Soviet Communist Party Twenty-third Congress in April 1966 seemed part of the deliberate underplaying of the significance, although Kosygin emphasized that the new system was a precondition of success for the 1966–70 Five Year Plan. By the end of 1966 one-third of the labour engineering force was governed by an arrangement under which wage increases were to be earned as bonuses. As this is extended to the entire economy, output indices are to determine the share of managers, engineers, and workers in the additional profits of all Soviet enterprises.

How successfully this will work in practice is another matter. But it will change the emphasis of the whole internal Soviet system of financing the economy. Hitherto this has been conducted as a vast cost-accounting budget exercise through the Government Bank and the main economic planning and controlling ministries and agencies, both central and regional. Beside this has been operated a national savings bank system designed primarily to hold down the surplus purchasing power of the mass of small wage-earners. In its fashion it has worked. But now Soviet industry will have to be financed by loans geared to a cash flow projection, while the 20% wage increases envisaged under the current plan coupled with a growing and widening range of consumer products will alter the pattern of Russian spending and saving. From the average 15% profit which industry is expected to show, not only must the bonuses and salary premiums be paid but two funds serviced, one for future capital investment and the other for social, housing, and cultural purposes. Over and above this, stockpile finance will have to be arranged at rates bearing some relationship to the prospects and turnover of individual enterprises competing against each other with installations of varying age and efficiency. The Soviet Government itself will have to compete with its own shops for savings, and a new range of interest-bearing incentives will gradually have to be introduced.

The new Soviet economic chapter will require financial and credit innovations which can only be met by some form of money market, even if officially controlled, between state directorates, agencies, and industries. A regulated 'reserve fund' announced in January 1967 appears to be the first step to this. At the Twenty-third Congress anxious voices were raised at the pressures which would cause managements to cut their labour force to maintain profit and cause local unemployment. Certainly labour mobility and with it even a worker bargaining factor may be created, given the extensive use of wage differentials to attract labour to new industrial areas and the continuing overall shortage of skilled workers.

Internal credit in turn will have to follow a closer alignment to Russian foreign trading activity, since the latest Five Year Plan involves the placing of orders abroad for both machinery and consumer goods on a greater scale than ever before. The first consequences have already been admitted. At the Congress, Kosygin announced: 'One of the big tasks in the new Five Year Plan is to increase production of the most readily selling goods for export.' Domestic and export price levels can no longer be held apart.

In November 1965 the Soviet bloc's International Bank of Economic Co-operation, set up two years previously to facilitate multilateral trade between Communist countries, announced that part of its capital would be re-denoted in 'convertible roubles' based on a gold value, while its members—Russia, the Eastern European satellites, and Outer Mongolia —would be allowed to convert part of their trading surpluses into gold or free currencies to finance trade with third countries. By June 1966 it was announced that the initial convertible capital would be the equivalent of 30,000,000 gold roubles, raised by the end of the year to 90,000,000 and would be available for settlements with non-member countries.[1]

The rouble thus theoretically enjoys the approximate status of a reserve currency within the Soviet bloc, and the establishment of a gold parity creates a closer link between domestic and external transactions—the latter had hitherto been balanced in non-Communist currencies and cleared or settled through the banking facilities offered by the City of London. The possibility of a deliberate association between the Soviet bloc and the international financial agencies of the non-Communist world may still be many years ahead, but the November 1965 step had become unavoidable. The International Bank of Economic Co-operation's attempts to settle credits and deficits between Communist countries by purely book-keeping transfers denoted in roubles had proved slow and clumsy, particularly when some major development occurred, such as increased Rumanian oil-sales to the West and a sudden Rumanian increased import capacity. Hungary and Czechoslovakia are again active international traders, buying products, equipment, and even ships in the West and selling or

---

[1] The free market rate for a ten-rouble gold piece varies between £3 2s 9d and £6 5s 0d.

using them in profitable transactions with Asia, Africa, and Latin America. Czechoslovakia is a full member of GATT, Poland an associate member, and Hungary has applied for observer status, having already openly demanded of the Soviet Union that the terms of trade between them must allow for Hungarian advantage.[1]

So from 1 January 1966 Russia and the Eastern European countries —through their economic policy co-ordinating agency, COMECON— have begun to base their trading prices, covering some two-thirds of intra-bloc exchanges, on the average main world market levels between 1960 and 1964. This relinking of the Eastern European trading and financial system to the West does not spell a sudden end to Soviet ascendancy. But it is only by agreeing to the innovations that Russia can maintain its voice, possibly even to the extent of accepting a wider convertibility link with outside currencies. And the development does weaken one of the four essential elements still common to all Communist regimes, namely an economic organization which prevents free choice in manufacture and commerce. Of the other three, the rule of a self-perpetuating party ready and able to resort to terrorism as a major instrument of authority, control by this party over the social and cultural lives of the people, and finally the advocacy—sincere or not— of a world society based on directed change in the nature of men, the last is weakened by the dying myth of world revolution. To the erosion of the supports is now added the Chinese challenge.

As the Fiftieth Anniversary of October Revolution dawned in 1967 Russia found herself leading a minority of the world's Communists. Russia's apocalyptic vision is fading—fortunately for the West— because within the Communist camp itself the myth of revolution has been accepted as unrealizable.

The ideological basis of a 'Cold War' no longer exists. In the residual confrontation between Russia and the United States both are uncertain in what final terms they can ever impose their will on the other. In the shorter term, Russian methods of weakening the will of an opponent may enjoy greater tactical success given the stronger roots of Slav identity and the growing neuroticism of the United States. The method of provoking the Americans to action and leaving them uncertain as to the outcome suits the Russian temperament as much as it bears hardly on the American. Doubt at the crossroads can be Europe's gain.

---

[1] Statement of 25 July 1966 by Hungarian Deputy Premier in charge of Eastern bloc trade.

11. Outlook

Europe's task of capital creation

Beyond the short-term problem of the English sickness and the medium-term one of an improved international credit mechanism looms the question of how to create a European capital market to support the process of technological development to back a renewed outward investment thrust, and to expand the convertibility of the world's currencies.

The threat of breakdown of the existing international monetary system comes rather from its possible misuse by world bodies than from its own deficiencies. The European endowment of financial skills is such that infinite adaptation is possible. Even a 'return to gold' with an increased price, new currency parities, domestic inflation and a somewhat spasmodic stimulus to world trade would not change the ratios of financial strength between the major industrial powers of the globe.[1] Gold would continue its present role of setting the order of preference of acceptability for different currencies so long as these remain substitutes rather than complements for each other.

The need for an expanding European capital market is not the narrow defensive one of 'keeping out the Americans'. This proves on examination to be a pseudo-conflict of interest. The 60% of American overseas investment going into Europe may at first sight appear to point to an American manufacturing emigration which could dominate the Continent. The giants' own statistics are in themselves impressive enough. General Motors, the world's biggest company, whose annual turnover exceeds by 10% the gross national product of the Netherlands, has a market capitalization of $20,118 millions, while that of International Business Machines is $13,411 millions. But the massive transplantation of resources and the recovery of assets and profits are only made

<hr>

[1] '. . . if all interest-bearing exchange were repatriated in exchange for non-interest-bearing gold, then with a *threefold increase* in the price of gold the total of reserves in the collective hands of the free world would rise by just under 50 per cent.' *International Liquidity*, Ian Shannon (Cheshire, Melbourne, 1965), p. 134.

possible for such enterprises by the co-operation of all industrialized states in an international credit and reserve system which no one country can dominate, although one or more could disrupt it. So far from being able to dominate governments, the American giants become hostages in the societies where they operate: the very size of their credit and financial needs makes them dependent on the approval and assistance of central institutions. When the American 'invasion' is set in perspective it is only $5\frac{1}{2}\%$ of total European spending on plant and equipment, and in France, the most resentful recipient, American investment is only 3.7% of the country's annual total; in Germany it is some 4%. The \$70,000 millions of United States' overseas investment is not mobilizable power. The partial withdrawal of the United States from the role of international banker between 1963 and 1966 illustrates the limiting factors.

But the investment continues, because the companies bring technological short-cuts to Europe and diffuse modern management methods. The needs of the electrochemical age leave no option. The heaviest foreign investment in France, with one of the most backward capital markets in Europe, has been in the chemical industry, 28.23% of 1965's total, and even in Germany, the home of modern industrial hydrocarbon processes, the main foreign participation is in oil and coal by-products.

European participation in material advance on an equitable footing with the United States is not a question of legal restriction nor a question of fifty-fifty formalized joint ventures, but the creation of a capital market to serve larger enterprises than European financial centres can at present handle. For taxation barriers to the free movement of funds, national credit policies conducted in the name of anti-inflation or credit squeeze, lack of encouragement to the private investor to turn to industrial shares have all contributed to hold back European resources which could have gone into large-scale modernization and development. The remedy against long-term capital flowing from deficit America to surplus Europe thus lies in Europe's own hands. Although the \$34,000 millions of European investment in the United States seems to balance statistically the American total of \$29,600 millions in Europe, it includes over \$20,000 millions invested since 1946 and which sought a better return than was held out in domestic markets. Restrictive investment policies only help to subordinate European capital needs to American domestic priorities!

Even the issue operations of the international capital market created between European centres by the use of Euro-currencies were in 1965 only \$1,300 millions, of which \$775,000,000 were in dollars and the remainder in European monies. This is less than London's equivalent of $1,700 millions of domestic capital issues in a year, and also demonstrates the relatively marginal nature of 'free' international investment funds, whatever their origin—Middle Eastern or Latin American—or made available through the Bahamas, Curaçao, Switzerland, or elsewhere. The 'international financier' no longer dominates the market: he may at most represent the balancing element between success or failure in an individual issue. If American demand on existing European capital markets is at times a disturbing element, its marginal nature can be contrasted with the magnitude of United States' domestic security issues—$32,000 millions in 1965 against a total of $9,100 millions for all EEC countries.[1] Although Europe may have accounted for 60% of the world's total of $118,000 millions of industrial exports in 1965, her mobilizable wealth does not yet reflect this.

Participation in this European task offers Britain a prospect of restoring its currency convertibility, overcoming its under-investment and also an alternative to the final surrender of its financial sovereignty to American-dominated world bodies. Whether the United Kingdom ever enjoys formal EEC membership or has to remain content with its OECD and EFTA roles, a British alignment in the European order of battle must be part of the treatment for its sickness. The 'world' is an inversion: it is Europe which is the outward challenge.

World order or order in the world?

And the acceptance of human diversity does not mean that Europe has to abandon the institutionalized notions of authority, liberty, equality, and welfare on which it pins its own identity. It only requires the historical recognition of the limits of their validity. And in the European tradition the neo-Grotian concept of an absolute *jus gentium* standing above the laws of peoples has always been under challenge. It never had any historical reality. The rival notion of international law as the ordered intercourse between rulers and states and governed by tolerance and prudence remains at the service of those who prefer such attributes to intolerance and dogmatism.

---

[1] According to EEC estimates available in 1966 and from which figures in this paragraph are also taken, the average annual total between 1960 and 1964 of all credit-raising operations including government and other bills, mortgages, etc., was: USA $54,000 millions, UK $7,900 millions, EEC $28,000 millions.

There is no moral order to which we can appeal, since goodness is a quality of men and not of actions. Admission of this is implicit when in the name of ideals or morality we abandon those who looked to us for protection, turn whole continents over to chaos, and denounce those struggling to maintain order and advance material welfare. *Our* motives are good, we claim; *theirs* are bad, they want to dominate. But there can never be reference to a moral balance sheet of world order since at any one point in time a moral decision is an affair of contemporary participation and not of numbers. If the Hoover Relief Organization had not saved the Russian people from starvation at the time of the great famine of 1921 the Communist system *might* have fallen apart, the millions massacred by Stalin *might* still be alive, Eastern Europe *might* not have been in chains, and China *might* not profess Communism today. History's most recurrent phenomenon, the seeming paradox of unintended consequences, can thus make a mockery of all intentions and methods. Under the emotional temptation to reject their history and abandon time in favour of universal ideas, Europeans must pause. The cross-sections of time are notoriously unreliable.

The notion of global unity, or a world order, is but another example of European mental convergences, reflecting nothing more than our own mind structure and given an illusion of autonomy by labels such as ecumene, numen, and the like. A rational authority controlling power relationships is a need of European rationality, but this is a different problem from that of maintaining peace in the world. Although the great powers may have the capacity to destroy all terrestrial life, they were unable to use this to influence the course of policy of the main disturbers of peace such as Nasser, Nkrumah, and Soekarno. If nuclear weapons have brought about a concentration of power which seems to have abolished any valid distinction between national and international security, there has on the other hand been a dispersal of power and control, where in practice peace would require concentration.

Not only does the pseudo-rationality of the United Nations fail to meet this situation: it has itself become an instrument of aggression and, as in the cases of Goa, Yemen, and Rhodesia, makes no pretence of neutrality. The great power confrontations such as Iran, Korea, and Suez where the United Nations was invited to produce the appearance of impartiality have been replaced by situations where the ambitions of small fry are given uncritical support.

Since Afro-Asian self-consciousness is by its nature divisive the consolatory alternative to world government of regional authorities, even functional, has even less substance. For where relationships are intuitive and subjective, antagonisms and conflicts will be at their fiercest. So it is Arab against Jew, Kurd, and Persian; Moslem against Hindu; Kikuyu against Somali; Haussa against Ibo; Chinese against Malays; Sumatrans against Javanese. Of such practical utility does regionalism appear to those inhabiting the 'regions' *we* have created in *our* minds that the three former British East African territories have disrupted the common currency, customs, and postal services bequeathed by the British, while Singapore Chinese and Malays have put an end to their common note-issuing and banking arrangements. To Europeans there may be nothing more functional than a postage stamp or bank note, but those embroiled in the intuitive power relationships of Africa and Asia sense otherwise.

But not all conflict need be the enemy of greater order. The political designs of outside powers were not frustrated in the Congo by the United Nations—as the Hammarskjoeld legend would have us believe —but by Mobutu disposing of Lumumba and ejecting the Russians with their fleet of transport aircraft intended to move Nasser's battalions on wide-ranging forays, and by General Abboud in the Sudan halting the passage of Egyptian and Russian weapons and funds to the Gizenga regime in Stanleyville. The long-drawn-out palavers of Africa can bring about symbiosis, if not rational compromise. Even the Arab preference for the quality of the thing rather than the thing itself brings its gain: the attributes of a particular virtue are more important in human situations than the notion of virtue. In the Indian subjectifying consciousness 'world order' easily finds a place: we provide it and they enjoy it. 'Our hunger is now a world problem,' beams the Indian official, proposing to do nothing about it. Only China possesses a system which is sufficient and closed.

Throughout history dissimilarity of political and economic systems has never been a barrier to co-operation nor an inevitable source of enmity, just as similarity does not necessarily bring amity. It is a measure of the monolithism of our present thinking that we should entertain such notions. In our colonial era we professed democracy at home and practised autocratic rule abroad, but the authoritarian rulers came home to quiet retirement in Cheltenham. Mankind now faces a long transitional dualism between self-conscious assertions of separate identity and a fundamental human need for participation. This will require from the West a willingness to accept political forms and relationships without precedent. Since the South Africans have at least tried to grapple with these needs, they may end up by influencing the course of events more than those who now condemn them. Europe's need, as with Britain, is to renew a tradition—that of setting out problems in terms of contrasts and asking embarrassing questions about emancipation, equality, and philanthropy, challenging them with authority, diversity, and identity. By reconciliation in new concepts the old skills will find new power.

And against Russian ambiguity imperturbability is also the effective weapon. In a system where personal power and position are ever-present preoccupations, the resistant attitudes of other countries force upon the Soviet leaders a continuing debate on the correctness of long-term courses of action and keep alive questioning of dogma and differences of opinion. If the dialogue with Russia is only half-way to reconciliation, the spectacle of chaos may tempt the Russians to reverse their present drift of thinking and decide that, after all, violence is still the midwife of history. So for Western Europe progress towards order in the world cannot be through its own disarmament. Europe may not be able to impose a world authority, but neither dare it become so weak that it has to acquiesce in world chaos. European skills are such that defence systems need not always be of the same order of cost and magnitude as the existing ones of the United States and Russia. Just as the United States has repeatedly opposed its interests outside Europe to those of its NATO allies the latter may have to give themselves the strength to do the same. The need for order in the world, if not for a world order, may require this.

New emphases of power

That emphasis does shift is clear enough from the immediate past. The victorious Britain of 1945 was the bankrupt of 1967, and the once-stricken Europe had become its creditors. The 'bipolarity of East and West' and a 'non-aligned Third World' are almost ancient history. The Sino-Soviet quarrel put American-Soviet antagonisms in a new perspective. Mao Tse-tung's regrettable twentieth-century version of the dynastic rectification of names robbed China's external revolutionary plans of any residual effectiveness. The growing contradiction between Marxist notions and their defective realization weakens further Russian claims to orthodoxy over other Slav peoples. Whether China's acquisition of thermonuclear weapons and working methods of delivery will force the United States and Russia to deal with her on an equal basis or sharpen the confrontation, a new limiting factor will in either case have been imposed on their policies: strategic nuclear weapons may prove to be something of an equalizer in international affairs.

With similar shifting emphasis, the anti-colonial struggle has yielded in one decade to the internecine intrigues and conspiracies of black dictatorships. The notion of development which was to have put the entire human race into reach-me-downs has lost all validity. With a gross national product greater than all that of Western Europe, the United States had to call on European forbearance to preserve its internal financial balance within its existing political system: its over-whelming conventional military strength was held in the field by Asian peasants. Human will and purpose remain the decisive factors.

Against this background it is not one single authority of doctrine or force which the world requires. It is an arbiter who enjoys a strength of his own. *Cui adhaero prae est* proclaimed Henry's device on the Field of Cloth of Gold. Diversity may hold no promise of eternal peace. It offers something better—a fresh field of action, where the individual has a sense of moving by his own volition into new human experience. And this is our sense of freedom and power.

Index